Two week loan
Benthyciad pythefnos

Please return on or before the due date to avoid overdue charges
*A wnewch chi ddychwelyd ar neu cyn y dyddiad a nodir ar eich llyfr os
gwelwch yn dda, er mwyn osgoi taliadau*

GOVERNING EUROPE'S NEIGHBOURHOOD

MANCHESTER
1824
Manchester University Press

EUROPE
IN
CHANGE SERIES EDITORS: Thomas Christiansen and Emil Kirchner

Katja Weber, Michael E. Smith, & Michael Baun
EDITORS

GOVERNING EUROPE'S NEIGHBOURHOOD

Partners or periphery?

MANCHESTER UNIVERSITY PRESS
Manchester and New York

distributed exclusively in the USA by Palgrave

Published by Manchester University Press
Oxford Road, Manchester M13 9NR, UK
and Room 400, 175 Fifth Avenue, New York, NY 10010, USA
www.manchesteruniversitypress.co.uk

Distributed exclusively in the USA by
Palgrave, 175 Fifth Avenue, New York,
NY 10010, USA

Distributed exclusively in Canada by
UBC Press, University of British Columbia, 2029 West Mall,
Vancouver, BC, Canada V6T 1Z2

British Library Cataloguing-in-Publication Data
A catalogue record for this book is available from the British Library

Library of Congress Cataloging-in-Publication Data applied for

ISBN 978 0 7190 7601 5 *hardback*

First published 2007

16 15 14 13 12 11 10 09 08 07   10 9 8 7 6 5 4 3 2 1

Typeset in Minion with Lithos
by Action Publishing Technology Ltd, Gloucester
Printed in Great Britain
by Anthony Rowe, Chippenham

Contents

*F*IGURES, *TABLES AND BOXES*

Figures

Tables

Boxes

Abbreviations

ACP	Africa, Caribbean and Pacific
BEPG	Broad Economic Policy Guidelines
BiH	Bosnia-Hercegovina
BMENA	Broader Middle East and North Africa
CARDS	Community Assistance for Reconstruction, Development and Stabilization
CBC	Cross Border Cooperation
CEEC	Central and Eastern European Countries
CEES	Central and East European States
CEPOL	European Police College
CFSP	Common Foreign and Security Policy
CIS	Commonwealth of Independent States
CoA	Court of Auditors
COREPER	Council of Permanent Representatives
DABLAS	Danube Black Sea Task Force
DG	Directorate General
EA	Europe Agreements
EAP	Environment Action Programme
EBRD	European Bank for Reconstruction and Development
ECE	East Central Europe
ECT	European Community Treaty
EDC	European Defence Community
EEA	European Economic Area
EECCA	Eastern Europe, Caucasus and Central Asia
EFTA	European Free Trade Association
EIB	European Investment Bank
EMAA	Euro-Mediterranean Association Agreements
EMP	European-Mediterranean Partnership
EMU	European Monetary Union
ENP	European Neighbourhood Policy
ENPI	European Neighbourhood Policy Instrument
EPC	European Political Cooperation
ESDP	European Security and Defence Policy
EUSR	European Union Special Representative
FATF	Financial Action Task Force
FDI	Foreign Direct Investment

FI	Freedom Index
FSU	Former Soviet Union
GAERC	General Affairs and External Relations Council
GTEP	Georgia Train and Equip Program
IBRD	International Bank for Reconstruction and Development
ICPDR	International Commission for the Protection of the Danube River
IFI	International Financial Institutions
IMF	International Monetary Fund
INTERREG	Interregional Cooperation Programme
IOM	International Organization for Migration
IPAP	Individual Partnership Action Programme
JHA	Justice and Home Affairs
JLS	Justice, Freedom and Security
LIFE	Instrument Financier pour l'Environnement
LNG	Liquefied Natural Gas
MCA	Millennium Challenge Account
MEDA	Mediterranean-European Development Agreement
MEPP	Middle East Peace Process
MES	Market Economy Status
MFA	Ministry of Foreign Affairs
NATO	North Atlantic Treaty Organization
NDI	National Democratic Institute
NGO	Non-Governmental Organisation
NIS	Newly Independent States
NNI	New Neighbourhood Instrument
NP	Neighbourhood Programme
NPF	Neighbourhood Project Facility
NTB	Non-tariff Barrier
OSCE	Organization for Security and Cooperation in Europe
PA	Palestinian Authority
PCA	Partnership and Cooperation Agreement
PfP	Partnership for Peace
PHARE	Poland and Hungary Aid for Economic Reconstruction
PLO	Palestine Liberation Organization
PPC	Permanent Partnership Council
PRSP	Poverty Reduction Strategy Paper
PSA	Production Sharing Agreement
REC	Regional Environmental Centre
RELEX	External Relations
SAA	Stabilisation and Association Agreement
SAP	Stabilization and Association Process
SCG	Serbia and Montenegro
SES	Single Economic Space

SFOR	Stabilisation Force
SGP	Stability and Growth Pact
SPF	Small Project Facility
SSOP	Sustainment and Stability Operations Programme
TACIS	Programme for Technical Assistance to the Commonwealth of Independent States
TIP	Trafficking in Persons
UNMIK	United Nations Mission in Kosovo
WMD	Weapons of Mass Destruction
WTO	World Trade Organization

CONTRIBUTORS

Michael Baun	Valdosta State University
Michael Emerson	Centre for European Policy Studies
Elisabeth Johansson-Nogués	Universitat Autònoma de Barcelona
Sandra Lavenex	University of Lucerne
Michael Leigh	European Commission
Sylvia Maier	Georgia Institute of Technology
Gergana Noutcheva	Centre for European Policy Studies
John Occhipinti	Canisius College
Michelle Pace	University of Birmingham
Frank Schimmelfennig	Swiss Federal Institute of Technology
Ulrich Sedelmeier	European University Institute
Michael E. Smith	University of St Andrews
Adam N. Stulberg	Georgia Institute of Technology
Milada Anna Vachudova	University of North Carolina at Chapel Hill
Katja Weber	Georgia Institute of Technology
Mark Webber	Loughborough University

Acknowledgements

Over the years we spent organising and editing this book, we benefitted enormously from the critical advice and support of colleagues and friends. Our most obvious debt is to the various contributors to this volume. This project was especially challenging in terms of finding authors with the right combination of expertise regarding the EU, its neighbouring regions, and certain functional policy issues, and our fellow contributors rose to the occasion with skill and dedication. Several authors managed to interview key players within the EU about the issues addressed in this volume and we are grateful for their input. We would also like to thank Brian Murphy, Jim Rosenau and Glenda Rosenthal for their participation in a workshop in Atlanta which helped outline the project, and we are indebted to Roy Ginsberg, Charles Lipson and Randall Newnham for lending a critical ear. Thanks are also due to our colleagues at the Sam Nunn School of International Affairs at Georgia Tech, the School of International Relations at the University of St Andrews, and the Department of Political Science at Valdosta State University for their valuable support and constructive feedback.

We also benefitted greatly from the feedback provided in response to various presentations at the annual meetings of the American Political Science Association, the International Studies Association, the Central and Eastern European International Studies Association, the European Union Studies Association, the European Consortium for Political Research, and the World International Studies Conference in Istanbul, as well as from the insightful comments by the participants of the University of Chicago Program on International Politics, Economics and Security seminar. We appreciate our colleagues' willingness to serve as sounding boards and critics.

We are also grateful for the generous financial support we received from the Commission of the European Union to host a series of workshops on the European Neighbourhood Policy.

Anthony Mason, our commissioning editor at Manchester University Press, skilfully guided us through the production process, and we appreciate the confidence in our work shown by the editors of MUP's 'Europe in Change' series, Thomas Christiansen and Emil Kirchner. Katja Weber is personally indebted to the Georgia Tech Foundation for travel support; Michael E. Smith would like to acknowledge the constructive criticism provided by the participants of a workshop on International Relations in Eastern Europe (Humboldt University, March 2006); and Michael Baun would like to thank the family of Col. Vernon Pizer for their generous support for research and travel activities related to this book. Finally, we would each like to add a special dedication to our families, whose unwavering support and love mean everything:

For Anne, Johannes and Samih	Katja Weber
For my parents, Carol and Charles	Michael E. Smith
For Edna Baun	Michael Baun

PART I

The conceptual and empirical background

MICHAEL E. SMITH AND KATJA WEBER

1

Governance theories, regional integration and EU foreign policy

The European Union (EU) represents one of the most complex experiments in regional integration since the advent of the modern state system in the seventeenth century. Over the past five decades, the EU has expanded its competencies in numerous policy domains, internal and external, while also increasing its membership from six to 25 member states. These two processes – the deepening of EU institutions/policies and the widening of EU membership – have long been linked in the EU's history since its first enlargement in 1973. This is especially true of its most recent enlargement, the most ambitious in the history of the EU, which brought ten mostly Central and East European countries (CEECs) into the system on 1 May 2004. However, while much attention has been paid recently to the internal dynamics of EU enlargement and the associated question of a constitution for Europe, this volume seeks to explore the external implications of EU enlargement. This expansion extended the EU's borders to some extremely unstable regions and thus challenges its external relations capabilities, as well as the effective functioning of its internal social, political and economic institutions. The EU's ability to manage its border areas will also have major consequences for regional and global stability, particularly in terms of the roles of market liberalisation and democracy promotion as mechanisms of peaceful change. Finally, these efforts raise important questions of foreign policy and international relations theory, especially concerning the role of institutions, incentive structures and military force in facilitating international cooperation.

The chief inspiration for our investigation is a major policy initiative launched by the European Commission, the EU's executive arm. On 11 March 2003, the Commission adopted a Communication outlining a new framework for relations with Russia, the Western Newly Independent States (NIS),[1] and the Southern Mediterranean countries[2] who would soon be sharing borders with the EU. More specifically, the Commission proposed that, 'Over the coming decades, the EU should aim to work in partnership to develop a zone of prosperity and a friendly neighbourhood – a "ring of friends" – with whom the EU enjoys close, peaceful and cooperative relations ... In return for concrete progress demonstrating shared values and effective implementation of political, economic, and institutional reforms, all the neighbouring countries should be offered the prospect of a stake in the EU's internal market' (European Commission 2003a). In this document, EU external relations Commissioner Chris Patten also noted that 'over the past decade, the Union's most successful foreign policy instrument has undeniably been the promise of EU membership', an instrument that by definition must be limited to European states. Given the asymmetry between the EU and the countries of 'wider Europe' with respect to economic wellbeing, domestic stability and security considerations, this approach to foreign policy with non-EU states is no longer sustainable. Hence, although the European Neighbourhood Policy (ENP) was largely modelled on the enlargement process, the EU needs to find new ways – beyond accession – to export stability, security and prosperity, and to develop a clear vision for positive relations with its neighbours.

The challenges the EU confronts with respect to minority issues, visa, border and trade policies, cross-border cooperation and security policies in hopes of stabilising its neighbourhood are enormous (Kempe and van Meurs 2002; Emerson 2003; Dannreuther 2004). And yet, it is clearly in the EU's interest to effectively manage its relations with its larger neighbourhood. Most importantly, the EU has to keep the heterogeneity of the eastern and southern neighbours – in terms of culture, language, religion, aspirations, and current relations with the EU – in mind when extending or replacing existing forms of cooperation with these countries. These plans, in turn, must still respect both the EU's own broad principles and values as well as the unique interests of each state incorporated into the neighbourhood initiative. And beyond Europe, these efforts also must take into consideration the activities of other interested parties, whether states (such as Russia and the US), regional organisations (such as NATO) or international institutions (such as the United Nations and the World Trade Organization).

Balancing these competing forces will not be an easy task, and we are only beginning to understand how certain problems of global order will intensify once the EU has reached its limit of new member states. Although the Commission has continued its plans for a new European Neighbourhood Policy Instrument (ENPI) in terms of identifying relevant target countries, policy issues and policy tools (European Commission 2003b), there is more scope for objectively analysing the prospects for these arrangements and their implications for global governance in light of theories of international cooperation and regional integration. In the rest of this chapter, we present a broad overview of the prospects for effective and efficient governance of the

European neighbourhood to provide some analytical structure for the problems and target countries covered in this volume. Our ultimate goal is to assess the EU's overall potential for promoting good governance with its 'near abroad' without being able to offer full EU membership to these countries as a key incentive for securing their compliance. To answer this question, we suggest it may be useful to synthesise at least four broad areas of ongoing research on European foreign policy. These involve:

1   The EU's past experience in handling its relations with important non-member states (Ginsberg 1989; Holland 1995; Smith 1995; Smith 1998; Cameron 1999; M. Smith 2001).
2   The EU's own unique sources of power and legitimacy in acting to organise the governance of the European neighbourhood (Crawford and Schulze 1990; Hill 1996; Cederman 2000; Ginsberg 2001; Schimmelfennig 2003a; M. E. Smith 2003).
3   The EU's specific policy initiatives in key functional areas such as border security, immigration, trade, human rights, energy, transportation, communications, etc. (Nuttall 2001b; Youngs 2002; Emerson 2003).
4   The experience of the enlargement process as a mechanism for inducing peaceful change among neighbouring countries (Jacoby 2004; Kelley 2004a; Schimmelfennig and Sedelmeier 2004; Schimmelfennig and Sedelmeier 2005a; Sedelmeier 2005; Vachudova 2005; Grabbe 2006).

With all of these related literatures we must further consider both sources of support and potential obstacles to the formulation and implementation of policy (Gordon 1997/98; Zielonka 1998).

Cooperation and governance

Before examining our approach to governance in detail, we should note the possibility of alternative modes of organizing cooperation among independent states. One of the most common themes in this literature views deliberate policy coordination in certain areas as an international public good. Since public goods tend to be underprovided due to problems of free-riding or buck-passing (among others), a dominant state, or hegemon, must provide the leadership, resources, and even punishments to induce cooperation in the absence of an effective global government (Kindleberger 1973; Krasner 1976; Keohane 1980). However, cooperation is possible in the absence of a hegemon, even when conflicts of interest seem to be present. Strategies of reciprocity, iteration and outright *quid pro quo* bargaining can often be applied in such circumstances (Axelrod 1984; Oye 1986); when such behaviours are embedded within a larger institutional framework the prospects for cooperation are even greater. This of course is the major contribution of international regime theory (Krasner 1983), assuming the existence of distinct issue-areas or policy domains (such as trade liberalisation or balance-of-payments financing) around which to organise such regimes. Related studies of global norm-creation, diffusion and internalisation also highlight the importance of common institutional frameworks in facilitating cooperation, even where no formal regime is present (Axelrod 1986; Nadelmann 1990; Cortell and Davis 1996).

Viewed from the broader perspective of theories of international cooperation, many of the problems to be covered by the ENP may be viewed as public goods, meaning they will be underprovided unless cooperation is deliberately organised. Fortunately the EU possesses certain attributes to help facilitate meaningful policy coordination with its new neighbours. As a regional centre of power or even a hegemon, the EU's most obvious source of influence is the membership incentive, as we have noted. Lacking a credible membership incentive, the EU must rely on its other sources of power: leadership/agenda-setting, programme funding or other side-payments, education/training, access to its market, security assistance, policy bargaining (or 'logrolling'), and similar measures. As a stable centre of gravity in Europe the EU also offers highly robust institutional mechanisms to facilitate regular norm transfer and policy coordination with its neighbours, as well as the prospect of continued positive relations through iteration and reciprocity. Indeed, the ENP as presented by the Commission makes explicit use of some of these mechanisms in hopes of eliciting good behaviour from its partner states.

While this volume pays close attention to this 'menu' of mostly material incentives on offer by the EU through the ENP, we also argue that there is a need to consider alternative ways of organising stable regional cooperation on the EU's borders. This is so for several reasons. The first is the problem of asymmetrical interdependence as represented by the EU and its apparently subordinate neighbours (Keohane and Nye 1977). While one might assume voluntary choice among the EU and its interlocutors, the fact remains that the EU is in a much stronger position than most, if not all, of its ENP participants. This makes such states highly sensitive to the possibility of coercion or even dominance by the EU in implementing ENP (Sedelmeier 2005; Vachudova 2005).[3] The EU therefore needs to create at least the appearance of equal status among participants in the ENP programme while at the same time preventing any intimations of eventual EU membership for those states. In doing so the EU will hopefully avoid the negative connotations normally associated with hierarchical relationships under anarchy, whether in the form of hegemony, empires, protectorates, spheres of influence or the like. Whether the EU can realistically achieve such a relationship through its ENP plan rather than through full or some form of partial membership is a major research question motivating this volume.

A more parochial but no less important problem in organising robust cooperation through the incentives noted above involves the assumptions of discrete issue-areas and fairly stable national interests when states negotiate. Given the wide range of topics covered in ENP, the EU's own evolving competencies over those topics, and the difficulties associated with national interest formation, it is difficult to imagine cooperation among these states taking the form of regular intergovernmental bargains over individual policy problems. Instead, the process of interest-formation for all parties is likely to be far more fluid and nuanced, and the policy coordination that results is likely to be far more complex and even incoherent than assumed by theories of cooperation based on intergovernmental bargaining. And given the high degree of interdependence found in the EU's neighbourhood, as well as the ambitious nature of the ENP agenda, all parties involved are likely to find it far more difficult to prioritise their competing and complementary interests, and to determine their individual 'payoffs' from alternative courses of action, than assumed by many theories of international cooperation (i.e. the so-called 'relative gains' problem in multilateral settings; see Snidal 1991).

Finally, these issues are not just conceptual or unique to the EU's current circumstances; we have the EU's own institutional history and the experience of other regional/international organisations to draw upon. For its part, the EU allows quasi-membership in its internal market for certain European states through the European Free Trade Association (EFTA), which includes Iceland, Liechtenstein, Norway and Switzerland. The EU's own formal accession process, which has been institutionalised in the course of three decades of enlargement, provides a kind of (temporary) second-class membership for future EU member states. The North Atlantic Treaty Organization (NATO) created its Partnership for Peace (PfP) programme in 1994 for the CEECs without offering them the benefit of a formal security guarantee. Other international organisations, such as the Organization for Security and Cooperation in Europe (OSCE), the Council of Europe, the United Nations (UN), and so on also offer a range of participatory frameworks to non-member states variously treated as partners, observers, associate members or associate partners. And where 'participation' is defined mainly through *operations* (such as NATO, OSCE, or EU military missions) rather than *access* (such as EFTA or the EU's single market), non-member countries can certainly participate on a case-by-case basis without any formal arrangements for doing so. Moreover, if the EU itself is becoming more diluted and decentralised, as some have argued, in the aftermath of the Constitutional Treaty rejection in 2005, then perhaps a 'Europe à la carte' with varying degrees of membership would be more effective and stable than formally limiting the EU's expansion through initiatives such as the ENP.[4]

This last question is especially important for the research presented in this volume. However, before speculating on the future of European enlargement and the merits of alternative forms of membership or participation through the mechanisms noted above, we need a more complete understanding of the ENP programme itself, as well as its relationship to similar EU programmes such as Association Agreements or Partnership and Cooperation Agreements (PCAs). We also need a conceptual framework to anchor our analysis of how ENP might actually work in practice, a framework that draws upon but also refines and extends the insights offered by existing theories of international cooperation and regional integration. Such a framework would attempt to add to our understanding of the possibilities and limits of creating a sort of 'halfway house' between 'normal' international/intergovernmental cooperation and the prospects of full EU membership. This task is taken up in the rest of this chapter.

Defining governance

To help structure the analyses of ENP presented in this volume, the contributors have collectively developed a governance perspective to explain the EU's attempts to handle potential problems in its near abroad. In fact, a large literature on governance structures already exists, spanning multiple disciplines.[5] Much of this literature was specifically developed to explain the EU's activities on behalf of its own member states (Bulmer 1994; Marks et al. 1996), which take it far beyond existing frameworks used to explain international cooperation. The EU is not merely a 'regime', nor a 'federal state', nor an 'international organisation', yet it does have a major impact on its member states and, increasingly, the outside world (Ginsberg 2001). In this section we re-examine and refocus the governance literature to ascertain how the EU can promote different forms of cooperation (defined here as mutually rewarding policy adjustment) with its neighbours without being able to extend the promise of EU membership, a major source of its regional power over the past three decades (Mayhew 1998).

Our approach to governance begins with Rosenau's description:

> governance is not synonymous with government. Both refer to purposive behaviour, to goal-oriented activities, to systems of rule; but government suggests activities that are backed by formal authority, by police powers to insure the implementation of duly constituted policies, whereas governance refers to activities backed by shared goals that may or may not derive from legal and formally prescribed responsibilities and that do not necessarily rely on police powers to overcome defiance and attain compliance. Governance, in other words, is a more encompassing phenomenon than government. (Rosenau 1992: 4)

Governance, moreover, does not always entail one-way control. Two-way or multi-dimensional designs are quite common and there is a vast literature on increasingly complex types of organisation. One common feature of these frameworks involves the relationship between vertical and horizontal loci of activity: 'multilevels' and 'networks'. For example, according to Marks et al. (1998: 273), 'EU policy is produced by a complex web of interconnected institutions at the supranational, national, and subnational levels of government comprising a system of "multi-level governance."' Sweet and Sandholtz (1998) also differentiate levels of jurisdiction spanning from the local to the supranational level, while Scharpf (2001) distinguishes between intergovernmental, joint and supranational decision-making. Similarly, Gstoehl (1995: 13) speaks of 'variable geometry', Eising and Kohler-Koch (1999) of 'overlapping policy networks', Johansson-Nogués (2003) of 'network governance', Lavenex (2004a) of 'external governance', and Emerson (2003: 4) of 'hub-and-spoke, cobweb, matrix and Rubik cube arrangements'.

Other scholars highlight factors such as the formality of rules and the inclusiveness or exclusiveness of the governance arrangements. Abbott and Snidal (2000) and M.E. Smith (2001) conceptualise institutional arrangements partly in terms of their degree of legalisation, i.e. hard versus soft law, while Dunsire (1993) differentiates between regulation and self-regulation. And more recently, Hooghe and Marks proposed to differentiate two types of multi-level governance design: 'Type I,' they explain, entails 'general-purpose jurisdictions, non-intersecting memberships, jurisdictions at a limited number of levels, and a system-wide architecture.' Type II is characterised by 'task-specific jurisdictions, intersecting memberships, no limit to the number of jurisdictional levels, and flexible design' (Hooghe and Marks 2003: 236).

For the purposes of our study we adopt, but as a starting point only, Heritier's encompassing definition of governance which implies 'every mode of political steering involving public and private actors, including the traditional modes of government and different types of steering from hierarchical imposition to sheer information measures' (Heritier 2002). While this formulation may make it difficult to distinguish, analytically, true 'governance' from mere 'politics' or 'influence', we prefer to begin with a somewhat more inclusive definition then to strip away unneeded factors as necessary to explore future case studies. Throughout this volume we will therefore pay close attention to four major governance themes:

1   The purposeful coordination of multiple players (both public and private) within a given multi-level social space (Jachtenfuchs and Kohler-Koch 1995; Heritier 2002).
2   The convergence of divergent preferences in ways that manage to respect the initial plurality of interests involved (Eising and Kohler-Koch 1999).
3   The application of both formal (i.e. legislation, legal obligations, case law, police powers, etc.) and informal (i.e. rules of thumb, best practices, professional norms, peer pressures, socialisation, etc.) rule-making and compliance mechanisms (Rosenau and Czempiel 1992; M.E. Smith 2001).
4   The deliberate transfer or diffusion of EU norms and rules to non-member states participating within the ENP programme, or 'external governance' (Lavenex 2004a; Schimmelfennig and Sedelmeier 2004; Kelley 2006).

Given these considerations, governance is not just about patterned relationships (Kooiman 1993: 2) or the provision of mere order or stability; it
involves a *particular type* of order (out of several possible types) that is further
subject to broader principles of inclusiveness, fairness, effectiveness and legitimacy (Sweet and Sandholtz 1998). The EU attempts, though not without
problems, to govern its own institutions by these principles, and it now hopes
to export this view to its near abroad and beyond.[6] This effort may be termed
'external governance'. We also should stress here that EU organisations such
as the Commission are not the only agents of governance of concern to this
study; we will therefore incorporate other actors or pressures from both
inside and outside the EU that may impinge upon these questions. Still, we
generally take for granted that the EU is the dominant focal point and
norm/rule creator for handling the major problems of concern to this study,
and that the Commission is often the lead actor in terms of both initiating
and implementing EU policies. The Commission's role, however, still varies
greatly across issue-areas, especially in the realm of foreign and security
policy. One subsidiary task of this project, therefore, may be to determine
whether the EU's effective governance of its neighbourhood necessitates an
expansion of Commission authority, such as through the creation of a formal
diplomatic service.

A continuum of cooperative institutional arrangements

Given the proclivity to move away from central state control and disperse
governance across multiple centres of authority, a great variety of institutional structures can be found in the international environment. And given
the range of possible solutions to collective action problems, we argue that
actors who have decided to regularly cooperate to promote security,
economic wellbeing, environmental standards, etc. – rather than to rely on
self-help or 'one shot deals' – have some degree of choice between different
governance structures that entail varying degrees of institutionalisation. This
focus on deliberate, conscious choice conforms to standard micro-founda-
tional assumptions about individual rationality found in most theories of
international cooperation: actors cooperate to solve their perceived collective
action problems or to protect their interests. However, while this 'functional'
or 'instrumental' rationality provides a very useful starting point for this
investigation, we remain open to other assumptions about rational motivations at the micro-level, such as rationales of hard power, social
skill/inclusion and appropriateness (see M.E. Smith 2003: Chapter 1).[7]

Assuming, therefore, that actors pursue governance in large part to solve
known or expected collective action problems, we might first propose a classification scheme ranging from hierarchical to non-hierarchical modes of
governance to give some structure to actors' choices. The history of interna-

tional politics is replete with such different institutional arrangements (see Weber 1997, 2000; and Weber and Hallerberg 2001). These arrangements can be viewed as occupying various positions on a continuum that ranges from relationships characterised by high autonomy to more structured relationships with significantly restricted autonomy (see Figures 1.1 and 1.2 on cooperative security and economic arrangements). The further an actor moves away from arrangements that allow for a high degree of manoeuvrability and toward the more restrictive arrangements, the greater its delegation of authority to a centralized structure, and the higher the costs of exiting the arrangement become. This suggests that the closer actors move on the continuum toward the arrangements that curtail their freedom of action, the more binding their commitment will be, both because the costs of defecting from a more structured arrangement are higher, and because the likelihood of defection is reduced. Bindingness – which entails the curtailment of sovereignty in

<--->

Informal Alliances/ Informal Security Communities	Formal Alliances	Confederations/ Formal Security Communities
(entente; nonaggression pact; consultation pact)	(oftentimes with internatonal organisations such as NATO)	(plans for an EDC/ESDP)

Figure 1.1   Continuum of cooperative security arrangements

<--->

General Trade Agreement	Economic Community; Association

Figure 1.2   Continuum of cooperative economic arrangements

In both cases, movement to the right means that:

> --------> Freedom of action, sovereignty, autonomy,
> manoeuvrability decrease

> --------> Costs of exiting the arrangement increase

> --------> Likelihood of defection decreases

> --------> Pressures for more cooperation/conditionality increase

Therefore:

=====>Governance arrangements become more binding and stable exchange for greater institutionalisation – is likely to decrease opportunistic behaviour, since it would be difficult as well as costly in terms of reputation and economic wellbeing (or security) for cheaters or defectors to find a replacement for a structurally sophisticated institutional apparatus. We can often detect this deontological change in terms of rule-making when commitments change from a weaker formulation ('ought' or 'should' or 'shall') to an explicit imperative ('will' or 'must').

A more binding commitment also often involves greater clarity and formality in terms of the rule-specification; in other words, a general norm or 'rule of thumb' or 'unwritten rule' becomes a specific, written rule (or even a law) as one moves along the continuum. Accordingly, rights and responsibilities become far more explicit and third-party dispute resolution, monitoring and sanctions become more common (M.E. Smith 2001). Given this conceptualisation, informal mechanisms like general trade agreements constitute economic arrangements on the less binding side of the continuum, while structurally more demanding mechanisms involving sophisticated arbitration mechanisms, supranational secretariats, specific behavioural targets or benchmarking, and monitoring or regulatory devices represent arrangements on the more binding side. A general trade agreement entails a commitment to remove some of the trade impediments between the parties involved in the agreement, and there is the assumption that a violation of the agreement would cost something.

Similarly, in the security realm, an alliance is a formal or informal relationship between two or more sovereign states that involves some measure of commitment to act jointly to bring about greater security. A confederation, association, or 'economic community', on the other hand, entails a deliberate banding together of actors to create a centralised political structure with genuine decision-making power. Such arrangements entail a much more formal relationship in which the parties agree to create sophisticated structural apparati to facilitate their cooperation and to constrain independent behaviour. Bindingness, therefore, as used in this study, measures the degree of structural commitment parties agree to make. To understand bindingness, one must scrutinise the specific institutional makeup of cooperative arrangements to ascertain how committed individual actors are to curtailing their discretionary powers. Before doing so, we should stress here that the continuum outlined above (ranging from coordination to subordination) is only one of many classification schemes of international governance, and we expect to make further refinements in future work on specific case studies.

Factors that influence the choice of governance types

In this increasingly interdependent world, where self-help often leads to suboptimal outcomes, actors have numerous incentives to cooperate. But which factors determine the type of cooperative structures chosen? Since different forms of governance are more efficient and acceptable in different circumstances, we next identify factors that are likely to influence actors' institutional choices. One immediate problem that arises is the wide coverage of issues within the ENP framework, which does not lend itself to simple generalisations about which kinds of rules are likely to result. As a first cut at this question, we can disaggregate the ENP sectors into three general areas: security cooperation, economic cooperation, and what might be termed principled cooperation. Preferences for institutional or governance structures will vary according to the inherent demands for these types of cooperation, as theories based on transaction costs have suggested (Williamson 1985; Weber 1997; Weber and Hallerberg 2001).

In the security realm, an (external) threat is instrumental in determining the nature and degree of a state's initial commitment to an alliance (Walt 1988). A related security motivation is the fear of exclusion from a cooperative security arrangement, even where a state faces no specific security threat. In other words, there are both 'push' and 'pull' factors – fears of attacks and abandonment – that might encourage states to join cooperative security arrangements (Christensen and Snyder 1990). In the economic realm, a (foreign) economic threat (i.e. competition or threats to flows of vital resources, such as oil) which endangers the survival or economic wellbeing of state and/or societal actors can be a major catalyst (a push factor) for institutionalised cooperative behaviour. The corresponding 'pull' factor is the incentive of guaranteed access to a rich economic market or shared strategic resources, especially if a state's own trading partners/competitors are making the same move.

In both cases, if the level of threat is low and the actors are viable with respect to the competition they face, there is no need for a strong commitment, and, if the actors choose to cooperate, an informal rather than a structurally sophisticated arrangement might be chosen. Such arrangements have low exit costs, usually do not require ratification by state actors, and can be easily modified or discarded (Lipson 1991). On the other hand, if the level of threat is high, actors are likely to prefer an arrangement that gives them greater assurance (i.e. one that is more binding, thereby reducing the risk of defection). These incentives for either security or economic cooperation might be measured in terms of relative military capability, geographic proximity, market share/access, trade balances, and threatening behaviour by other states (such as a Russian threat to deny energy supplies). Other factors such as uncertainty, high asset specificity (or low asset mobility), and a need for regular transactions may increase the desire of actors to institutionalise their commitments to each other (Williamson 1979, 1985; Weber 1997). In these cases, actors also may institutionalise a corresponding dispute-resolution mechanism such as the European Court of Justice or a joint EU–partner country commission (Sweet and Brunell 1998) to further bind themselves.

It is more difficult to measure transaction costs and push/pull factors in the area of principled cooperation, such as human rights or cultural exchanges; therefore in this realm actors may need to justify the desirability of more binding arrangements in terms of broader values or goals rather than in terms of narrow self-interests. Although such 'aspirational' institutions can be difficult to analyse in terms of standard instrumental rational choice motivations (Botcheva and Martin 2001), they play an increasingly important role in the EU's conception of itself as a global actor and will deserve more attention in certain cases covered in this volume. In addition, EU agreements with non-member states now require explicit support of such principled goals (chiefly human rights and democracy; the so-called 'democratic conditionality clause') as a condition for economic cooperation (Szymanski and Smith 2005).

To summarise, then, both a high level of threat and high transaction costs are often *necessary* to bring about a structurally sophisticated institutional arrangement (they are separately necessary), but neither is *sufficient*. We therefore should be sensitive to governance arrangements that arise because of other factors in addition to (or even instead of) calculations about power or threats, such as normative concerns, institutional inertia, collective identity, socialisation processes (both elite and public), or even symbols, language, and rhetoric. This open-ended approach will allow us to explain variation across the many policy sectors covered by the ENP programme. It also may shed light on cases (if any) where governance arrangements involving Europe either develop without a clear security or economic threat, or fail to emerge despite a clear security or economic threat.

Three caveats must be added before moving on. First, the EU's status as a major centre of gravity in Europe must be qualified in light of functionally-related competitors, such as NATO, the OSCE, or Russia's own Commonwealth of Independent States, that could serve as substitutes or even spoilers to an EU-focused arrangement. We should therefore consider whether non-member states like the ENP partners are able to play these institutions off one another (i.e. 'forum shop') in terms of solving specific collective action problems or merely pursuing their own self-interests. Second, we must keep in mind that the initial incentives for pursuing a particular agreement may change over time (from negotiation to ratification to implementation, for example) in light of changes in preferences, institutional legacies in the form of PCAs, enlargements, or the Euro-Med programme (which involve path-dependency or lock-in effects), and changes in functionally-related institutions or policy-domains. In this sense we should recognise that any governance arrangements, even the most formal and binding, must allow for some degree of flexibility if they are to maintain their effectiveness and legitimacy.

Third and perhaps most importantly, it likely will be necessary to modify the above assumptions in light of the asymmetrical nature of EU–ENP relations as noted above. As the richest market in Europe and the most highly developed international institution, the EU may possess more influence over some issues and countries than we might expect of a typical bilateral relationship between equals. The EU is able, by virtue of its mere size and numerous competencies, to offer stronger incentives for pursuing cooperation than most non-member states on its perimeter. Our assumption of a certain degree of *voluntary action* on the part of ENP partners will therefore require further refinement in certain areas. Clearly, one can think of scenarios where actors are coerced to behave in a certain manner and where they need punishments (sticks) or incentives (carrots) to cooperate (see Dietz 2000: 5).[8] How the EU's inherent power as a negotiating partner varies across issues and external interlocutors will deserve much greater attention as the ENP initiative develops.

In fact, one of the primary questions for this study is whether the EU is capable of placing relations with its new neighbours in a framework that does not allow full integration/membership *and* does not generally involve the use of hard power instruments, whether military or economic, or the threat of exclusion. In other words, will the EU permit a true partnership of equals here, or will it resort to its traditional foreign policy instruments (and even the prospect of membership, whether full or partial), such as the threat of exclusion in case of violations of political conditionality or other defections? And will this new ENP framework be as effective as traditional foreign policy tools in terms of solving the problems the EU expects to face in the near future? Although the EU has shown increasing sophistication in its agreements with important non-member states, largely through the use of specific framework agreements (which combine economic, political, and some soft security cooperation measures into package deals[9]), the new ENP proposals are more ambitious. Therefore we will need to think carefully about how to incorporate these traditional instruments of EU foreign policy into our analytical framework as presented in the discussion above.

The plan of the book: cases and questions

Since actors prefer different forms of institutionalisation in different issue areas, this volume is organised around sector analyses which, as Kooiman puts it, 'seem, for the time being, to be the most appropriate level for doing research' (Kooiman 1993: 262). Moreover, we need to remain cognisant of the fact that, with respect to many issue areas, 'from trade and investment to human rights and the environment, individuals and private groups are the actors most responsible for new international agreements' (Abbott and Snidal 2000: 450). Based on the Commission's own proposals (European Commission 2003b) and recent work by other scholars in this area (Emerson 2003; Dannreuther 2004; Pardo 2004; Albi 2005; Smith 2005; Kelley 2006), we have commissioned a series of case studies to highlight a wide range of EU activities in terms of delivering external governance to its new neighbourhood.

The rest of the volume is organised as follows. Chapter 2 provides a general overview of the origins of the ENP based on an initial blueprint drawn up by then-EU External Relations Commissioner Chris Patten and High Representative for the Common Foreign and Security Policy (CFSP) Javier Solana. This chapter is followed by seven major case study chapters (Chapters 3–9) presented in the order they appeared in the Commission's proposals for the ENP. Each of the individual ENP sectoral policy domains actually comprises multiple 'sub-policy' goals, which provide some useful case study variance for theoretical analysis. Additional variance was built into the chapters by requesting that the authors, if possible, examine at least two different target regions/countries for their analyses, ideally one in the east and another in the south-east or south. We also asked our contributors to pay close attention to other important actors, particularly Russia, depending on their specific cases. Finally, we have included three additional analytical chapters to round out the volume. While proximity alone favours the EU as the major player among its perimeter states, we also need to examine the ENP's possible impact on America's policies toward these countries. Accordingly, Chapter 10 examines the implications of the ENP for both transatlantic relations and global governance. Chapter 11 will take a critical view of the entire project, in terms of both its theoretical component and ENP's specific policy goals. Chapter 12 presents the Commission's view of these issues and of the prospects for the ENP in light of recent trends. Finally, the Conclusion to the volume will attempt to summarise and synthesise the arguments presented in the various case studies.

As this volume does not claim to present a single theory of external governance but only offers a definition and some conceptual elements for developing governance theory in light of the ENP, our case study authors have enjoyed a fair degree of autonomy in determining which variables and factors to highlight in explaining their particular policy sectors. However, we have specifically identified a range of common questions regarding external governance and the ENP. For example, *within each case*, we have asked the contributors to examine a number of questions:

1   To what extent does the EU's past relationship, if any, with that issue/partner country inform current efforts, in both positive and negative ways? And to what extent will it be possible to structure the relationship on a new foundation? Here we can draw upon the literature on EU relations with key non-member states (such as Russia) as well as analyses of existing cooperative frameworks, such as PCAs, Euro-Med, INTERREG, PHARE, and TACIS.

2   What balance is being proposed/developed by the EU and the partner

country in terms of the various dimensions of governance noted above (which includes specifying the role, if any, of the Commission and other EU organisations)? To what extent do they initially agree or disagree (i.e. the bargaining space) and what are the chances for resolution?

3   How can we measure and explain the emergence and implementation of the target issue/country in terms of governance principles (legitimacy, transparency, accountability, compliance, effectiveness) and mechanisms (carrots and sticks, hard and soft power, hard and soft law)? And to what extent might implementation be affected by both voluntary and involuntary defection?

4   To what extent do broader power asymmetries (in military, economic, normative, informational or other terms) and threat perceptions (security and economic) play a role in explaining the outcome?

5   What determines the specific constellation of actors and their power resources in each policy domain/target country? Are the dynamics of cooperation stimulated by 'top down' priorities set by government officials or 'bottom up' activities of firms and citizens, or some combination of the two? And to what extent does the interaction between these elements – transgovernmental political collusion and transnational social/economic market behaviour – condition the legitimacy or effectiveness of the resulting governance mechanisms?

Finally, we have decided to address the following questions *across all cases* covered by the ENP:

1   Are there inherent differences across issue-areas in terms of collective action problems and effective or appropriate governance structures (military defence, security, economics, environment, infrastructural issues, etc.)?

2   What are the prospects for coordinating/prioritising all sectors into coherent governance frameworks, whether in terms of agreements with single countries, broader regions, or smaller sub-national units (public and private)?

3   To what extent can the EU incorporate provisions for future evaluation/revision of its ENP initiative? How can we determine whether the new ENP measures are likely to be robust and self-sustaining or stagnant and ineffective?

4   How do the EU's efforts toward its neighbourhood compare to those of other global actors, such as the UN, the US, Russia, NATO, the OSCE, and others? Do the EU's efforts mutually reinforce, conflict with, or have a negligible impact on the efforts of others (i.e. a 'sphere of influence' type of division of labour)?

Conclusion

Having successfully negotiated the most extensive enlargement of the EU in its history, European officials must now think very carefully about securing the perimeter of one of the richest markets on earth. This task presents a challenge almost equal in scope to enlargement itself, yet it also presents the EU with a highly unique opportunity and potential source of power. The EU's single market, and the institutional foundation on which it is based, might yet serve as the most important source of regional stability on the continent if Europe's enthusiasts can manage to organise a wide variety of relationships and policy problems on the basis of coherent common principles. Europe has been the flashpoint for, or inspiration of, some of history's most violent and revolutionary ideas, conflicts, and political movements, and the EU's new neighbourhood instrument might be a rare opportunity to permanently alter the course of Europe's troubled history.

In doing so, the EU can be expected to draw upon its long experience with the complex governance of its own member states. The question is whether this experience can be adapted in the service of EU foreign policy and exported to states that may have virtually no chance of joining the EU. We have outlined a conceptual framework for analysing this question, focusing on the EU's ability to set the agenda and structure the incentives for institutionalised cooperation in security, economic, and principled issue-areas. While the EU's capacities as a global actor still vary widely across these fields, European officials (especially within the Commission) have increasingly managed to use the attractions of access to the single market as leverage in the pursuit of other EU goals, such as democratisation and human rights. The Commission's penchant for uniform 'package deals' with non-member states, where market access is conditioned on upholding the EU's political principles, is firmly institutionalised as a key foreign policy tool. We can expect this process to continue with the creation of a new neighbourhood instrument and its application to virtually all states that border the EU.

The challenge of external governance lies in reconciling the EU's desire for protecting its core political principles with the wide variety of states and political/economic problems found on its perimeter. While the EU has relaxed certain common standards among its own member states (such as the criteria for euro membership and the various 'opt outs' allowed in some EU policy domains), it often has been less willing to be flexible with candidates for accession. Even the newest EU member states have accused the EU of holding them to standards that older member states cannot meet. The incentive of EU membership has led the CEECs to put up with this 'second class' treatment, but this incentive is lacking for the new border states. Only a more detailed analysis of specific issue areas and target states will shed more light on how the ENP might balance common principles with flexibility/differentiation, which is one of the tasks of this volume.

A second challenge for the EU and those who study it lies in situating the EU as the new centre of gravity for Europe within the larger global context, namely in terms of America's hegemonic status, Russia's regional dominance, and the future of key global institutions, such as the UN and the WTO, that strongly depend on transatlantic support. Will the ENP project increasingly conflict with American policies at the regional and global levels, or will it allow transatlantic relations to be placed on a new foundation of mutual cooperation? And will the EU be content with its status as a junior partner to America or will it instead attempt to challenge American dominance and even facilitate the creation of a bipolar or multipolar system? The EU's approach toward its bordering non-member states will be an extremely important test case of its ability to manage a variety of problems and thus answer these questions. To the extent that the EU's approach to such problems ultimately differs from America's (and Russia's) often heavy-handed (and contradictory) policies, we may be witnessing the emergence of a new approach to hegemony, or even a form of 'benevolent imperialism', whereby a dominant actor attempts to govern its periphery by the same principles of democratic legitimacy and the rule of law found within itself. Whether these classical liberal principles of global order will be furthered or frustrated by the harsh conditions assumed by realists remains to be seen, and we hope to explore this fundamental question of global governance further in the rest of this volume.

Notes

1 Ukraine, Moldova, and Belarus. Russia chose not to be a participant in the formal ENP programme, which was later extended to include the southern Caucasus (Armenia, Azerbaijan and Georgia).

2 Algeria, Egypt, Israel, Jordan, Lebanon, Libya, Morocco, Palestinian Authority, Syria and Tunisia.

3 America's relationship with its own 'neighbourhood' is instructive on this point, as it often insists on unilaterally 'certifying' its weaker partners (such as Mexico) according to its own standards of good behaviour (for example, on counter-drug cooperation) rather than allowing more of a bilateral dialogue on such matters.

4 For recent speculation on this point, see Cottrell 2005.

5 For an overview, see Hooghe and Marks 2003.

6 For example, the Commission's 'White Paper on European Governance' (2001a) cites five principles of good governance that the EU should respect: openness, participation, accountability, effectiveness and coherence. This document further argues that the EU 'should seek to apply the principles of good governance to its global responsibilities. It should aim to boost the effectiveness and enforcement powers of international institutions.' The debate over the EU's proposed constitution also addresses principles of good governance.

7 Specifically, a logic of hard (i.e. material) power conforms to realist-based theories (where the power and interests of large states largely determine outcomes). A logic of normative appropriateness comes into play when new institutional elements are defined in terms of existing ones. Ambiguities, inconsistencies, and contradictions within institutions (and between institutions with similar goals) must constantly be

resolved. Finally, a socio-cultural logic may also emerge, in the sense that actors learn to reorient their attitudes and behaviour to an institution's norms as they regularly participate in the system. Actors (particularly ones new to the institution, as occurs during enlargement of the EU) must constantly adjust their own perspective to that of the institution to be viewed as legitimate participants.

8   For a continuum that includes governance structures that resulted from coercion, see Lake 1999, especially pp. 17 and 27–31. He, for the most part, focuses on 'control' and 'power asymmetries' and largely discusses situations in which one party gains greater decision-making authority over another. Instead of examining mutually advantageous relationships, where parties voluntarily curtail their autonomy and delegate authority to a cooperative structure that benefits all, he emphasises 'subordination' and 'domination'.

9   The EU's recent 'Global Agreement' with Mexico is instructive; see Szymanski and Smith 2005.

Elisabeth Johansson-Nogués[1]

2

The EU and its neighbourhood: an overview

In May 2003 the Thessalonica European Council formally launched the new European Neighbourhood Policy (ENP). This marked the culmination of a year of feverish activity after the General Affairs Council, in April 2002, first invited the CFSP High Representative, Javier Solana, and then EU External Relations Commissioner, Chris Patten, to draw up the initial blueprint for a new ambitious foreign policy initiative. This plan would encompass all of the countries neighbouring the enlarged EU to the east and south. The May 2003 European Council would not, however, entirely conclude the policy process set in motion. New developments in the European Union's geographical vicinity in Thessalonica's aftermath would mean that the incipient policy would have to adapt and adjust as new demands arose.

This chapter sheds light on the early evolution of the ENP, first discussing the different stimuli that led the EU to create it. At the most patent level, the initiative came about as a result of the reflection in the latter stage of the Eastern enlargement process that the EU was on the verge of obtaining a new set of neighbours along its eastern borders, with all the correspondent implications of this. However, other factors also came into play in the formative years of this new neighbourhood policy. After outlining the motivational origins of the ENP, this chapter explores the policy formation process between 2002 – when the first proposals were aired – and late 2005. During this time period, ENP drafts succeeded counter-drafts by the Council, the European Commission and national delegations, and the documents reveal an interesting dialogue in terms of how the EU conceives the nature of its relations with its closest geographical neighbours, and, what is more, how these relations are best managed. The end result, as we will see, is a plural policy with unusually broad EU backing.

The 'neighbourhood' finds its way onto the EU's agenda

The Eastern enlargement is without doubt the most obvious reason why the ENP came about. The decision at the Helsinki European Council in 1999 to change tack in the Eastern enlargement process was a first important step for the Union to liberate itself from a matter which had consumed substantial quantities of both the EU and the member states' institutional energies for close to a decade. The post-Berlin Wall deliberation among the member states to admit ten Central and Eastern European countries (CEECs) to the EU had been a drawn-out affair. The process was full of tensions, hampered by internal pay-offs and, for some time, subject to considerable uncertainty regarding scope and timetable (Friis 1997; Friis and Murphy 1999; Torreblanca 2003). The issue was, however, to be settled more or less satisfactorily at the Helsinki Summit in December 1999, where it was decided to open negotiations with all remaining candidate countries, as well as with Malta. Hereafter the Eastern enlargement would take on a more technical quality (Commission-led), and the member states found that the Council meetings could be employed to deliberate other foreign policy pursuits.

As the EU member states now began to look beyond enlarging their borders to the east, and to take stock of existing relations with neighbours such as Russia and the Mediterranean countries, they became concerned. Public patience regarding matters of justice and home affairs (see Chapter 7) was growing particularly thin in the late 1990s. Reports of corruption and transborder organised crime, trafficking in everything from drugs to arms and human beings, had become a mainstay of news programmes and on the covers of newspapers across Europe. Crime and illegal immigration had increasingly become associated with the Western Balkans and Eastern Europe. The electorates in European member states began to demand more preventive measures by their respective governments.

Even more troubling, violence was on the rise in the Middle East with the outbreak of the Second *Intifada* in late 2000. The Middle East Peace Process, launched in Madrid in 1991, thus seemed inevitably derailed. September 11 prompted further calls for measures against global terrorism and the international networks of money laundering that sustain it. The attacks in New York and Washington also triggered considerable soul-searching in countries like France, Germany and the Netherlands regarding the integration of Muslims living in their societies, and prompted a widespread feeling that the EU needed to improve relations with its Arab neighbours.

As these deficient relations with the EU's neighbours came to be highlighted, there were also a set of subtle forces at work within the European Union. Beginning in late 1999, a re-evaluation of the Union's role as an international actor was under way. Some analysts have noted that the conclusion of the Kosovo crisis had come to mark a psychological turn-around in the EU's foreign policy in that the EU-15 managed to remain remarkably united, despite the member states' numerous concerns (Ginsberg 2001; Crowe 2003: 536). Other scholars have provided a more sombre reading of the Union's involvement, but still agree that the aftermath of the Kosovo conflict conspired to converge 'in such a way as to impart new momentum to the development of [the] European foreign policy and to raise the possibility of an almost revolutionary change in member state commitments' toward such a policy (M. Smith 2003: 556; see also Howorth 2000; M. Smith 2001). There was thus a new, growing confidence among EU leaders that the Union could, and indeed should, play a more decisive role in foreign policy pursuits, especially when it comes to its geographical vicinity.

Following Kosovo, and the entering into force of the Amsterdam Treaty (May 1999), the member states reflected upon recent developments at the Cologne European Council (1999):

> The European Council recalls that at its Vienna meeting it called on the Council also to prepare common strategies on Ukraine, on the Mediterranean region, specifically taking into account the Barcelona process and the Middle East peace process, and on the western Balkans. The six months since the Vienna meeting have, in various ways, again clearly brought out *the importance of all these regions to the European Union not only as partners in its external relations but also for the stability and security of our continent and its immediate neighbourhood* [emphasis added].

The term 'neighbourhood' had thus made its entrance on the Union's agenda as a concept, signalling the intention to design a more coherent and strategic approach towards third countries in the EU's immediate geographical vicinity.

The Common Strategies, purportedly the basis for such a new strategic approach, would, however, shortly afterwards prove fairly unsatisfactory instruments to advance that objective. The three Common Strategies adopted for Russia (1999), Ukraine (1999) and the Mediterranean (2000) essentially restated the existing bilateral or regional relations without adding anything decisively new, nor did they provide the Union with more than a blurred vision of how these relations would henceforth develop (Haukkala and Medvedev 2001; Spencer 2001). Solana in 2001 severely criticised the utility of Common Strategies as tools against third countries (*Financial Times*, 23 January 2001).

Adding insult to injury, the Common Strategies also accentuated the simmering rivalry between member states regarding the EU's prioritisation of different neighbourhoods (Barbé 1998). Different member states lobbied for their own 'backyards' and, when needed, blocked the smooth functioning of other regional EU foreign policy initiatives, in their competition for scarce technical and financial resources. Both the Mediterranean and the Baltic Sea region, consequently, had become 'rim areas' to the European centre, which were essentially 'competitors in the bid for favours from the Union's structural funds and neighbourhood policies' (Stålvant 2001: 5).

These were the circumstances when, in January 2002, Britain submitted a proposal to the Commission suggesting a differentiated, ambitious and long-term approach to the new eastern neighbours, in particular Belarus, Moldova and Ukraine. In a letter to then Commission President Romano Prodi, British Foreign Secretary Jack Straw proposed offering 'a kind of special neighbour status' to these ex-Soviet republics (Haukkala and Moshes 2004: 15). According to press reports, Straw's vision seemed to be mostly motivated by London's concern over cross-border crime and illegal immigration, i.e. security at the enlarging borders of the EU. As seen from the perspective of the Blair government, the host of new challenges, purportedly arising as a consequence of the Eastern enlargement, put in relief the limitations and lack of sophistication of the EU's existing relations with the Western NIS (*Radio Free Europe*, 18 April 2002; *European Report*, 13 July 2002). As Jack Straw's letter was being circulated, there was no denying that the Union's links with the Western NIS (Partnership and Cooperation Associations) had been largely steeped in the straitjacket of the EU's view of the former Soviet Union's space as largely within the dominion of Moscow. This thinking was now beginning to be seen as outdated in various European capitals and in need of an urgent overhaul.

Tracing the birth of a policy

The British proposal one month later was followed by a Swedish 'non-paper' authored by Anna Lindh and Leif Pagrotsky, then the Swedish Minister of Foreign Affairs and the Minister for Trade, respectively. The Lindh-Pagrotsky dispatch largely concurred with the British letter drawing the EU's attention to the importance of an Eastern policy. Yet the Swedish document went one step further, calling for 'a broader and more active policy towards our neighbours in the bow-shaped area ranging from Russia and Ukraine *to the Mediterranean*' (Lindh and Pagrotsky 2002: 2; emphasis added). Moreover, the text makes clear that the Swedish ministers felt that the Common Strategies set up for Russia, Ukraine and the Mediterranean countries were too vague and general and that a new policy was urgently needed. The ministers thus suggested that, in view of the Strategies' prompt expiration date (by 2003 and 2004 respectively), the EU should opt for a different course, namely to integrate the Union's immediate neighbours into a European economic and social partnership (Lindh and Pagrotsky 2002: 4).

At the General Affairs Council on 15 April 2002 a first official exchange among member states took place in regards to 'wider Europe'. The Council concluded that the matter should be studied further, and tasked the High Representative and the External Relations Commissioner to draw up a primary proposal (Council of the European Union 2002a). The results of the petition would a few months later take the form of a joint letter addressed to the Danish EU Presidency.

In their memo, Javier Solana and Chris Patten sketched out the bare essentials of a medium-term strategy for closer relations with third neighbouring countries. The Solana-Patten communiqué examined the existing and differentiated relations between the Union and its neighbours, dividing the EU's geographical vicinity into three main areas: the Western Balkans, the Mediterranean and the new Eastern neighbours (Western NIS and Russia), classifying them according to their relations with the Union: potential to join, no potential to join, or somewhere in between. The letter concluded that the initial focus of the new policy should be on the Western NIS.

The Solana-Patten memo was the first coherent blueprint outlining the new policy. The letter is visionary, revealing a willingness to look to the medium and longer term. It recommends the creation of an 'economic and political space' surrounding the Union and even the extension of new contractual relations to neighbouring countries if necessary. The objective of this new EU policy should be to safeguard 'stability, prosperity, shared values and rule of law' along the EU's borders (Solana and Patten 2002: 2). The joint letter was officially presented to the General Affairs and External Relations Council (GAERC) on 30 September, where the ministers decided, however, to concentrate their efforts on Belarus, Moldova and Ukraine, although they noted that, 'beyond the question of Eastern neighbours, the broader question of "wider Europe" deserved consideration' (Council of the European Union 2002b).

The September GAERC, nevertheless, only gave cursory treatment to this new neighbourhood initiative. Accession negotiations with the Eastern candidate countries were at a decisive stage and took precedent over most other matters. Moreover, as the Eastern enlargement was taking more concrete shape, a series of outstanding EU–Russian issues became increasingly more urgent to deal with. This meant that, apart from enlargement, the Danish Presidency in late 2002 was to be kept busy with settling Russian grievances in terms of trade, visas, Kaliningrad etc. arising from the enlargement process.

The baton of the new neighbourhood initiative, however, was picked up by the Council organs, such as the Council of Permanent Representatives (COREPER), the Political and Security Committee and COEST (a unit dealing with Eastern Europe and Central Asia), which debated the initiative on different occasions from September to November. These meetings helped to flesh out the policy. A more thorough discussion among ministers took place in the GAERC on 18 November. This Brussels Council meeting now took the geographical coverage of the initiative a step further, recommending that the policy should target Ukraine, Moldova and Belarus, but also be 'seen in conjunction with the EU's strong commitment to deepening co-operation with the Russian Federation' (Council of the European Union 2002c). Moreover, the Council returned to the Lindh-Pagrotsky suggestion that it might 'subsequently reflect on those elements which could be relevant for relations with partners in other bordering regions', in a clear reference to the

Union's southern Mediterranean partners (Council of the European Union 2002c).

The serene language of the GAERC conclusions as to which countries would eventually be included in the new neighbourhood scheme suggested a long timeframe for reflection before further action would be taken. Not surprisingly, many observers were caught off-guard, when, in little more than a week, a greatly expanded list of new neighbourhood countries was confirmed. A few weeks later, Romano Prodi outlined a policy which was no longer reserved to the eastern neighbours. As proposed by Patten and Solana earlier, the policy now also included the Mediterranean (Prodi 2002a and 2002b). The initiative 'Wider Europe' thus began its transition to 'proximity policy' when the Commission's President insisted that the new policy was to be opened to all EU non-candidate neighbours. Prodi significantly broadened a previously modest policy into a strategy, insisting on the creation of a 'ring of friends' around the EU-25's outer border that would stretch from Russia to Morocco. He also made clear that the policy would be the most generous in the Union's history, where interested neighbouring countries would be offered integration in concrete EU programmes and the Internal Market to a degree distinguishable from member states only by the fact that they 'shared everything but institutions' (Prodi 2002b).

The Copenhagen European Council, a few weeks later, confirmed this new policy focus by inextricably linking the Eastern enlargement with the new neighbourhood and fixed the geographical limit of the policy to Moldova and Ukraine in the east, and the Euro-Mediterranean partners in the south. The Copenhagen Summit marked in many ways the end of the first phase of political discussions among member states regarding the neighbourhood initiative. The European Commission was then tasked with creating a coherent and detailed plan for how the Union should proceed in its relations with the eastern and southern neighbours. The Commission's Communication *Wider Europe – New Neighbourhood Initiative* was consequently presented on 11 March 2003. It echoes the main proposals earlier outlined by Prodi, such as offering progressive integration into the Internal Market and its regulatory structures (health, consumer and environmental protection), including those pertaining to sustainable development (European Commission 2003a). Moreover, the new neighbourhood policy also opens the door to enhanced trade relations, supports WTO accession and intends to intensify cooperation in a host of other areas ranging from 'terrorism to air-borne pollution'. The Union's approach to realise these goals would, as EU Enlargement Commissioner Günter Verheugen stressed during a speech in London just days before the Communication was published, essentially 'build on the experience of [the Eastern] enlargement' and hence be 'progressive, differentiated and conditional' (*European Report*, 5 March 2003).

The public reaction following the presentation of the Commission's Communication was mixed. Among the most vocal critics were both EU member states and some neighbouring countries contemplated in the initiative. Three issues in particular drew much attention: first, there was doubt with regards to the meaning of the principle of 'differentiation'; second, there was the reference to the progressive introduction of freedom of movement of persons; and finally, there was the issue of whether the new neighbourhood policy would close the door to prospective applicant countries.

First, the principle of differentiation, as expressed by the Communication, was essentially intended to assuage the fears of neighbouring countries, e.g. Morocco, striving for more advanced relations with the Union, by reiterating that they would all be treated with due attention to their individual circumstances in the framework of the new policy. However, a few weeks later the principle of differentiation had become a key concept to alleviate growing tensions within the EU on this same point. After the official presentation of the 11 March Communication, some EU members became concerned that the new neighbourhood policy would not pay sufficient homage to their wishes to keep their interests regarding their respective near neighbourhoods high on the EU agenda. There were also some who were alarmed that the new policy would serve to dilute advances already achieved with certain third countries.

On 14 April, 2003 the CFSP High Representative nevertheless made clear to the GAERC that the principle of differentiation was a crucial element of the new policy and would have to be applied rigorously. Solana signalled that different countries would have to be treated differently as circumstances warranted – e.g. Ukraine needed a boost along its way towards democracy and market economy, Moldova needed help to resolve its Transnistria conflict – and the Barcelona Process upgraded economic and political relations with the EU (*European Report*, 16 April 2003). This meant that although there was one policy, with one final objective (cooperation), prioritisation of one country over another according to member states' wishes would still be possible. The principle of differentiation therefore became the flag around which the member states could rally. Moreover, there was relief that each individual neighbouring country would be able to move as fast or as slow as it saw fit, and that future upgrading of relations with countries proving determined to reform would be judged on an individual basis.

Second, the proposal in the Commission's Communication to offer to third neighbouring countries a gradually eased regime of freedom of movement of persons would be highly controversial for a number of member states. The granting of a more liberal EU visa regime allowing for tourism and facilitating temporary labour permits has long been demanded by some EU neighbours such as the Southern Mediterranean countries (Johansson-Nogués 2004: 246). However, the majority of EU member states are currently reluctant to grant such concessions, fearing negative reactions by their electorates. The Portuguese government, for instance, presented at the 16 April GAERC a note of caution *à propos* the ENP stating that the EU must proceed 'extraordinarily carefully' in regards to this matter (*European Report*, 16 April 2003).

In a follow-up press conference, Verheugen defended the inclusion of freer movement of persons in the Communication, explaining that, although he was aware of the concerns of some member states, the measure was conceived for the long term (*European Report*, 16 April 2003). Verheugen added that the EU would need to find a balance between internal security concerns (immigration) and reaching out to neighbouring countries, extending to them credible and real concessions which could act as true carrots for reform. The matter has since been toned down. The final 16 June GAERC conclusion omitted any reference to the free movement of persons from third countries, and the current formula simply speaks of an enhanced cooperation with partner countries 'on matters related to legal migration' (Council of the European Union 2003a: vi).

Finally, reactions from third countries to the Commission's Communication were also forthcoming. For some of them the document reaffirmed the lack of potential for accession, at least in the short to medium term. This announcement would generate renewed outcries from Ukraine and Moldova, the two Western NIS that have, off and on, expressed their interest in joining the EU. Kiev had already voiced its complaints when the new neighbourhood initiative was first mooted in 2002. For Kuchma's Ukraine, wanting to keep the European door open as an ace up his sleeve in relations with Moscow (Wolczuk 2004), the Communication's verdict represented a considerable diplomatic setback.

However, the very language of the 11 March Communication on the topic of further enlargement reflects the extreme reluctance felt by many member states – and even within the EU Commission itself – of extending any further EU membership invitations. The large and taxing Eastern enlargement was in early 2003 yet to be completed, i.e. the accession agreements had still not been signed. Moreover, Bulgaria and Romania had been left for a later round, predicted for 2007–8, and after them the Western Balkan countries and Turkey are apparently next in line. This already extensive invitation list of prospective members made several European leaders uneasy about further countries joining the Union. Indeed, tempers had already been running high late in 2002, with a hotly disputed debate in the European Convention and off-the-cuff comments by its delegates and other European personalities speaking out in favour of or against further EU enlargement (*El País*, 4 March, 2003).

As the ENP took more concrete shape upon the publication of the Commission's 11 March Communication, it came time to formally present the new neighbourhood policy to the countries contemplated in it. For this reason, the Greek EU Presidency hosted, first, a special enlarged European Conference in Athens on 17 April 2003, attended by Moldova and Ukraine, and about a month later, the Southern Mediterranean partners were briefed on the ENP at a regular Euro-Mediterranean minister meeting. Ana Palacio, then Spanish Foreign Minister, had earlier during the spring requested the Union to consider a joint 'neighbourhood conference', basically demanding that the Mediterranean partners should also attend the European Conference in Athens. This proposal had, however, encountered resistance from some northern EU members, Luxembourg prime among them (*European Report*, 16 April 2003). The reasons behind the Principality's reluctance are unclear, but one might assume that they are related to some (southern and northern) member states' reluctance to blur the distinctions between continental 'Europe' and non-European Mediterranean countries. Symbolically the European Conference, launched as an institutional forum for EU pre-accession states in 1997, also has such close associations with EU membership that one might infer that inviting the Union's Southern Mediterranean partners would have given rise to yet further speculations on where the borders of Europe effectively lie.

The two presentations of the new neighbourhood policy cleared the way for the official launch of the policy at the Thessalonica European Council in June 2003. As expected the heads of state warmly endorsed the findings of the preceding GAERC, stating that the Wider Europe initiative provides a 'good basis for developing a new range of policies towards Ukraine, Moldova, Belarus, Algeria, Egypt, Israel, Jordan, Lebanon, Libya, Morocco, Palestinian Authority, Syria, Tunisia' and serves to 'reinforce the EU-Russia strategic partnership' (Council of the European Union 2003a: vi).

From 'Wider Europe' to a 'European Neighbourhood Policy'

The Thessalonica European Council thus opened the door for the Commission to take over the more technical set-up of the policy and begin preparing its eventual implementation. In the hands of the Commission, the policy would, in late 2003, see a quiet transition away from its initial name 'Wider Europe – New Neighbourhood' to its present denomination of 'European Neighbourhood Policy'. The change purportedly came about as a reaction to the negative imagery associated with the former term (Interviews, Commission, 4 July 2005). It can be inferred that both for institutional and historical reasons the term 'Wider Europe' was increasingly deemed politically incorrect. Wider Europe – originally devised to denote the Union's Eastern European neighbours – had with the expansion of the scope come to include a set of non-European countries in the southern and eastern Mediterranean. The term became suspect, suggesting that the very label 'Wider Europe' might imply a new conceptualisation of what 'Europe' meant and perhaps entail a subtle relaxation of EU membership requirements.[2] In fact, the 'Wider Europe' seemed to confer a certain belonging to the European continent, even to countries properly not European in the geographical sense.

For those EU member states most enlargement-averse, 'Wider Europe' seemed to give too much leeway concerning new EU bids (e.g. Morocco, Israel) and compromise the Union constitutionally with respect to Article 49 (*International Herald Tribune*, 27 June 2003; *El País*, 13 May 2004).[3]

Historically, the term Wider Europe was in hindsight deemed objectionable as well, given the connotations that such an expression carries with it, especially for a set of countries which still have not forgotten their colonial subjugation. The name of the new policy, thus, in countries like Algeria or Tunisia, revived fears of new forms of post-imperial colonialism. Such allegations might seem preposterous to most students of the contemporary European Union; however, it should also be noted that a return to imperialism (albeit in a benign form) is precisely the recipe Robert Cooper, a then close aide to the Blair government, has advocated the EU should apply in an influential article published in a British daily (Cooper 2002). These reactions against the name of the new neighbourhood policy produced an impetus within European institutions to look for a more neutral name: European Neighbourhood Policy.

At the same time as the budding neighbourhood policy was beginning to take more concrete shape, new developments beyond the EU's borders in different ways came to impinge on the policy. First, the 'Rose Revolution' in Georgia in late 2003, which ushered in Mikhail Saakashvili as the temporary leader and in early 2004 confirmed him as elected president, meant that the pressure on the EU to re-evaluate its relations with the three small Southern Caucasian countries would be stepped up. Different international and European observers suggested the EU take a lead in providing support for the 'born-again' democracy. Their pleas were echoed by the European Parliament, a longstanding supporter of greater EU involvement in the Caucasus (see e.g. European Parliament 2003). The EU foreign ministers in January 2004 responded by tasking the Commission and Solana with examining how the three Southern Caucasus countries could be included in the ENP. A recommendation was inserted in the ENP Strategy Paper presented by the Commission on 12 May 2004, but a final decision was not forthcoming until the GAERC held in Luxembourg on 14 June 2004 (Council of the European Union 2004).

The decision to include this trio of countries in the ENP marked a decisive highpoint thus far in the EU's relations with Armenia, Azerbaijan and Georgia (cf. Chapter 4). Although there had been several attempts over the years by different member states to create a closer policy with these three Caucasus republics, the proposals had been met by relative indifference by most member states (*RFE/RL*, 30 January 2004). The Caucasus was considered too unstable, too far away from the EU-15 territory and too closely bound into Russia's concept of its 'near abroad' to have a real bearing on EU interest. However, as the BTC oil pipeline (Baku-Tbilisi-Ceyhan) – stretching from Azerbaijan to the Turkish post of Ceyhan, passing through Georgia –

was nearing completion (finally inaugurated in May 2005), the Southern Caucasus took on a new relevance for the European Union. Moreover, the Union will eventually, once Bulgaria and Romania join the EU, share the Black Sea seaboard with Georgia (and by extension with the rest of the restive Southern Caucasus). The logical conclusion of such a shared Black Sea border thus inevitably begged the establishment of a more ambitious EU framework for relations with these countries.

Apart from the proposal to include the Southern Caucasus trio, the Commission's 2004 ENP Strategy Paper also contained a surprise. Presented only days ahead of the first summit between Russia and the enlarged EU, the Strategy Paper proposed a clearly differentiated status for Russia compared to the rest of the EU's neighbours. Russia, which had been included in the ENP by Romano Prodi's 'ring of friends' speech in 2002, had from the start been visibly reluctant to become part of this initiative. The 2004 ENP Strategy Paper clearly bowing to Russian preferences instead awards Russia a special standing in which the EU and Russia – as agreed at the St Petersburg Summit in May 2003 – would explore a distinct joint scheme, the so-called 'Four Common Spaces' (Council of the European Union 2004).

The decision must been seen in light of years of recurrent indecision within the EU on how to best deal with the Russian Federation. Russia, for its size, historical greatness and energy supplies distinguishes itself clearly from smaller EU neighbours (see Chapter 8). Different formulas have been discussed over the past decade, some of them proposed by Moscow, in a view to angle for 'a special relationship with the union – like the one it already has with NATO' (*The Guardian,* 18 April 2003). While most member states were against what would have entailed a 'Council plus', or a 'COREPER plus' formula, and a too close involvement of Moscow in internal EU affairs, they are also well aware of Russia's importance as an energy supplier and export market.

The special treatment of Russia in relation to the new neighbourhood policy would become yet another diplomatic 'bucket of cold water' for Ukraine in relation to the ENP. Much larger than the other two Western NIS (Belarus and Moldova) and many Southern Mediterranean countries, and strategically placed for energy transits, Ukraine always sought a special status with the Union and, if possible, at par with Russia. The Commission's ENP Strategy Paper and the 14 June GAERC clearly break with the EU logic employed hitherto, inherent both in the 1998 PCAs (virtually identical) and the gesture to adopt the two Common Strategies on Russia and Ukraine in 1999. This relative parity seemed to reward Ukraine with just such a privileged status alongside Russia (Kuzio, 2003: 17). However, the new neighbourhood policy deflated that vision in Kiev, leaving Ukrainian diplomats complaining bitterly about their country being placed in the same category as chaotic, impoverished Moldova and Belarus, and, what is worse in the eyes of the Ukrainian governmental elite, in the same category as the non-

EU eligible Southern Mediterranean countries. EU–Ukrainian relations seemed perceptibly downgraded several notches.

The sensitivity in Kiev of being assigned a second-rate ranking has not dissipated even after the 2004 'Orange Revolution'. If the new Ukrainian government under Viktor Yuschenko had expected the pro-democratic groundswell bringing him to power to produce a quick volte-face by the Union in terms of extending a possible membership perspective to his country, he was to be disappointed. Addressing the European Parliament on 23 February, Yuschenko argued in favour of an enhanced relation with the Union and reiterated Kiev's long-standing ambitions of EU accession maintaining that '[t]he format of our ties should proceed from the recognition of Ukraine as an inalienable part of united Europe' (RFE/RL, 24 February 2005). However, the Union has so far insisted on dissuading Yuschenko and other neighbouring governments from lodging membership applications. Brussels insists that the ENP remains for the time being the only road open for closer EU–Ukraine relations. In an attempt to show support for the new regime, however, the Union has refurbished the ENP Action Plan, originally negotiated with the outgoing Kuchma government. The revamped EU–Ukrainian Action Plan now additionally contemplates a set of measures to improve trade relations, provide more aid, and possibly ease the current visa regime.

The EU's dealings with Yuschenko's Ukraine can be interpreted as marking the passage of maturity of the ENP. The member states' desire to promote the ENP as the principal framework for proceeding with EU–Ukrainian relations is obviously a disappointment for Kiev's 'European aspirations'. Nevertheless, one could infer that this reconfirms the ENP as an important policy conduit in the Union's dealings with its neighbours. The very fact that alternative sources of policy are not sought, neither existing with a view to strengthen them (e.g. Common Strategy) nor through tabling new, special schemes just for Ukraine (e.g. membership perspectives), demonstrates that the EU institutions and member states believe that the ENP, as it develops further, will be the main neighbourhood instrument for the European Union, at least in the short to medium term. This passage to maturity was captured well by Commissioner Benita Ferrero-Waldner when she proclaimed 2005 as the year of 'delivery of the ENP' as the first Action Plans entered into their implementation phase.

Switching the ENP into first gear?

The work on the elaboration of the Action Plans[4] had begun shortly after the Thessalonica European Council. For the Commission the new policy would mean a daunting and complex task, spanning the institutional expertise of many different Directorates General (DGs) and their specialised departments. As a consequence, Thessalonica would give way to a specialised 'Wider

Europe Task Force' set up in the seat of the Commission, drawing together officials predominantly from DG Enlargement and DG External Relations.[5] One of the first jobs of the new Task Force became drafting partner-specific Action Plans for Moldova, Ukraine and five Mediterranean partners (Israel, Jordan, Morocco, the Palestinian Authority and Tunisia). In the drafting process the Task Force would initially employ the same methodology as in the Eastern enlargement process, i.e. once a template was sketched out, each partner country was contacted directly to solicit feedback.

This method would in the case of the ENP, however, get the Commission into trouble. Testimony to how new and ambitious the ENP was compared to previous framework policies was the fact that the policy combined Commission–Council competencies in such a fluid way as to blur clear distinction. The Action Plans were drafted by the Task Force to group issue areas under six major headings: political dialogue and cooperation; economic and social cooperation and development; trade related issues, market and regulatory reform; cooperation in justice and home affairs; transport, energy, information society, environment and science and technology; and finally, social policy and people-to-people contacts. The Action Plans envision, in other words, cooperation both in the economic as well as in the political and security field (CFSP, ESDP and JHA). What would unnerve the Council in the early months of 2004 was that the Commission in its ongoing consultations with the ENP partners had seemingly made itself the Union's interlocutor not only for first pillar, but also for second pillar matters. This caused a momentary turf-battle over competency and delayed the Council's official approval of the first round of seven Action Plans until December 2004 (Interview, Commission, 4 July 2005).

With the Council's blessing finally extended, the Action Plans were remitted for their final adoption in the respective bilateral EU–partner Association or Cooperation Councils. All seven Action Plans in the first round were adopted during the first semester of 2005, automatically giving way to the implementation process. In accordance with the principle of 'joint ownership' espoused by the ENP, sub-committees within each Council have since been set up to promote and monitor the execution of the Action Plan. Revisions, if needed, will be undertaken within a period of two years of the Plan's original adoption.

As for the remaining eligible ENP partners, the 2590th GAERC on 14 June 2004 invited the Commission to begin initial explorations with Egypt, Lebanon and the Southern Caucasus with a view to draft ENP Action Plans (Council of the European Union 2004). The Action Plans with Armenia, Azerbaijan and Georgia were subsequently adopted in late 2006, and those with Egypt and Lebanon in early 2007.

Apart from elaborating Action Plans, the Wider Europe Task Force had to create a new financial instrument for the ENP. Germany initially questioned the need for another financial mechanism given the existence of the MEDA, PHARE and TACIS assistance (*European Report*, 16 April 2003). However, Berlin eventually gave in when it was reassured that the new mechanism would not translate into a Commission budget increase, at least not in the short term. Hence, on 1 July 2003 the Commission proposal was revealed. The new financial instrument cleverly evolves in two distinct stages. In the first stage (2004–2006), the so-called 'European Neighbourhood Programme', targeting primarily cross-border cooperation, disposed of an estimated €955 million drawn together from unutilised resources of the INTERREG, MEDA, PHARE-CBC, TACIS-CBC and CARDS programmes. In the second stage a 'European Neighbourhood and Partnership Instrument' has been created and bestowed a proper budget line of its own. As a consequence MEDA, PHARE and TACIS as distinct financial assistance programmes will disappear in 2007, by which time the 2007–2013 financial perspective is scheduled to enter into force. It has been argued that this arrangement will better homogenise resources spent in the east and the south of the Union's borders, and potentially increase transparency and control over how the Commission's budget is spent. Moreover, the existence of a single financial instrument might help to boost cohesion and consistency in the EU's external relations and over time come to counteract the previously noted parochial, 'knee-jerk' competition among different member states to maximise financial assignments to the different rim areas of the European Union.

Prospects, by way of conclusions

The Thessalonica decision by the EU to launch new relations with its immediate geographic neighbours suggests that, after years of inaction and hesitancy, the EU has become convinced that it needs to play a larger role to secure peace and prosperity on the European continent. Indeed, one might argue that with the ENP the EU seeks to establish a form of external governance to make the vast hinterland beyond its borders more manageable. However, the consolidation and success of the ENP will depend on a host of factors that will be explored in greater detail in the subsequent chapters of this volume.

As we have seen, one of the most prominent features of the neighbourhood policy is the plural manner in which it was conceived. The fact that the ENP has evolved in a fashion which has allowed extensive input from member states and European institutions from the very start of the policy formation process is perhaps one of the strongest points speaking in favour of ensuring that the ENP will have a longer half-life than some of the Common Strategies. The openness of the formative stage of the policy process has allowed EU member states and institutions to introduce matters close to their interests (e.g. special bilateral relations, visas, EU membership, etc.), thus ensuring that the ENP today appears to enjoy a broad policy backing within the EU. However, one should also note that the very plural character and all-encompassing scope of the ENP could turn into its Achilles' heel over time. The ambiguous or hybrid nature of the ENP, as a catch-all policy, makes it difficult to establish any sure and fast markers on which to determine the success of the policy. Can the policy be judged a success if it manages to transform one country (e.g. Ukraine) but not the rest? Will it be seen as successful if it promotes market reform in a couple of ENP partners, while making no progress in terms of human rights or reducing cross-border trafficking of humans and illicit goods? Since political interest is fickle, the current momentum behind the ENP can only be sustained if the main policy stakeholders see their interests satisfied. This will be one of the greater challenges for the ENP in the years to come.

Moreover, the policy gestation process for the ENP has been unusually long, especially in comparison to other EU framework policies. However, although the ENP is now well into its implementation phase, it would be premature to proclaim that all the major controversies surrounding the policy have been resolved. Apart from the conclusion of the next round of Action Plans, the next important step will be to see how the 2007–2013 foreign affairs budget will finally be distributed in relation to specific issue areas. The proposals from the Commission to augment the external action budget line in the coming financial perspective did not fly with the December 2005 European Council (Council of the European Union 2005). The Commission's original suggestion had allocated the ENPI €14.9bn, but the outcome of the 2005 financial battle within the Union was to cut that number down by a fifth, endowing the ENPI for 2007–2013 with the more modest sum of approximately €12bn. The credibility of any policy resides to a great extent in matching objectives with resources, and hence the great unknown regarding the ENP's future and the EU's ambition to better manage its neighbourhood, is whether the newly assigned financial means will be sufficient to make the policy a success.

Notes

1   The author wishes to acknowledge the useful help and input on this chapter by the three editors of the volume, as well as Esther Barbé, Dag Hartelius, and numerous officials in Brussels who were very forthcoming in their answers. Any remaining errors are the sole responsibility of the author. The author also wants to acknowledge the financial support by CHALLENGE – The Changing Landscape of European Liberty & Security European project.
2   Article 49 (TEU) holds that any *European* state may apply to become a member of the European Union, provided that it complies with the objective membership criteria.
3   It is also worth noting that the term 'Wider Europe' never translated well into the non-English communitarian official languages (Interview, Commission, 4 July 2005).
4   An Action Plan is essentially a non-binding political statement of intent committing the two partners to cooperation in a determined timeframe.
5   The Task Force has since been dissolved. The ENP is currently coordinated by External Relations' Directorate D.

PART II

The European Neighbourhood Policy in action

3

Shared values: democracy and human rights

In the Commission's ENP Strategy Paper (European Commission 2004a), 'democracy and good governance' and 'the promotion of human rights' appear in two ways. First, together with stability, they are two of the overarching goals of the entire policy and a condition for cooperation in other areas. Second, they are two specific issue-areas of cooperation alongside others. Since a stringent political conditionality might prevent functional cooperation in other issue-areas, or the quest for efficient cooperation in those other issue-areas might compromise political conditionality, there is a potential source of goal conflict and inconsistency within the ENP. Does the EU generally privilege its value commitments in its external relations, and does it treat all partner countries according to the same standards? The most relevant question, however, is that of effectiveness. Can we expect the ENP to have a positive impact on democracy and human rights in the partner countries? This chapter will address both questions.

The inclusion of democracy and human rights is neither new nor specific to the ENP. As human rights have become 'settled norms' of contemporary international society over the past decades (Frost 1996: 104–11), political conditionality has become a general feature of EU external relations in the course of the 1990s and all ENP participants have been subject to political conditionality in one form or another in their previous institutional arrangements with the EU (Riedel and Will 1999; K.E. Smith 2001). Thus, endogenous institutional and identity-based factors primarily account for the origins of this policy domain in the ENP. They are no guarantee of effective impact, however.

Research on the use and effectiveness of political conditionality in the accession process strongly suggests that a credible membership perspective has been a necessary condition for an effective EU impact on domestic change. It has not been sufficient, however. Even when a membership perspective was credible, high domestic political power costs of adaptation to

EU conditions have blocked compliance. Since most ENP participants are without a membership perspective and generally governed by authoritarian regimes for whom the political power costs of complying with democratic and human rights rules are high, these findings strongly suggest that the ENP will not have a significant impact on democracy and human rights in the ENP participants.

To address the questions about goal conflict, consistency, and effectiveness empirically, this chapter will draw on general human rights data as well as an illustrative case study, the trafficking of women and children for sexual exploitation. Since policy instruments similar to the ENP, such as Partnership and Cooperation Agreements (PCAs), have been in place for at least ten years in EU relations with Eastern Europe and the Mediterranean, data such as the Freedom House ratings as well as the Trafficking in Persons Report (TIP) published annually by the US State Department give us a rather good general picture regarding the correlation between EU political conditionality and democratic or human rights improvements in the ENP participants.

The analysis shows that EU political conditionality vis-à-vis the ENP participants has been neither consistent nor effective in the past. Indeed, in light of the inconsistent enforcement of human rights conditionality clauses that reflects institutional constraints and conflicting national interests, some authors even speak of a 'credibility crisis' of the EU regarding human rights (Clapham 1999: 630). The lack of consistency suggests that political conditionality has indeed suffered from conflicting functional goals of improving and institutionalising relations with the neighbouring countries. The lack of effectiveness confirms the relevance of the incentive and cost factors identified in previous studies. As long as membership incentives are absent and the ENP participants are governed by authoritarian regimes, there is no reason to expect that the ENP will have a more positive impact on democracy and human rights in the partner countries in the future.

Democracy, good governance and human rights in the ENP

With regard to the issues of democracy and good governance, the ENP does not constitute a break with previous EU policies toward non-member countries (Alston 1999; Fierro 2002). First, the ENP is based on the EU's commitment to promoting core liberal values and norms beyond its borders, albeit with greater support for democracy and good governance than for human rights. Second, the EU uses political conditionality as the main instrument of norm promotion. Finally, direct democracy assistance complements political conditionality as a secondary instrument, with diplomatic tools, such as declarations and demarches, mostly used to express discontent with human rights violations (K. E. Smith 2001).

In its ENP Strategy Paper, the Commission invokes the EU's general value commitments: 'The Union is founded on the values of respect for human dignity, liberty, democracy, equality, the rule of law and respect for human rights. These values are common to the Member States ... In its relations with the wider world, [the Union] aims at upholding and promoting these values.' In addition, the Commission calls attention to the fact that 'the Union's neighbours have pledged adherence to fundamental human rights and freedoms, through their adherence to a number of multilateral treaties as well as through their bilateral agreements with the EU'. These mutual commitments form the basis for the dual role of democracy and human rights in the ENP, first, as a pre-condition for participation in the ENP and, second, as an objective of ENP actions (European Commission 2004a).

On the one hand, the ENP offers a 'privileged partnership with neighbours', which 'will build on mutual commitment to common values principally within the fields of the rule of law, good governance, the respect for human rights, including minority rights, the promotion of good neighbourly relations, and the principles of market economy and sustainable development'. Under the ENP umbrella, the EU draws up and negotiates Action Plans for each partner country. Given the various regional contexts and the highly different political and economic situations of the partner countries, the EU's and the partners' priorities and interests will vary strongly, and so will the content and the objectives of the individual Action Plans. In addition, however, the Strategy Paper stipulates that differentiation should 'be based on a clear commitment to shared values' and that the 'level of ambition of the EU's relationships with its neighbours will take into account the extent to which these values are effectively shared'. What is more, the Strategy Paper outlines a clear political conditionality for the participation in the ENP of neighbouring countries that are not yet considered worthy. With regard to Belarus, for instance, it promises to 'reinforce its lasting commitments to supporting democratic development ... When fundamental political and economic reforms take place, it will be possible for Belarus to make full use of the ENP.'

On the other hand, the Strategy Paper outlines 'a number of priorities' for the individual Action Plans 'intended to strengthen commitment to these values. These include strengthening democracy and the rule of law, the reform of the judiciary and the fight against corruption and organised crime; respect of human rights and fundamental freedoms, trade union rights and other core labour standards, and the fight against the practice of torture and prevention of ill-treatment; support for the development of civil society; and co-operation with the Criminal Court.' Finally, the Commission hopes to promote its fundamental values and norms as a result of 'deeper engagement' in a great variety of issue areas and activities (European Commission 2004a). Thus, the ENP contains all the elements of previous EU policies toward non-members.

Since the end of the Cold War, the EU (then EC) has made assistance and institutional ties conditional on the fulfilment of democratic and human rights standards. Whereas democracy and human rights have become most prominent as the *sine qua non* conditions of accession to the EU in the Copenhagen Criteria of 1993, they have also featured regularly as preconditions for negotiating lower-level agreements like the PCAs with the successor countries of the Soviet Union. In addition, the EU added a clause to each cooperation agreement, the so-called 'basic clause', later replaced by the 'essential elements' clause, which stipulated a suspension of the agreement if partner countries fail to comply with these principles.[1]

In their Barcelona Declaration, the EU and its Mediterranean Partners also declared an intention to 'develop the rule of law and democracy in their political systems' and to 'respect human rights and fundamental freedoms and guarantee the effective legitimate exercise of such rights and freedoms'.[2] Further, 'Respect for human rights and democratic principles are an essential element of the Euro-Mediterranean Association Agreements and the architecture of each Agreement is such as to enable it to be suspended in the event of major human rights violations.'[3]

Thus it may be argued that endogenous institutional and identity-based factors primarily account for the origins of this policy domain in the ENP. First, the affirmation of democracy and human rights as essential components of the ENP and the political conditionality of the ENP follow from the EU's identity as an international community of liberal democratic states. It is most clearly stated in Article 6 of the Treaty on European Union: 'The Union is founded on the principles of liberty, democracy, respect for human rights and fundamental freedoms, and the rule of law, principles which are common to the Member States.'

Second, Judith Kelley (2006) points to institutional factors that explain the high degree of policy continuity. Many of the Commission officials responsible for designing and implementing the ENP have previously worked on enlargement and relations with the CEECs. What is more, the Commission appears to regard the ENP as an opportunity to maintain and expand those foreign policy competencies that it gained and used in the course of Eastern enlargement.

ENP action plans and the promotion of democracy and human rights

Does the ENP add anything new to the 'acquis' of democracy and human rights promotion? Where the Strategy Paper speaks of the ENP's 'added value, going beyond existing cooperation', it does not define new objectives or institutions but rather stresses an increase in focus, intensity, and funding of cooperation, thus providing higher incentives to realise the 'full potential' of existing agreements (European Commission 2004a: 7–9).

A look at the existing Action Plans shows that they are much more detailed, concrete and specific with regard to democracy and human rights promotion than any previous documents. For instance, whereas the Association Agreement with Morocco only contained the general democracy and human rights clause (Article 2) and did not even mention these issues in the Political Dialogue section, the Action Plan enumerates 30 objectives to be achieved in the short and the medium term.[4]

All ENP Action Plans make explicit references, ranging from quite specific to more general, to the need to strengthen democracy, the rule of law and human rights.[5] Demands vary from unequivocal prescriptions for the protection of quite specific rights – for example, freedom of the media and expression, national minority rights, prohibition of torture, gender equality, children's rights, and international justice for Ukraine (European Commission 2004c: 5–6) and religious freedom, gender equality and stepping up the fight against transnational organised crime, including trafficking in human beings, for Moldova (European Commission 2004b: 3) – to more general calls for enhancing the status of women and freedom of expression for Jordan (European Commission 2004d: 3–4) and the 'promot[ion] and protect[ion of] rights of minorities' and the 'promot[ion] [of] evaluation and monitoring of policies from the perspective of gender equality' for Israel (European Commission 2004e: 4). Furthermore, all Action Plans stress that governmental policies must be brought into compliance with international and European standards, and promote adherence to and ensure implementation of core UN and Council of Europe Conventions.

The detail and specificity of the ENP Action Plans certainly constitutes a step forward and a value added in the cooperation between the EU and the ENP participants. It provides the promotion of human rights and democracy with more focus and establishes a basis for more concrete EU monitoring of progress and compliance. It cannot be taken for granted, however, that these objectives can be implemented effectively. First, since a stringent political conditionality might prevent useful functional cooperation in other issue-areas, or the quest for efficient cooperation in those other issue-areas might compromise political conditionality, there is a potential source of goal conflict and inconsistency within the ENP, and it is an open question whether such a conflict will be generally resolved in favour of the EU's value commitments. It is a second open question under which conditions even a consistent strategy of democracy promotion by political conditionality will be effective.

Theoretical expectations

Whereas it is too early to study any impact of the ENP on respect for democracy and human rights in the target countries, there is something to be learned from the analysis of EU political conditionality in the candidate countries for EU membership and from the past record of EU relations with today's ENP participants.

Studies on the impact of political conditionality in the Central and Eastern European candidate countries for EU membership come to broadly similar conclusions:[6] credible EU membership incentives and low domestic adaptation costs have been individually necessary and jointly sufficient conditions of compliance. First of all, EU demands for compliance with human rights and democratic rules have generally not been effective in the candidate countries unless the EU provided a credible membership promise and presented compliance as an explicit condition of accession (or the beginning of accession negotiations).

However, even when accession conditionality was credible, it did not automatically result in candidate compliance. The liberal democratic norms, which are the subject of political conditionality, usually limit the autonomy and power of governments. They prohibit certain undemocratic and illiberal practices on which a government may rely to preserve its power – such as suppressing opposition parties or civic associations, curbing the freedom of the press, or rigging elections. Moreover, they may change power relations between governmental actors – such as increasing the independence of courts or limiting the political influence of the military. Finally, above all in the case of minority rights, they affect the composition of the citizenship and empower certain social and ethnic groups. This may erode the social power base of governments and, in their opinion, threaten the security, integrity, and identity of the state. Whenever compliance with EU conditions would lead to *de facto* regime change and risk the incumbent government's loss of power, target governments failed to comply. They have valued the preservation of their political power higher than EU membership.

What follows from these findings for EU relations with non-candidate neighbouring countries? In general, both the necessary and jointly sufficient conditions of effective EU impact are absent. First, the absence of a membership perspective strongly reduces the external incentives of compliance. Second, most of the non-candidate neighbouring countries are authoritarian or autocratic states. Only domestic uprisings such as the ones in Serbia (2000), Georgia (2003), and Ukraine (2004) provided, in principle, new access points for the democracy-consolidating effects of EU political conditionality. If, however, the EU does not offer a credible membership perspective, it is unlikely to make use of this potential, and if it does, it will need to move beyond the ENP framework. Thus, the – rather overdetermined – expectation is that EU political conditionality in the context of the ENP will not be effective.

Will EU political conditionality in the ENP participants be consistent at least? Again, previous findings and theoretical considerations point toward negative expectations. First, studies of EU democracy and human rights promotion beyond candidates for membership generally come to the conclusion that EU policy has been inconsistent, fragmented and often undermined by strategic or economic goals (Riedel and Will 1999: 742; K.E. Smith 2001; Youngs 2001: 90–1).

Second, it can be assumed theoretically that identity-based values and norms become the more politically relevant in relations with external countries the closer these countries move toward membership. Membership of the EU is a constitutive or constitutional issue and, as such, more likely to be affected by questions of identity and fundamental values than issues of functional cooperation, regulation and distribution (Schimmelfennig 2003a). Conversely, in its relations with countries that are not considered potential future members, the EU is less normatively constrained and can treat democracy and human rights more expediently. As a result, consistency will be low.

EU association and human rights in the ENP participants

How consistent and effective have EU political conditionality and institutional association been in the past with regard to the ENP target countries? To address this question, we use the Freedom Index (FI), the summary rating provided annually by Freedom House for civil liberties and political rights.[7] Table 3.1 presents the relevant data for the ENP participants.

To assess the conditions and effects of EU association, we begin the analysis with the starting dates of negotiations for the PCAs and the Barcelona Process (column 2). For the Eastern European countries, PCAs have been the highest form of contractual relations with the EU, and the first negotiations began at the end of 1992 (with Russia). In the Mediterranean region, the Euro-Mediterranean Conference in Barcelona in November 1995 marked the starting point for the negotiation of Euro-Mediterranean Association Agreements (EMAA), the rough equivalent to the PCA in the East. The Freedom Index for 1992 and 1995 respectively (FI1) serves as a baseline for evaluating the effects of association on democratisation in the ENP participants.

Column 3 lists the years in which the EU signed a PCA or EMAA with the ENP country; column 4 reports the Freedom Index for this year (FI2). D1 in column 5 calculates the difference in FI ratings between FI1 and FI2. It is a measure of the improvement (positive values) or deterioration (negative values) that has occurred between the start of the association process and the signing of the agreements. Columns 6 to 8 do the same for the period between the signing of the agreements and their entry into force.

Column 9 presents the Freedom House data for 2004. They serve to calculate the difference (D3) in column 10 between the current state of political rights and civil liberties (FI4) and the state of liberal democracy when the agreements went into force (FI3) and thus to measure the effect of EU agreements after conditionality ceased to play a role. Finally, column 11 lists the

Table 3.1   Democratic developments in ENP participants

	FI1 1992/95	Agreement signed	FI2	D1 (FI1–FI2)	Agreement in force	FI3	D2 (FI2–FI3)	FI4 2004	D3 (FI3–FI4)	D (FI1–FI4)
Belarus	3.5	1995	5	−1.5				6		−2.5
Moldova	5	1994	4	1	1998	3	1	3.5	−0.5	1.5
Ukraine	3	1994	3.5	−0.5	1998	3.5	0	3.5	0	−0.5
Armenia	3.5	1996	4.5	−1	1999	4	0.5	4.5	−0.5	−1
Azerbaijan	5	1996	5.5	−0.5	1999	5	0.5	5.5	−0.5	−0.5
Georgia	4.5	1996	4	0.5	1999	3.5	0.5	4	−0.5	0.5
Algeria	6	2002	5.5	0.5				5.5		0.5
Egypt	6	2001	6	0	2004	5.5	0.5	5.5	0	0.5
Israel	2	1995	2	0	2000	2	0	2	0	0
Jordan	4	1997	4	0	2002	5.5	−1.5	4.5	1	−0.5
Lebanon	5.5	2002	5.5	0	2003	5.5	0	5.5	0	0
Libya	7							7		0
Morocco	5	1996	5	0	2000	5	0	4.5	0.5	0.5
PA[a]		1997			1997			5.5		
Syria	7	2004	7	0				7		0
Tunisia	5.5	1995	5.5	0	1998	5.5	0	5.5	0	0
Average	4.83		4.79	−0.11			4.36	0.14	4.97 (4.5)−0.05		−0.1
Std. Dev.	1.44		1.24				1.23		1.27		

[a] Note that Freedom House data are not readily available for the Palestinian Authority (PA), which is not a sovereign state. Thus the table only includes ratings for the PA for 2004.

difference in FI ratings for the entire period from the start of the PCA and Barcelona processes until 2004.

What inferences can we draw from these data? First, the starting points for the ENP participants have been very different. With a rating of 2, Israel is the positive outlier; Libya and Syria are the negative extremes with ratings of 7. The average ENP country had a rating of 4.83 at the beginning of the process, representing the lower end of the 'partly free' category. Briefly put, democracy was generally weak to absent in the ENP participants; there was vast room for improvement triggered by EU association policies.

If EU political conditionality were consistent and effective, we would see both less varying and lower FI ratings for those countries that signed PCAs and EMAAs. However, the average FI2 ratings are only slightly better than the average FI1 ratings (4.79 as compared to 4.83). The changes in ratings (D1) show that most of the states that signed an agreement with the EU experienced no change at all between the start of the association process and the signing of the agreement. The situation improved in three countries but it actually worsened in four of them. On average, the change is slightly negative (−0.11). The standard deviation improved (from 1.44 to 1.24) but, just as at the beginning of the process, FI ratings varied between 2 and 7 for the ENP participants that signed an agreement. That is, with the exception of Libya, the EU did not implement any noticeable and consistent political condition-ality ahead of signing agreements with its neighbouring non-candidate countries. The only discernible pattern appears to be that the most autocratic systems tend to sign association agreements later (Syria in 2004, Algeria and Lebanon in 2002, and Egypt in 2001 – but see Tunisia 1995). What is more, the first stage of the association process has had no positive impact on the overall human rights and democracy situation in these countries.

The second phase to be analysed lasts from the signing of agreements to their entry into force. Due to the fact that agreements for some of the most autocratic states have not (yet) entered into force (Belarus, Algeria, Syria), the average FI rating improves to 4.36 and the worst rating in the group changes from 7 to 5.5. Thus, we see a small effect of a slightly more discriminatory conditionality policy of the EU. We also see a small positive effect on the political situation in those countries whose agreements with the EU have entered into force. Five countries experienced an improvement in FI ratings between signing and entry into force and only one country (Jordan) suffered from a deterioration of the rating resulting in a small average improvement of 0.14. However, these are only interim results that should not be overinter-preted. If the EMAAs with Algeria and Syria enter into force in the absence of a marked improvement of the political situation in these two countries, the minor positive effects will probably disappear altogether.

What is more, the small improvements in those countries with agree-ments in force have not lasted. Four out of 11 associated countries (all in Eastern Europe) experienced a net deterioration of the political situation after the PCAs entered into force. In 2004, the average FI rating for the associated countries (FI4) dropped to 4.5 (from 4.36 upon entry into force). The average change (D3) was slightly negative (–0.05). That is, if there was any improve-ment due to political conditionality between signing and entry into force of the agreements, this improvement was more than compensated by negative developments later.

This finding is confirmed if one looks at the overall effectiveness of the impact of EU policy on the ENP participants in the last decade. The average FI rating for this group of countries in 2004 was 4.97 as compared to 4.83 at the beginning of the association process, and the average change (D) was slightly negative (–0.1) for the entire time period.

A representative case study on a key human rights issue will serve to further support our argument. We chose trafficking of women and children for the purpose of sexual exploitation for three reasons: first, several ENP participants – Ukraine, Moldova, Georgia and Belarus – have among the worst track records in the world as source countries of trafficked women and children. Second, the heinous nature of the crime has put the spotlight of international attention on these countries and raised expectations that, in exchange for closer economic and political cooperation with the EU, they would be willing to aggressively confront trafficking. Third, the EU has shown remarkable commitment to combating sex-trafficking through devoting financial resources and logistical assistance to these countries and explicitly including the need to combat trafficking in individual ENP Action Plans. Therefore, the willingness ENP participants have shown to address sex-trafficking is a good indicator of the effectiveness of EU human rights policy.

Case study: the ENP and the trafficking in women and children for sexual exploitation

Sex-trafficking as a global phenomenon
Each year, an estimated one to two million women and children are lured or coerced into sexual exploitation by human traffickers, almost always members of organised crime cartels, and held in slavery-like conditions (King 2004).[8] According to the Moscow-based anti-trafficking NGO, *Angel Coalition*, Moldova, Ukraine and Russia – the former two being ENP participants – are the main source countries for trafficking into Western Europe – 'approximately 50,000 to 100,000 Moldovans, over 100,000 Ukrainian and 500,000 Russian women are active in prostitution outside their home countries, with as many as eighty percent victims of trafficking'[9] – generating an average of seven billion US dollars per year for organised crime, ranking only behind drugs and arms sales. Reflecting a growing awareness of the enormous social costs of trafficking, the human tragedies behind this phenomenon and the global threat posed by organised crime, the campaign against trafficking in women has gained increasing momentum in the past ten years (Bales 2000; Hughes 2001; Hochschild and Ehrenreich 2004; King 2004). In response, the United Nations, the European Union, the Council of Europe, and the United States have taken a leading role in eliminating sex-trafficking and adopted a significant number of programmes that seek to combat trafficking by simultaneously targeting the perpetrators and aiding the victims of this crime.

The EU strategy to combat sex-trafficking
The European Union has been actively involved in the development and implementation of a comprehensive, multidimensional approach towards the prevention of and fight against trafficking in human beings since the mid-1990s. In light of hundreds of thousands of women smuggled annually into Western Europe for purposes of sexual exploitation, particularly from countries that were positioning themselves for accession at the time, such as Poland, Latvia, the Czech Republic and Hungary as well as countries that now make up the European Neighbourhood, including Belarus, Ukraine, Moldova, and Georgia, the European Union devised its first European Strategy to fight against human trafficking in 1996. This Strategy, which exists in its basic form to this day, utilises a three-prong 'prevent, punish and remedy' approach (European Commission 2001b, 2001c, 2001d).

Specifically, it combines the criminalisation of all aspects of human trafficking through the adoption of anti-trafficking laws on the European and domestic levels ('punish') with the implementation of programmes to prevent women from becoming victims of trafficking (for instance, through information and awareness-raising programmes) to assisting victims both in the source and target countries, through temporary visa and witness protection programs, provision of shelter, medical and psychological services as well as of facilities assisting in the repatriation and reintegration of survivors ('remedy') (European Parliament 1996).

The most effective, and comprehensive, EU anti-sex-trafficking programmes are the initiative and exchange programs, STOP I and STOP II,[10] and the anti-violence initiative (now programme) DAPHNE. STOP I (1997–2001) and STOP II (2001–2006) provide financial and logistic support to individuals and organisations directly involved in the fight against and prevention of trafficking in humans, such as law enforcement personnel, judges, social workers and activists. With a budget of €6.5 million, their multifaceted programmes are designed to establish networks and cooperation between all individuals and groups responsible for anti-trafficking activities. During the nine years of its existence, the more than 120 STOP projects included international conferences against sex-trafficking, pilot studies with Poland and Hungary on the root causes of sex-trafficking, police training seminars, and the creation of a legal network.

DAPHNE, created in 1998, recognises the need for a multidimensional approach and thus focuses on combating violence against women and children and a national legislative review to bring domestic laws in line with EU goals in the struggle against trafficking (European Commission 1999). It is one of the most successful EU-funded social programmes and has provided for €5 million yearly (€50 million for 2004–2008) to support multi-disciplinary, multi-national actions to combat all forms of violence against children and women. Since 1997, DAPHNE has supported almost three hundred individual projects involving six hundred different organisations, including NGOs, research institutions and local authority departments. Projects undertaken range from direct assistance to victims (for example, shelters for abuse victims) and training programmes for different groups, to awareness-raising campaigns and information exchange.[11] The biggest achievement of DAPHNE-supported local NGOs, such as *La Strada* in Poland and the Czech Republic has been their effective lobbying for changes in these countries' criminal codes to criminalise trafficking and for better government support of their activities. Simultaneously, in cooperation with the International Organization for Migration (IOM), the EU Commission has carried out an awareness-raising campaign on sex-trafficking in Ukraine and undertaken feasibility studies for programmes in Belarus and Moldova.

The European Union did not limit itself to programmatic approaches, however. It clearly recognised the need to institutionalise the criminalisation of human trafficking on the level of domestic, EU and international law. It did so in three ways: first, it encouraged member, candidate and PCA states to change their criminal codes to make any aspect of human trafficking a crime and to significantly increase sentences for traffickers. All EU member states have done so, but not all candidate and ENP participants have followed suit. Indeed, the need to adapt domestic laws to conform to international legal principles is explicitly stated in the Action Plan for Moldova and is consistently encouraged in the annual TIP reports by the US State Department for Azerbaijan, Ukraine, Egypt and Lebanon.

Second, the EU made the elimination of sex-trafficking official EU policy and included it in Article VI of the 1999 Treaty of Amsterdam, renewing its commitment at the European Council Summit in Tampere the same year. Additionally, in 2002 the Council of the European Union adopted the Commission's proposal for a *Framework Decision to Combat Trafficking in Human Beings*. This decision is rather progressive in that it offers a harmonised definition of trafficking and provides for uniform sentences of no less than eight years' imprisonment for traffickers. Earlier that year, the Commission had put forward a proposal to grant temporary one-year residency visas to victims of trafficking provided the victim cooperated with the authorities to apprehend the traffickers. Most EU member states have implemented this decision.

On the level of international law, the EU signed and ratified the United Nations *International Convention on Transnational Organized Crime* (aka the 'Palermo Convention') as well as its second *Optional Protocol on Trafficking in Persons, Particularly Women and Children* in 2000. Ratification of the Palermo Convention is doubly significant. First, the Convention is the first international agreement to recognise the need for international cooperation to confront the transnational danger emanating from organised criminal gangs and to impose a legal obligation on ratifying states to take verifiable steps against such gangs. Second, the Optional Protocol is the first international agreement to recognise the magnitude of human smuggling and to compel ratifying states to undertake a whole array of legal, political and social reforms to confront this problem effectively. The significance of the Convention and Protocol is underlined by the fact that the Action Plan for Moldova explicitly stated that both documents needed to be ratified and implemented.

Table 3.2 shows the signatures and ratifications of the Palermo Convention and its second Optional Protocol by countries covered by the Neighbourhood Policy. Of the sixteen ENP members, eight have signed and ratified both documents. Four have signed both the Convention and the Protocol but not ratified it, the crucial step before it can be enforced domestically. The reason for their non-ratification (as for the non-adoption of numerous stricter domestic anti-sex-trafficking laws) is continued domestic resistance by corrupt lawmakers and lobbying by law-enforcement officials close to criminal gangs. Only Moldova and the Palestinian Authority have not

Table 3.2 Signatures and ratifications of the Palermo Convention and the
Optional Protocol

	Palermo Convention	Optional Protocol
Belarus	2003	2003
Moldova	not signed	not signed
Ukraine	2004	2004
Armenia	2003	2003
Azerbaijan	2003	2003
Georgia	signed in 2000, not ratified	signed in 2000, not ratified
Algeria	2002	2004
Egypt	2004	2004
Israel	signed in 2000, not ratified	signed in 2001, not ratified
Jordan	signed in 2002, not ratified	not signed
Lebanon	signed in 2001, not ratified	signed in 2002, not ratified
Libya	2004	2004
Morocco	2002	not signed
PA	N/A	N/A
Syria	signed in 2000, not ratified	signed in 2000, not ratified
Tunisia	2003	2003

Source: United Nations Treaty Database: http://untreaty.un.org/English/access.asp.

signed or ratified either document. Surprisingly, Morocco, which has been commended by many Western countries for its aggressive stance against human trafficking, has not yet signed or ratified the Optional Protocol. It will be interesting to see if, and to what extent, the European Union will try to persuade Morocco to ratify this crucial document.

The ENP action plans and sex-trafficking
Significantly, fighting against sex-trafficking and organised crime featured prominently in the Action Plans of the pre-accession strategies for the new Eastern European member states and does so again in the Action Plans for the ENP participants. For example, the Action Plan for Ukraine (European Commission 2004c: 20) makes specific mention of the significance of combating sex-trafficking, stating, 'The first EU–Ukraine JHA Ministerial Troika of November 2002 assigned priority in cooperation on Justice and Home Affairs to readmission and migration, border management, money laundering, trafficking in human beings, drugs as well as corruption, prevention and fighting sexual exploitation of women, children, and child pornography.'

Likewise Moldova is encouraged to 'develop an appropriate legal framework for the prevention of, and the fight against, trafficking in human beings and for addressing the problems faced by victims of trafficking' and 'to ratify relevant international instruments ... to prevent, suppress and punish trafficking in persons, especially women and children' such as the UN Convention against Transnational Organized Crime and its protocols (European Commission 2004b: 5). Furthermore, the Moldovan government is urged to enhance 'the Moldovan law enforcement authorities ... [to] prevent and fight sexual exploitation of women, children and child pornography' (European Commission 2004b: 22). Clearly recognising the causal relationship between women's inferior economic and social status and their vulnerability to sex-trafficking, both Action Plans also urge the assurance of equal treatment of men and women in society and economic life (European Commission 2004b: 6; 2004c: 5). However, at no point is the protection of human rights, generally speaking, or an aggressive confrontation of sex-trafficking, a *conditio sine qua non* for the improved cooperation, nor is it listed as a 'priority for action' area.

The effectiveness of anti-trafficking laws and programmes in the European neighbourhood

The question now arises as to the effectiveness of EU human rights policy regarding sex-trafficking in ENP participants. A serious drawback is that neither the European Union nor individual countries systematically collect data on how many women are trafficked, deported and repatriated, or on the number of trafficking cases, convictions and sentences for traffickers. Therefore the most comprehensive and reliable source for analysing a country's efforts to eliminate trafficking are the TIP Reports, published annually since 2001 by the US Department of State. The TIP Reports collect information of each country's annual anti-trafficking activities in the categories 'punishment', 'prevention' and 'protection'. For instance, the Reports describe, to the extent collected and reported by individual countries, any legal changes, the number of criminal cases involving trafficking activities, traffickers convicted over the last year, length of sentences, government activities and support for anti-trafficking measures by non-governmental or international organisations.

On the basis of this information, the TIP Reports classify almost all countries into four tiers, in descending order of compliance with their anti-trafficking obligations. A listing in Tier 1 means that the country fully complies with international obligations and makes every effort to eliminate trafficking. Tier 2 signifies that a country 'does not fully comply with the minimum standards for the elimination of trafficking', but is 'making significant efforts to do so'.[12] Tier 2–Watchlist encompasses countries that do not fully comply with minimum anti-trafficking standards and need to increase their efforts. A Tier 3 classification means that a country does not comply with minimum standards and is not making an effort at improvement. All OECD countries as well as Taiwan, the Republic of Korea and Ghana are classified in Tier 1. Most other countries are in Tier 2 or Tier 2–Watchlist. Only a few countries such as Cuba, Burma and Bangladesh are listed in Tier 3.

Table 3.3 shows the TIP rankings of all ENP participants for each year from 2001 to 2005, as well as the overall change in ranking, if any. When the State Department began to collect data in 2000–2001, most ENP participants were ranked in Tiers 2 and 3, with an 'average' ranking of 2.42, and numerous ENP participants did not report any data at all. Over the next four years, the number of non-reporting countries decreased from nine to four, and most ENP participants have been consistently ranked in Tier 2 and Tier 2–Watchlist. Belarus, Lebanon and Israel managed to improve their ranking from Tier 3 to Tier 2 as a result of their more decisive anti-sex-trafficking efforts. The only real success story is Morocco, which has aggressively pursued an anti-sex-trafficking policy for the past four years and is ranked in Tier 1, the only ENP country and the only Middle Eastern country with this classification. However, Ukraine, Armenia and Georgia have slid back from Tier 2 to Tier 3 or Tier 2-Watchlist. Nonetheless, by 2005, the 'average' ranking for an ENP country had slightly improved from 2.42 to 2.04, a decrease in ranking by 0.38. It appears that the coordination of European and American actions had a synergetic effect. While the EU concentrated on support for grass roots efforts as well as legislative and programmatic reforms, the US focused on the prosecution and punishment of traffickers, and clearly, some progress has been made in both categories.

Indeed, 2004 seems to have been a watershed year for anti-sex-trafficking activities. Numerous ENP participants signed and/or ratified the Optional Protocol and some countries took serious steps against trafficking.

Table 3.3 TIP rankings of ENP participants

	PCA in force	2001	2002	2003	Protocol ratified	2004	2005	Change
Belarus		3	3	2	2003	2	2	−1
Moldova	1998	2	2	2	–	2	2	0
Ukraine	1998	2	2	2	2004	2	2.5	0.5
Armenia	1999	ND	3	2	2003	2	2.5	0.5
Azerbaijan	1999	ND	ND	ND	2003	2.5	2.5	0
Georgia	1999	2	2	3	–	2.5	2	0
Algeria		ND	ND	ND	2004	ND	2	0
Egypt	2004	ND	ND	ND	2004	2	2	0
Israel	2000	3	2	2	–	2	2	−1
Jordan	2002	ND	ND	ND	–	ND	ND	ND
Lebanon	2003	3	3	2	–	2	ND	−1
Libya		ND	ND	ND	2004	ND	2	0
Morocco	2000	2	2	1	–	1	1	−1
PA	1997	ND	ND	ND	–	ND	ND	ND
Syria	–	ND	ND	ND	–	ND	2	0
Tunisia	1998	ND	ND	ND	2003	ND	ND	ND
Average		2.42	2.37	2		2	2.04	−0.38

Source: Trafficking in Persons Reports 2001–2005: www.state.gov/g/tip/rls/tiprpt/.

Developments on three different levels – official government positions, awareness-raising and legal enforcement – are of particular significance. For instance, in May 2004, the Azeri president ordered all government bodies to implement Azerbaijan's National Action Plan, appointed the Deputy Minister of Internal Affairs as National Coordinator for Trafficking and ordered consular officials to report trafficking cases to international organisations (TIP 2005, Country Narrative on Azerbaijan). Georgia set up a comprehensive National Action Plan and funded a new anti-trafficking unit that will be active throughout the country (TIP 2005, Country Narrative on Georgia). Even President Lukashenka of Belarus, one of the countries with the worst trafficking records, signed a decree in spring 2005 to combat trafficking in persons. As a result, most countries provide some anti-trafficking training to police and have created new task forces. Another positive development is the increasing cross-border cooperation between countries to aid the repatriation of smuggling victims and to break organised crime groups. For instance, Moldova participated in the 'Mirage 2004' operation that enabled law enforcement officials to initiate nine anti-trafficking cases, and Israel worked with Russia, Ukraine and Belarus to crack international smuggling rings and to facilitate the repatriation of smuggled persons (TIP 2005, Country Narratives on Moldova and Israel).

Additionally, most countries have begun awareness-raising campaigns. For instance, Armenia now includes anti-trafficking discussions on local talk shows, and Belarus and Georgia air anti-trafficking public service announcements prepared by international organisations free of charge on state television stations. The Lebanese government produced and distributed brochures about the rights and duties of migrant workers and cooperated with two large international NGOs to set up a shelter for trafficking victims (TIP 2005, Country Narratives on Armenia and Lebanon).

On the level of legal reform some progress has also been made, but serious deficiencies remain. For instance, most ENP participants have amended their legal codes to include a prohibition of trafficking in persons. Those who have not, such as Azerbaijan, Ukraine, Egypt and Lebanon, use charges of slavery, rape and coercion into prostitution as the basis for charges. Maximum penalties for trafficking generally have been set to carry sentences of between four to eight years' imprisonment, although some have been as long as twelve (in Georgia) or even sixteen years (in Moldova). However, many countries, especially in the Caucasus region, apply articles that carry much lower sentences, for instance for pimping, resulting in suspended or very short sentences or corrective labour. Therefore, while overall numbers of trafficking-related convictions increase, the deterrence factor is low due to the light sentences. Furthermore, while prosecution rates are significantly improving, conviction rates are generally low, which is another indicator of a lack of a serious political will to take on the traffickers. For instance, Belarus prosecuted 290 trafficking cases in 2004 (up from 191 in 2003), but only 26 persons were convicted for trafficking. Israel investigated 602 cases, arrested 103 suspects and handed down 28 convictions. Moldova investigated 274 trafficking cases in 2004, and convicted 23 individuals (TIP 2005, Country Narratives on Belarus, Israel and Moldova).

Regarding victims services, the TIP Reports consistently point to under-funding of anti-trafficking and victim protection services, including shelters, healthcare facilities, and witness protection programmes, and a general absence of formal referral mechanisms. Most follow-up work is done by local NGOs, often in cooperation with international organisations. In Israel, for instance, victim services are still inadequate: there is only one shelter with fifty beds. Trafficked women are classified as illegal foreigners and subject to deportation unless they cooperate with the police against their traffickers, in which case they receive visa extensions, medical, legal and psychological care (TIP 2005, Country Narrative on Israel).

In sum, the two main problems in all ENP participants are, firstly, the absence of a sincere political will to determinedly confront human trafficking, and consequently, secondly, the lackadaisical enforcement of anti-trafficking statutes. The reason for the non-enforcement of the statutes is the high level of corruption and the close relationship between traffickers, legislators and law enforcement officials. For instance, the 2005 TIP Report explicitly states that 'indications of official collusion and complicity among government offi-cials hampered the government's efforts to adequately tackle Armenia's trafficking problem' (Country Narrative on Armenia). Likewise for Moldova 'it is widely suspected that the Anti-Trafficking Unit limited the number of cases it investigated due in some instances to pressure from complicit officials at higher levels in the government' (Country Narrative on Moldova).

Therefore, despite concerted efforts by the European Union, the United States and the United Nations, neither global supply nor demand has declined markedly. Clearly the main obstacle to effective action against sex-trafficking is its complex, multidimensional nature. At the root of the problem lies the pervasive, social, economic and political marginalisation of women: limited access to equal political representation and economic opportunities, a wide-spread image of women as expendable sexual objects, a sense among the police forces that victims are complicit in their victimisation, and the connec-tion between government officials and organised crime groups make the adoption of effective programmes that address the cause of the phenomenon, and not just the symptoms, particularly costly and thus undesirable for the countries in question. In effect, what would be required are comprehensive women's empowerment programmes that significantly improve the social, political and economic status of women. Understandably, such a fundamen-tal restructuring of social relations goes beyond the ability or desire of the European Union.

Conclusion

In sum, the EU has had no significant positive impact on the overall political and human rights situation in its neighbouring non-candidate countries.[13] As we have shown, neither the degree of civil rights and liberties, as measured by the Freedom House Index, nor the problem of sex-trafficking has improved to any significant degree. This result confirms the expectation derived in the previous section on the basis of the external incentives model and of earlier studies on the EU impact on candidate countries. Whereas it is much too early to declare the ENP as an instrument of democracy and human rights promotion failed, there is every reason to be sceptical about its prospects. Although political conditionality was introduced to the ENP as an institutional and identity-based legacy of Eastern enlargement and general external relations principles, it lacks the prerequisites of effectiveness: a credible membership promise, a consistent application of conditionality, and domestic conditions of impact in the target countries. Thus, the political conditionality in the ENP is likely to remain a ceremonial affirmation of basic EU values and norms without major practical consequences – and to deepen the credibility crisis of the EU in this issue-area.

In our opinion, the EU has two basic choices in overcoming this situation. On the one hand, the EU could turn toward a more consistent application of political conditionality in the ENP participants. This would certainly enhance the credibility of the EU's value-based stance and its human rights policy. However, even normatively consistent policy is unlikely to lead to higher effectiveness in the absence of a membership perspective and favourable domestic conditions in the target countries. Rather, it would force the EU to forego potentially beneficial cooperation on issues of mutual economic and security interests. On the other hand, the EU could simply abolish political conditionality in its relationship with non-candidates for membership, while continuing the promotion of human rights and democracy as a field of cooperation alongside others. Whereas such a policy would probably not result in a more effective promotion of democracy and human rights, it would be more consistent and interfere less with cooperation in other issue-areas.

Notes

1   This clause, however, has never been invoked (Fierro 2002).
2   See Barcelona Declaration at: http://ec.europa.eu/comm/external_relations /euromed/bd.htm, accessed 21 July 2006.
3   See http://ec.europa.eu/comm/external_relations/euromed/news/memo04_275.htm, accessed 21 July 2006.
4   'EU/Morocco Action Plan', available at: http://ec.europa.eu/world/enp/pdf /action_plans/morocco_enp_ap_final_en.pdf, accessed 21 July 2006.

5   See the ENP Website with links to all ENP Action Plans: http://ec.europa.eu/world /enp/documents_en.htm#2, accessed 21 July 2006.

6   See Kubicek (2003); Kelley (2004a); Schimmelfennig (2005a); Vachudova (2005); Schimmelfennig, Engert, and Knobel (2006).

7   The Freedom Index combines the ratings for 'civil liberties' and 'political rights' and ranges from 1 (best) to 7 (worst). See www.freedomhouse.org. Kelley (2006) uses other data and comparisons but comes to similar conclusions.

8   According to the UNDOC, four million individuals are trafficked each year for the sex industry and sweat-shop, domestic and construction labour as well as begging. For more information, see www.unodc.org/palermo/convmain.html, accessed 31 January 2006.

9   www.angelcoalition.org/trafficking.html, accessed 2 April 2005.

10 http://europa.eu.int/comm/justice_home/project/stop_en.htm, accessed 4 February 2006.

11 For a detailed overview of STOP and DAPHNE activities, see: www.europrofem .org/06.actio/action_en/03act_en.htm#DIRECTLY, accessed 19 January 2006.

12 This is standard terminology used by the US State Department.

13 One must be highly cautious with regard to causal attributions. Even if the situation had improved in the ENP participants, it would have been difficult to claim that this had happened *because of* EU policy. Conversely, we do not argue that EU policy was responsible for the lack of improvement.

Michael E. Smith and Mark Webber

4

Political dialogue and security: the CFSP and ESDP

Political dialogue arrangements are apparent in numerous EU agreements with third countries, including some well beyond Europe. These mechanisms provide the EU and its partners with institutionalised frameworks for managing diplomatic relations and, in some cases, organising cooperation in foreign policy matters. On paper at least, the ENP replicates and, in some senses, extends these provisions, offering the ENP partners a role in the CFSP/ESDP policy domain. In this chapter we analyse the origins, content, implementation and implications of this aspect of the ENP programme. Our goal is to realistically assess the prospects for meaningful cooperation in light of the EU's past experience, ENP policy tools, and the various security-related problems found in the border areas. While we commend the EU for reaching out to these countries rather than adopting a 'fortress Europe' mentality, we also raise serious questions about whether the EU has the political will, institutional means, and material resources necessary to provide the ENP with a real 'value added'. We also ask how the EU, if forced to choose, might prioritise among several competing ENP goals: normative (human rights and democracy), political (security), and economic (market access and financial aid). Finally, one must consider the impact of the ENP political dialogue arrangements with key non-participants, whether outside of Europe (the US) or closer to home (Russia).

Origins of the policy domain

Political dialogue frameworks with non-member states have deep roots in the EU. The first arrangements under European Political Cooperation (EPC) in the early 1970s involved the Arab countries. Indeed, during the 1973 October

War in the Middle East and the associated oil crisis, the Arab states themselves requested a more comprehensive framework for their talks with the Europeans. However, at the time there were no provisions in the EC/EPC for any regional or group-to-group dialogue, except perhaps for the EC's limited Association Agreements and Yaoundé/Lomé conventions, which were strictly confined to economic issues (Edwards and Regelsberger 1990). Thus, the EU had to improvise in creating the Euro-Arab Dialogue. In so doing it institutionalised one of the most important norms of EU foreign policy: promoting regional cooperation or integration along EU lines in troubled areas of the world (Nuttall 1990).

With this precedent set, the EU gradually expanded its activities. The political dialogue with Central America after 1984 was one such effort, and from the early 1990s the EU developed a network of relations embracing the whole gamut of former communist states. This effort involved considerable differentiation in the form of Europe Agreements (EAs) with EU candidate states, Partnership and Cooperation Agreements (PCAs) with the majority of states in the former Soviet Union (FSU), and Stabilisation and Association Agreements (SAAs) with Croatia and Macedonia in the early 2000s. All these arrangements, however, shared to varying degrees provisions for political dialogue (most extensively in the case of EAs and SAAs where this overlapped with accession preparations), and their proliferation and complexity provided a key rationale for the current ENP programme.

In anticipation of the 2004 enlargement, political concerns were paramount in the Patten-Solana joint letter of August 2002 (see Chapter 2). The very first item in its list of 'concrete measures' was a reinforced political dialogue 'where the aim should be to enrich the quality of discussion rather than multiplying the number of high-level meetings'. It also alluded to enhanced responsibility for the ENP partners in regional security matters, possibly through new 'Neighbourhood and Proximity Agreements', while 'closer cooperation on ESDP/crisis management could also be envisaged' (Patten and Solana 2002).

This idea was promoted further by two important EU decisions taken in 2003 relating to ESDP: agreeing to take over NATO's conflict prevention operation in the Former Yugoslav Republic of Macedonia, and expressing a willingness to do the same regarding the NATO Stabilisation Force (SFOR) in Bosnia. These operations would provide important precedents for concerted EU external action. At this time the EU was also increasingly concerned with the possibility of war in Iraq and its link to the ongoing peace process in the Middle East (European Council 2002b). These two factors – war with Iraq, and the prospect of actual ESDP military operations – combined with broader issues concerning the impact of enlargement (see Chapter 2), helped synthesise the debate on the emerging neighbourhood policy, both in terms of geographic coverage, but also importantly its political objectives.

Content: political dialogue and security in the ENP

The condition of the EU's neighbourhood will have profound and long-term repercussions for the status of the EU and, within this context, the ENP is premised on stabilisation and engagement rather than quarantine and distance. This suggests a view of the EU as a strategic actor, capable and willing, in the words of the European Security Strategy, of enhancing the security of the Union by promoting in its *geographic neighbourhood* 'a ring of well governed countries [...] with whom we can enjoy close and cooperative relations' (Solana 2003: 13). As such, this can be viewed as the *ultima ratio* of the CFSP and its ESDP offspring. Not only is the ENP a logical extension of CFSP concerns – as Wallace (2003: 27) has suggested, a CFSP 'that did not have at its core a coherent strategy towards the EU's immediate neighbours would be a contradiction in terms' – but the vast area covered by the initiative provides plentiful opportunities for the application of the EU's political and military instruments.

Political dialogue consequently forms a central part of the ENP. The General Affairs and External Relations Council (2003) noted the importance of 'shared responsibility for conflict prevention and conflict resolution' among ENP partners and the EU. In a fifteen-item list of 'incentives' to further ENP goals, it prioritised 'more effective political dialogue and cooperation', 'intensified cooperation to prevent and combat common security threats', and 'greater cooperation in conflict prevention and crisis management'. The Commission's ENP Strategy Paper of May 2004 notes a similar ambition, this time adding specific locales of activity, namely 'improved coordination within the established political dialogue formats [...] the possible involvement of partner countries in aspects of CFSP and ESDP, conflict prevention, crisis management, the exchange of information, joint training and exercises and possible participation in EU-led crisis management operations' (European Commission 2004a: 13). Putting flesh on this skeleton of cooperation, the proposed Action Plans drawn up by the Commission at the end of 2004[1] envisaged commitments by ENP partners to 'certain essential aspects of the EU's external action, including [...] the fight against terrorism and the proliferation of weapons of mass destruction (WMD), as well as efforts to achieve conflict resolution' (European Commission 2004f: 3). These plans represent 'an offer ... of much deeper cooperation and progressive integration into certain EU policies and programs, depending on the fulfilment of commitments', in part to prevent 'a new dividing line being drawn across Europe following enlargement' (Ferrero-Waldner 2004).

The specific content of political dialogue under the ENP might be viewed positively on a number of counts. The Action Plan with Moldova, for instance, devotes an entire section to the sensitive separatist problem of Transnistria. That with Israel, meanwhile, notes the aim of 'reaching a comprehensive settlement of the Israeli/Palestinian conflict and a permanent two-state solution'. The ENP also brings to bear a conceptual framework and set of priorities, however grandiose, in an area where previously the EU was charged with lacking strategic vision (Tanner 2004: 147). The initiative recognises the security interdependence of the EU and its neighbours and involves a belated but necessary turn of attention to sub-regions (the South Caucasus, for instance) where EU involvement had long been perceived as negligible. The region as a whole has been the subject, in some cases, of already intense CFSP action (as with the Middle East Peace Process (MEPP)) and roughly overlaps in geographical terms with planning assumptions regarding the scope for ESDP military crisis management operations (Missiroli 2003: 31). To some commentators, the ENP might also permit the EU to project its assets as an international actor. Such assets include a perceived neutrality in areas (the South Caucasus again) where it is untainted by prior involvement, the 'democratic legitimacy' of its foreign policy actions such that they are welcomed locally rather than shunned as neo-colonial, and the experience of its member states in resolving conflicts in ethnically complex societies (Grigorian 2003: 140; Harris 2004: 103; Emerson 2004c: 60–1).

These positives aside, there are a number of necessary questions that can be asked. A first and obvious point concerns 'value added'. What, in other words, is to be gained from the ENP which was not already provided by existing arrangements? In practical terms, the ENP is premised on varying levels of bilateral relations with individual partners: the principle of differentiation. It does not, therefore, provide new opportunities for multilateral political dialogue. The Barcelona process or Euro-Mediterranean Partnership (EMP) already provides this in the Mediterranean but a clear opportunity exists among the former Soviet partners for EU-led multilateralism which the ENP has failed to exploit. Further, the ENP offers little new thematic content. With the possible exception of the South Caucasus, ENP areas of attention reflect initiatives already recently set in train. Thus in the Mediterranean, the ENP stands alongside the EMP, the 2000 EU Common Strategy on the Mediterranean, the 2002 Valencia Action Plan of Euro-Mediterranean Foreign Ministers and the 2004 document 'EU Strategic Partnership with the Mediterranean and the Middle East', all aimed at invigorating political and security dialogue. In this light, the ENP can at best be seen as an opportunity to refocus and synthesise attention, particularly where existing political dialogue between the EU and partners has been perceived as weak and ineffectual, as in the case of the EMP for example (Balfour 2004: 9).

In institutional terms as well the basis of relations with individual partners differs little from its previous stance. In the case of Ukraine for example, the ENP Action Plan adds nothing beyond vague exhortations of 'improvement' to the provisions outlined at the Nice (December 2000) and Seville (June 2002) European Councils on participation in ESDP operations (EU–Ukraine Action Plan). The Action Plans with the Euro-Med partners, meanwhile, specify points of contact with the EU on CFSP and ESDP, but this is simply to repeat what the December 2004 Presidency Report on ESDP referred to as 'modalities for dialogue and co-operation with Mediterranean partners' already existing 'within the framework of the Barcelona process' (European Council, 2004).[2] In fact, Morocco is the only Mediterranean ENP partner to participate in an ESDP operation. Even here its involvement in EU Operation Althea in Bosnia is not a new commitment but merely a continuation of the Moroccan contingent attached to NATO's SFOR mission.

To questions regarding institutional continuity, one might also add the issue of incentive structure. In one sense, partner involvement is encouraged by involvement in the fashioning of programme priorities, or joint governance. Whereas previous framework documents with ENP partners had been the sole preserve of EU institutions, notably the Commission, the ENP Action Plans have involved negotiation of a sort. The resultant Plans consequently reflect the principle of differentiation noted above in which, according to the Commission (2004g), 'each partner will choose how far it wants to deepen its political and economic ties with the EU'. The pursuit of cooperation by this logic rests in part on the fact that the partners are led by their own priorities. The monitoring of implementation meanwhile is to occur jointly, albeit through existing bodies under PCA or Association Agreement auspices. While all this is suggestive of some form of equal relationship, the asymmetry of power between ENP partners and the EU noted in Chapter 1 means that the broad terms of partnership are set by the Commission. Crucially, however, EU leverage in setting these terms is diluted somewhat by the lack of a membership perspective within the ENP. All this has made for opportunities for bargaining but with often bland outcomes.

Thus, while negotiations on some Action Plans have entailed prolonged and difficult exchanges (interviews, July 2004), the end result is invariably a rather predictable sounding set of 'Priorities for Action'. Within this framework, certain seemingly significant incentives are on offer including possible concessions on trade (greater access to the EU internal market) and migration (see Chapters 6 and 7). As Emerson (2004b: 15) has noted, the modus operandi here is seemingly one of 'positive conditionality' – an absence of punishment for non-compliance and the use of rewards for good performance. Yet previous initiatives are instructive here: conditionality has not been seriously applied to the Mediterranean countries in order to promote democratisation, and within the former Soviet Union only Belarus has received censure for its undemocratic practices (Kelley 2006).

But how might this work in the less quantifiable sphere of political dialogue? Here, the precedent of the accession states is perhaps instructive. The application in these cases of 'positive conditionality' to the chapters on external relations and CFSP during accession negotiations proved largely trouble-free. The rate of alignment with CFSP positions increased as membership drew closer (Regelsberger 2003: 3–7), and as such the process could be said to reflect both a rational logic of membership conditionality as well as a process of social learning. This elite socialisation into the EU foreign/security policy culture has been documented for most EU member states (Manners and Whitman 2000; Smith 2000) and may be expected to continue for the recent accession states, though it does take considerable time and experience.

Because the ENP, by contrast, lacks the 'ultimate reward' of membership it is conducted in a much less intensely institutionalised setting. Consequently, while CFSP alignment even among the acceding states had an often symbolic and declarative quality, that with the ENP partners may be even more hollow as both the incentives for constructive engagement and the barriers to defection are fewer and less substantive. A further difference resides in the scope for independent action. Among the acceding or candidate countries the constraints of accession, as well as the impact of post-Cold War 'Westernistic' norms of market economics, democracy and international integration (Waever 2000: 43–4), meant that few had the inclination to pursue foreign policies markedly out of step with EU preferences. Among the ENP partners, by contrast, these processes are much weaker and, in some cases in the southern Mediterranean, largely absent. Consequently, there are a sufficient number of states (including Israel, Syria and Algeria) that have robustly independent foreign policies capable of conflicting with the EU. Some also have alternative poles of attraction (Russia in the case of Armenia and Belarus, and the US in the case of Israel). The significance of the latter depends on the degree to which EU external policy is itself at odds with the preferences of the relevant regional power (the US or Russia) and thus the degree to which EU–ENP partner political dialogue requires the partners to strike a balance between the two. This is particularly noteworthy in the cases of Israel and Georgia, as we shall see below.

Implementation

Students of policy analysis typically appreciate that even if a policy has been rationally conceived it is rarely implemented in a fully coherent and effective manner (Webber, Smith et al. 2002: 79–80). Implementing the ENP could well be the most difficult test case ever of the EU's ability to achieve coherence in its foreign policies. The ENP exemplifies what Stetter (2004: 724) has referred to as 'a cross-pillar setting in EU foreign affairs' given that it aims explicitly to aggregate a wide range of policies across 'all three "pillars" of the Union's present structure' (European Commission 2004a: 6). Building coherence and effectiveness have been constant themes in public scrutiny of EU external action (for instance on the part of the European Parliament and the European Convention) and also in academic analyses (M.E. Smith 2003: 210–20). In fact, one can distinguish between no less than four types of coherence, as outlined in Table 4.1.

Table 4.1   Types of coherence/consistency in EU foreign policy-making

	Vertical (or 'Europeanisation')	Horizontal
Institutional (or procedural)	National policy-making mechanisms support/conform to common EU policy-making mechanisms.	EU foreign policy-making mechanisms are uniformly applied across policy areas/time.
Policy (or substantive)	National policies support/conform to common EU policies.	Various EU policies conform to broad goals or principles.

Source: Adapted from Smith 2004: 747. Also see Krenzler and Schneider 1997 and Nuttall 2001a.

Regarding horizontal coherence (both institutional and policy), Del Sarto and Schumacher (2005: 37–8) have noted, for instance, the seeming disconnection between the ENP, the EMP and the Strategic Partnership with the Mediterranean and the Middle East. A second example relates to Ukraine, where the 'Orange Revolution' of late 2004 has challenged the EU to upgrade its relationship with Kiev while maintaining the delicate balance between Ukraine's new-found aspiration for membership and the more limited ambitions of the ENP. Although it may be asking too much of the EU to coordinate its multi-faceted foreign activities given its decentralised policy-making structure, the case could be made that the importance and complexity of the relationship with Ukraine (and other ENP partners) requires even greater long-term strategic oversight (i.e. horizontal institutional and policy coherence) currently lacking in the EU given the spread of attention across EU institutions. The office of an EU Minister for Foreign Affairs backed by the proposed External Action Service offers promise in this regard (Crowe 2005: 5–10) but progress here has been stalled by the seeming demise in 2005 of the EU Constitutional Treaty.

As for vertical coherence, here attention has been given to the discrepancy between the policy views of Brussels-based institutions and those of individual EU member states, as well as divergent positions among the member states themselves (Everts 2002: 30–7). This has a particular relevance in relation to the ENP given a geographic coverage that touches upon the foreign policy interests of several EU members. Throughout the 1990s there was a clear split in priorities between those who favoured a Mediterranean orientation in EU external relations (France, Italy and Spain) and those who gave preference to an Eastern agenda (Germany and Finland). To some extent, this pattern has continued and as such has complicated the ENP, especially in light of whether to use the ENP as a 'waiting room' for accession to the EU. Ukraine has been particularly controversial, in that some member states (Hungary, Lithuania, Poland and Slovakia) support its accession to the

EU while a majority (most notably France) are more lukewarm to the idea (Schneider and Saurenbach 2005: 3–4).

Turning to issues of effectiveness, here we follow the distinction used throughout this volume between procedural and substantive effects. The former relates to how far partners regard their participation in the ENP as desirable and thus, by extension, how far they welcome the ENP as demonstrating a readiness on the part of the EU to act in particular issue areas. A first indication here is the ENP Action Plans given that these were negotiated with partners. The presence of extensive references to CFSP/ESDP-related topics in the Action Plans with Ukraine, Moldova and Israel might thus be suggestive of a recognition of EU efficacy, in some cases (Ukraine and Georgia) reinforced by a long-term expectation of EU membership. Yet the Action Plans are a not entirely reliable guide, partly because they reflect EU preferences over those of partners, and partly because they are the product of discursive habits stemming from several years' worth of bilateral and multilateral political communiqués.

The particular positions taken by individual ENP partner countries are as significant as the Action Plans. Here, differing degrees of involvement are apparent. Among the post-Soviet ENP partners, Ukraine has participated in ESDP operations and has been the site (from December 2005) of an EU Border Assistance Mission along its frontier with Moldova. Georgia, meanwhile, has been the location of an ESDP rule-of-law mission, and Moldova has increasingly viewed EU involvement in the Transnistria conflict as a more constructive alternative to long-term OSCE mediation and Russian involvement. Even Armenia, traditionally a stalwart of Russia, has come to recognise the benefits of its ENP status, in this case as a means of pressing its case over border and other disputes with Turkey (Gorvett 2005). Among the Mediterranean partners, some governments have welcomed the possibilities for political dialogue offered by the ENP, but generally these political aspects have attracted little attention. The ENP has not been viewed as a significant departure from the EMP, some ENP partners are suspicious of the regional purposes of CFSP and especially ESDP, and they feel also that the EU is too passive on regional issues, notably the Israel–Palestine conflict, but also conflicts in the Western Sahara and Algeria (Biscop 2004: 30–1).

Substantive effectiveness refers to how target problems are being addressed. In this respect the measurement of success is hard to pin down, but one might reach judgement by reference to two criteria: first, whether or not the EU itself has identified an issue as worthy of action, and second, the EU's unique impact, if any, on an issue. These criteria avoid the fallacious all-or-nothing suggestion that the 'solution' of an issue is the only measure of policy success. The first criterion has already been hinted at by reference to the content of political dialogue, which can be taken as indicative of political will on the part of the EU. Yet by the same token, the absence in ENP Country Reports/Action Plans of any mention of the Western Sahara dispute in

Morocco, of a meaningful role for the EU in the Nagorno-Karabakh dispute in Armenia/Azerbaijan, or for that matter of an EU interest in Lebanon's dispute with Israel, suggests either a deference to the diplomatic efforts of other international actors or a recognition of the limits of EU influence.

As for impact, this according to Ginsberg (2001: 51–4) can be judged in terms of how the EU can alter the behaviour of non-EU actors, which, in turn, may influence an issue upon which the EU has concentrated. Given the infancy of the ENP it is too soon to make reliable judgements in these regards. There is also an analytical problem of isolating ENP effects from those which relate to existing policy instruments. Bearing these considerations in mind, in relation to CFSP/ESDP the impact of the EU might be viewed in terms of categories surveyed by Ginsberg (2001: 51–5). For the EU to be of any consequence 'presence' is first required (Allen and Smith 1990), in the physical sense of an active participation in the issue at stake, and in terms of the demonstration of 'actorness', which, in turn, involves coherence (see above), recognition (an acceptance by others of EU competence), authority (a political and legal basis upon which to act) and autonomy (an approach that is distinct from that of other actors) (Caporaso and Jupille 1998, cited in Ginsberg 2001: 47). One must then add the EU's unique external power resources (or incentives), such as market access or denial. It is worth noting here that these factors signify obstacles to action as much as facilitators of it. A lack of recognition (the indifference or opposition of local parties) or autonomy (being 'crowded out' by other external actors), for example, would suggest limits to EU impact. These considerations inform the short case studies of the following section.

The ENP in action: comparing the south and the east

How does the EU expect to incorporate foreign/security/defence affairs into the specific ENP Action Plans, and how does it differentiate among its political goals according to the ENP partners? Here we attempt to shed light on these questions by contrasting two major regional targets of the ENP: the Middle East and the FSU.

The Middle East
As we have already noted, the Middle East has been the object of sustained attention by the EU. To a large extent, the Israeli-Palestinian conflict is at the heart of European interest in this region, although related concerns such as secure oil imports and border controls certainly play a role. The questions that then arise are whether the ENP represents a real departure from past practice (such as the Euro-Arab Dialogue and the EMP) and the extent to which the EU has made a uniquely positive impact on the politics of the region.

It is clear that the EU has devoted an increasing amount of resources –

political and economic – to the Middle East. However, determining whether the EU has had a demonstrable impact on the region is more problematic. Ginsberg's comprehensive analysis reports that EU foreign policy actions have had a considerable to significant[3] impact on the Palestinians (87 per cent of total actions, 1990–99) and on the Israelis (75 per cent of total actions) but no significant impact on the MEPP itself, with a considerable impact on just five occasions (28 per cent of total actions). Ginsberg concludes that the EU impacts the MEPP indirectly through actions directed at the two main protagonists. As he puts it, although the EU often plays a role secondary to that of the US, and has made its share of mistakes, the EU has nonetheless effectively applied a wide range of its policy tools: 'diplomacy and good offices, trade concessions and investment, technical and development expertise, humanitarian and refugee assistance, electoral support, multilateral aid coordination, and bilateral grants and subsidized loans for running costs, infrastructure, and institution-building designed to build the foundations of civil society and conditioned on respect for the rule of law and human rights' (Ginsberg 2001: 106).

Activities toward the Middle East have been embedded since 1995 in the broader EMP, or Barcelona process, involving initially twelve partners.[4] Reinforced in June 2000 and May 2003, the EMP involves bilateral Association Agreements as well as a complex institutional infrastructure from ministerial level on down to administer the various relationships. As usual with such arrangements, the Commission plays a special role in organising the meetings and managing the entire project, which involves billions of euros in financial aid delivered through dozens of policy sectors. Despite these initiatives, the Barcelona process has suffered frequent criticisms: its largely bilateral character has done little to build multilateral and regional cooperation;[5] it has not made effective use of EU market access to leverage greater cooperation with these countries; its aid delivery has been sporadic; it has not managed to facilitate stronger confidence-building mechanisms in the region; and it has never invoked the provisions for political conditionality despite many violations of human rights and democratic principles by certain EMP partners (Barbé and Izquierdo 1997; Spencer 2001; Youngs 2001; Philippart 2003; Emerson and Noutcheva 2004b).

The last two criticisms are especially salient for the topic of this chapter: political dialogue and security. In this domain, and relative to the EMP framework, the ENP does provide for greater attention to human rights and democracy as well as cooperation in foreign/security policy and conflict prevention. This also builds upon one of the key goals of the EU's Common Strategy on the Mediterranean: to establish a common area of peace and stability through a political and security partnership.[6] As always, the MEPP is a key focal point of the political/security aspects of these initiatives and of the recent ENP Action Plans, which mention several general political goals: 1) facilitating efforts to resolve the Middle East conflict; 2) cooperation on non-proliferation of WMD and the fight against terrorism; 3) conflict prevention and resolution in the region and beyond; 4) promoting the protection of human rights; 5) improving the dialogue between cultures and religions; and 6) cooperating in the fight against anti-Semitism, racism, and xenophobia.

Yet the specific priorities for action under these headings are still quite vague; they stress 'dialogue' and 'strengthening of cooperation' without actually detailing expected behavioural changes or the benchmarking/monitoring mechanisms to encourage those changes. There are some key omissions and contradictions within them as well. We have already noted above the lack of attention to the Western Sahara dispute in Morocco or Lebanon's dispute with Israel. The Israeli-Lebanon conflict of mid-2006 again exposed divisions within the EU over the MEPP, and the ENP consequently played no role in mitigating the dispute (as of yet). In addition, the Israel and PA Action Plans provide virtually no concrete recommendations on the MEPP other than stating the goal of 'resolving' the conflict. The PA Action Plan mentions the political constraints arising from the separation barrier and settlement activity in the occupied territories; the Israel Action Plan makes no such references. And neither mentions the refugee question or the status of Jerusalem; nor do they even touch upon emerging conflicts over other matters, such as control of water resources, or suggest possible crisis prevention mechanisms. Although very comprehensive in other areas, the MEPP issue is in fact one of the weakest aspects of the Israel Action Plan on political dialogue. Even on WMD, certainly a priority security topic for the region, the Action Plans provide no specific details concerning WMD export controls and dual-use technologies. There are key differences as well: the Action Plans for the PA and Jordan mention the objective of 'pursuing a mutually and effectively verifiable Middle East zone free of WMD'; that with Israel mentions no such goal. The Israel Action Plan also goes into some detail about possible joint action under CFSP/ESDP and the fight against terrorism; such provisions are much weaker in the PA and Jordan Action plans.

Certainly such variations and omissions are to be expected to some extent given the principles of differentiation and joint ownership, yet we must wonder whether these Plans are in fact improving the coherence of the ENP or are instead working at cross-purposes to each other. Moreover, these 'reforms' are in fact added to the existing EMP Association Agreements and must be implemented through them. As there is virtually no precedent for intensive political/security cooperation with the countries of this region under the EMP, one must remain sceptical about the real value added of the ENP in this area. This is not for a lack of ideas or trying on the part of the EU; the Commission's strategic guidelines on the human rights and democratisation aspects of the Euro-Med relationship go into some detail about the specific ways that political dialogue can be enhanced in both institutional and substantive terms (European Commission 2003c). Yet these ideas did not appear with the same force or clarity in the ENP Action Plans negotiated with the Euro-Med states only a year later; the principle of 'joint ownership' of the ENP had allowed them to be watered down considerably. Instead, the Commission might be able to use the regular country reports to unilaterally monitor progress under the ENP Action Plans and make appropriate recommendations to the Council for re-negotiating them, but whether the Commission will use these 'powers' remains to be seen.

By one set of standards as presented in this volume, then, the ENP seems to add little value where political dialogue is concerned. Procedurally, the EMP framework had already established a highly complex network of meetings and joint bodies. The ENP adds the Action Plans and the prospects of negotiated access to the EU's single market. Substantively, the ENP raises the possibility of greater cooperation in foreign/security policy and conflict prevention/resolution, an area lacking in the EMP, yet there are no details and no legacy of joint action to help facilitate this goal. However, these are largely unrealised external governance tools that were in place long before the ENP in the form of Association Agreements and similar pacts. Since the EU has made it quite clear that it will trade with these countries as necessary but neither give them full access to the single market (as the major incentive) nor cut off trade or aid in the face of non-compliance (as the major disincentive), it seems the ENP provides no new or effective methods to facilitate greater political cooperation.

But we also must examine the ENP in light of two other factors. The first involves the inherent intractability of the problems of this region, if one can even call it a 'region'. The fact is that some political problems are virtually unsolvable by outsiders such as the EU until a great deal of domestic political change occurs within the partner countries. It took over 20 years for Israel (and the US) to even negotiate with the PLO; why should we expect the two-state solution to evolve on a shorter timescale? And considering the interplay between history, territory, culture, and security among the EMP/ENP states, any discussions with the EU on political issues that do not immediately result in violence or stalemate might be viewed as a great success. By this measure – do the partners 'feel good' about their relationship? – the EMP/ENP is quite remarkable for the wide range of issues it raises with these various states even while keeping in line with the EU's own priorities and norms.

A second measure is simple counterfactual reasoning: suppose the EU had never attempted to systematically engage with this region with an increasingly ambitious set of common standards since the 1970s? It is quite possible, though of course difficult to prove, that violence and human rights violations in the region would have been more intense or widespread had the EU relied on *ad hoc* bilateral agreements with various Middle Eastern countries and had it not taken the PLO as seriously as it did in 1980. And considering America's reputation in the region today, the ENP at a minimum will keep the lines of communication open and at a maximum may provide a viable alternative to military force and occupation as a means of bringing about long overdue political reforms in these states. Such reforms may then improve the prospects for regional conflict resolution. The EU's proximity alone will require it to be far more engaged with, and sensitive to, the political needs and realities of the region as compared to the US, which can afford to take a 'hands off' approach whenever its political leadership chooses to do so.

The former Soviet Union

Compared to the Middle East, where the EU has a long history of engagement, the ENP's attention to the FSU is fairly recent. Indeed, prior to the adoption of the ENP plan the area of the FSU seemed ill-suited for political cooperation with the EU despite the legacy of PCAs, the TACIS programme, and EU strategic partnerships with Russia and Ukraine. In Russia democratic progress had stalled, and the region as a whole had become characterised by personalist semi-authoritarian regimes while a series of unresolved territorial conflicts continued to complicate domestic politics and inter-regional relations. Within this context, the main tool of EU policy, the PCA, was increasingly regarded as inadequate. Yet the EU lacked the influence exerted by conditionality through enlargement it had successfully employed in east-central Europe. With the exception of the three Baltic countries, prior to 2003 none of the Soviet successor states was actively demanding membership and no one in either the Commission or among the EU member states (with the curious exception of Silvio Berlosconi's championing of Russia) was prepared to countenance it. Within the EU, meanwhile, there was also a lack of political will to push for greater engagement with the FSU (Lynch 2003a: 182).

However, after 2001 several factors coalesced to promote greater EU attention toward the region. First, domestic pro-EU political reorientations took place in Ukraine (as noted above) and in Georgia (the 'Rose Revolution' of November 2003). Second, the September 11 terrorist attacks on the US elevated the strategic importance of the South Caucasus for the US and NATO, as well as for some key EU member states (the UK and France notably) who already had a direct stake in ongoing conflict resolution efforts under UN and OSCE auspices. Third, the 2004 EU enlargement acted as a framing event for the ENP (see Chapter 2). The prospect of Romanian accession in 2007 similarly necessitated a serious attention to neighbouring Moldova, while the decision in December 2004 to approve accession negotiations with Turkey required some consideration of the fact that the country borders on all three states of the South Caucasus and enjoys close relations with Azerbaijan. Finally, energy security came into play in that many EU member states hoped to diversify their sources of supply beyond Russia's natural gas reserves. Here the EU has backed the modernisation of pipelines carrying oil and gas from the Caspian basin and has made energy security a component of the 2003 European Security Strategy and the ENP initiative (see Chapter 8).

Given these considerations, Ukraine and Moldova were included in the

ENP from the outset. Russia itself preferred to stay outside the ENP initiative in favour of pursuing the 'four common spaces' of cooperation agreed with the EU in 2003.[7] The states of the South Caucasus were initially left out but belatedly included in mid-2004 (see Chapter 2). It might also be noted that there was a broad political purpose at work here. Having been wary of the multiple problems in the South Caucasus, the Commission's view, subsequently endorsed by the Council, was that the ENP could contribute to the promotion of domestic governance and regional stability. It would be clearly wrong, however, to suggest that the enhancement of political dialogue has been entirely dependent on the ENP process. Many of the factors listed above pre-date the ENP or run autonomously of it. In order to explore this relationship further, we now turn to a brief consideration of an indicative case, that of Georgia.

In the post-Soviet period Georgia has been a beneficiary of relations with the EU. Total EC economic assistance between 1992 and 2004 amounted to €420 million. EU–Georgia political dialogue, meanwhile, is structured by the relevant PCA (EU–Georgia Partnership and Cooperation Agreement, 1999) which entered into force in 1999. This commits the two sides to work toward 'an increasing convergence of positions on international issues of mutual concern' and a 'resolution of regional conflicts and tensions'. The Cooperation Council established by the PCA has met annually and has typically involved the EU presidency and the Georgian Foreign Minister; parallel meetings have been held with the EU Troika. These meetings were usually the occasion for the EU to exhort Georgia toward greater efforts at resolving its internal security situation, reducing corruption and ensuring political stability. Yet it was clear by 2003 that neither side was fully satisfied with the relationship. The murder in December 2001 of a German diplomat serving with the Commission was described by one Commission official as 'the lowest point in the history of EU–Georgia relations' (European Parliament 2004) and led to a temporary suspension of EU assistance programmes. The Cooperation Council meeting of October 2002 noted the poor implementation of PCA provisions and that future EU aid would be conditional on an improvement in internal security.

An EU political role had not been absent up to this point. From 2000 attention had turned to Georgia owing to spill-over from Russia's offensive against Chechnya (launched in 1999) and US concern after 9/11 that the Pankisi Gorge had become a haven for international terrorism. Between July 2000 and June 2003, the EU adopted five CFSP Joint Actions on Georgia aimed at supporting the work of the OSCE Border Monitoring Operation on the Georgia–Russia border (part of which abuts Chechnya) and OSCE efforts in the province of South Ossetia. These initiatives did shift EU policy up a gear, but were nonetheless small-scale, modest in impact, and hardly indicative of an autonomous EU involvement (Devdariani and Hancilova 2002, 10–11). Recognition of the need for the EU to do more was clearly evident on the Georgian side. At a meeting of the EU–Georgia Parliamentary Cooperation Committee in June 2003, the Georgian Ambassador to the EU, as well as expressing 'concern' at Georgia's exclusion from the ENP, went on to suggest that the EU ought to 'play a more constructive political role in the South Caucasus and take on a more mediatory role between Russia and Georgia'. Georgian parliamentarians, meanwhile, criticised the EU for premising its policy toward Georgia on 'goodwill' rather than concrete actions and being too passive in the face of Russian destabilisation (European Parliament 2004). In the wake of the 'Rose Revolution' of 2003, newly elected president Mikheil Saakashvili adopted a much more overtly pro-EU policy (including a clearly articulated case for EU membership). In parallel, a Commission for European Integration was created aimed to further on the Georgian side implementation of the PCA.

The EU response to these developments was positive. In late 2003 and early 2004 Georgia was visited on several occasions by the EU's Special Representative for the South Caucasus Heikke Talvitie, by Commission President Romano Prodi and HR-CFSP Javier Solana. In July 2004, at the request of the Georgian Prime Minister, the Council established a rule of law mission to Georgia (EUJUST Themis) to assist in reform of the criminal justice system. While modest in size, scope and duration (the mission was terminated in July 2005), EUJUST Themis was notable for being the first ESDP-related operation to be launched anywhere in the FSU. In September 2005, meanwhile, a small EU team began work in advising and 'mentoring' the Georgian border guard. And during 2005–2006, the Commission undertook a number of economic rehabilitation projects in the war-ravaged Abkhazia region (Lynch 2006: 64–5).

These initiatives were taken outside the ENP framework, but the ENP itself foresaw in Georgia's case a reinforcement of political dialogue. The ENP Action Plan with Georgia under negotiation in 2005, for instance, envisaged an enhanced EU role 'in the resolution of conflicts and enhanced regional cooperation' (European Commission 2005f). The ENP process, moreover, has clearly raised Georgia's expectations of EU action. During a visit to Brussels in March 2005, Georgian Foreign Minister Zarubishvili-Kashia suggested that the EU set up its own border monitoring mission in Georgia to replace that of the OSCE[8] and play a greater role in settling the conflicts in Abkhazia and South Ossetia (Lobjakas 2005).

There are, however, significant obstacles to a greater role for the EU under the CFSP/ESDP fields. The belated inclusion of the South Caucasus in the ENP cannot disguise the constraints on policy toward the region, a site of failing states, weak governance and civil conflict. The appointment of the EU Special Representative and the small-scale ESDP missions in Georgia mark an important precedent but are relatively unambitious in scale. The former entails no direct involvement in mediation efforts and thus lacks visibility and impact by comparison with other interested actors (Russia, the US, the UN, the OSCE and more recently NATO). The latter, meanwhile, have skirted Georgia's urgent need for tools of civilian crisis management and so unlike ESDP missions in the Balkans have involved no EU role in policing or maintaining the peace. Further, the reliance on an EU mentoring role for Georgian border guard training rather than an EU border guard mission proper to replace the OSCE effort suggests a debilitating sensitivity to Russian interests – something the EU has long been criticised for in its dealings with Moscow on the Georgian issue (Ghebali 2004: 286–7; Leonard and Grant 2005: 8).

While the South Caucasus has its advocates in both the Commission and the EP,[9] and while there are significant factors working to raise its regional significance (see above), the EU member states have yet to undertake a concerted engagement there. The generous view here might be that the ENP is something of a breakthrough but that it premises regional stabilisation and domestic governance on predominantly economic and social levers. Political dialogue is an adjunct to this, but regarded as secondary. The less generous view would point to a lack of priority born of member state divisions, negative perceptions of the region, a reluctance to fashion a partnership with Russia for regional conflict settlement and a deference to the growing security role of the US and NATO in the region (Lynch 2006: 55). Political dialogue by this view is considered desirable but still very limited in its possibilities, especially in relation to the actions of other interested parties.

Conclusion

The EU's political dialogue arrangements, whether in the ENP or elsewhere, are largely a case of missed opportunities and unrealised potential. This is true whether examining the Middle East where the EU has a long legacy of involvement or the FSU areas where it is attempting to build new bridges. In both cases the EU seems unwilling (though not unable) to make full use of its range of incentives to guide change in these areas. And this is the crux of the matter: the ENP *as a general framework* is geared toward creating a 'ring of friends' on the EU's periphery though open dialogue, which suggests an emphasis on stability, yet the *specific elements* of the ENP Action Plans are far more suggestive of promoting changes within and among these partners, changes that would almost certainly undermine stability, at least in the short term. So if forced to choose between stability and change towards these states, and between withholding or exerting the EU's considerable power resources over them, the EU will almost always choose the former options.

Thus on the basis of overall effectiveness the ENP is not particularly inspiring in the area of political cooperation, though it may help facilitate this goal indirectly through the other policy domains examined in this volume. Cooperation in economic affairs, energy security, immigration, and civil society building may yet produce important spill-over effects to improve the political dialogue from the 'bottom up' (citizens, NGOs and firms) rather than from the 'top down' (government representatives). Even at the government level the ENP certainly raises the prospects of more 'activity' with these important neighbouring states: more meetings, more financial aid, more agreements, more goals. International cooperation on anything is virtually impossible without a reservoir of trust and a means of communication; ENP political dialogue arrangements certainly preserve those features. And the framework may go further in the long term by adding more subtle socialisation and normative incentives onto the existing structure of material incentives (trade and aid) that provides the backbone of the ENP Action Plans (Kelley 2006). This of course will take time, while the EU itself will be preoccupied with completing the enlargement process and handling the fallout from the French and Dutch rejections of the Constitutional Treaty (which had mentioned developing a 'special relationship' with neighbouring countries). The EU will also face continued competition from the US and Russia in promoting its vision for the ENP partners, competition that may undermine the coherence and effectiveness of the ENP entirely.

Yet in the final analysis the EU has no other choice but to engage with its neighbouring states, whether through the ENP framework or otherwise. Geography is at least partly destiny, and the EU's bordering states are not going to disappear. Nor are they likely to remain as stable as the EU seems to hope. Thus the ENP programme may ultimately attain greater prominence by virtue of as yet unforeseen exogenous stresses forced upon it rather than through the innocuous diplomatic niceties outlined in the various ENP Action Plans. As is always the case in EU foreign policy, incremental steps are very important, as are learning-by-doing and the symbols and rhetoric involved in creating the EU's global identity (M.E. Smith 2003). The ENP, like most EU foreign policy initiatives, certainly upholds these traditions while moving the EU ever so slightly in new directions: procedurally, substantively, and geographically.

Notes

1   With Israel, Jordan, Moldova, Morocco, the Palestinian Authority, Tunisia, and Ukraine.
2   Details of these arrangements can be found in Biscop (2004: 30).
3   'Significant impact' involves primary, direct influence on non-member states, with a major beneficial or adverse impact on their vital interests resulting in a change of behaviour/policy of the non-member state that can be empirically-verified (Ginsberg 2001: 53).
4   Algeria, Cyprus, Egypt, Israel, Jordan, Lebanon, Malta, Morocco, Syria, Tunisia, Turkey and the Palestinian Authority. The agreements with Algeria and Lebanon still await ratification; that with Syria has not been signed.
5   Or even sub-regional cooperation, for example among the EMP partners of the Mashreq (Egypt, Jordan, Lebanon), the Maghreb (Algeria, Libya, Mauritania,

Morocco and Tunisia), and the Agadir group of 'like-minded' states (Morocco, Egypt, Jordan and Tunisia).

6   Although a draft 'Euro-Mediterranean Charter for Peace and Stability' could not be adopted in November 2000 due to the problems of the MEPP.

7   Russia, however, remains a beneficiary of Community funding under the European Neighbourhood and Partnership Instrument given the similarity between the policy concerns of the common spaces and those of the ENP.

8   The mandate of the OSCE operation was not renewed in December 2004 owing to the exercise of a veto by Russia.

9   The Committee on Foreign Affairs has issued reports advocating the formation of a regional stability pact for the Caucasus.

GERGANA NOUTCHEVA AND MICHAEL EMERSON

5

Economic and social development

With its new European Neighbourhood Policy, the European Union has begun to develop a further ring in a widening set of economic policy regimes that gravitate around it. There are now no less than six rings to this system. The purpose of this chapter is to trace the emergence of this proliferating 'export' activity, and to consider whether with the ENP it has reached the outer limits of its viability.

The first ring is the 'old EU', which first defined the rules of the internal market and economic and monetary union in the 1980s and then applied them in the 1990s. This stock of laws, norms and rules became known as the '*acquis communautaire*', i.e. meaning effectively the 'acquired jurisdiction of the European Community'. In a second ring, the EU's internal market was extended to the European Free Trade Association (EFTA) states, to form the European Economic Area (EEA) in 1994, with the adoption of virtually the whole of the internal market *acquis*. This was a case of extension of the system to states with the most advanced governance standards. The third ring saw extension of the *acquis* to the new member states acceding in 2004. In this case the new member states from Central and Eastern Europe were at the same time completing their regime change out of communism. The fourth ring consists of the Western Balkan states, which are not yet accession candidates, and for whom the Stabilisation and Association Process (SAP) was devised. This involves a substantial but less complete or rapid adoption of the *acquis*, but the political incentive of accession to the EU in the long term is still present. These are also cases of post-communist regime change, but with the addition of severe post-conflict and state-building agendas.

The ENP, initiated in 2003, thus represents the fifth and largest ring, embracing six former republics of the Soviet Union in Eastern Europe (excluding Russia) and the ten Southern Mediterranean states of the Barcelona Process. This also involves the post-communist transition for the post-Soviet states, but the same policy is addressing the culturally different challenges of modernisation of the Arab world. Both groups of states have serious weaknesses of political and economic governance to resolve, and the EU *acquis* is only selectively being introduced, depending on the will and aptitudes of each state individually. Most of the neighbouring European states look for a long-term prospect of EU accession, but this is not encouraged by the EU itself.

Last but not least, Russia alone occupies the sixth ring, with a set of 'common space' agreements signed with the EU in 2005. These are more limited still than the ENP in commitment to convergence on EU norms, and there is no demand by Russia for the prospect of EU membership, but there is a more ambitious geo-strategic content.

This chapter focuses mainly on the emerging ENP, but places it in the perspective of the other rings in the EU's spectrum of arrangements for exporting its norms and rules of economic governance. The comparison between these several regimes, all belonging to the same family, allows us to examine both the extent and limits of this complex and growing process. Looking across the rings, we observe that the EU economic regime has extended its outreach to all categories of countries, but the degree of acceptance of EU economic norms and the speed of adoption of EU economic rules are diminishing in the areas further away from the EU core. In the immediate vicinity, the EFTA ring, a high level of economic standards existed prior to the countries' full inclusion in the single market and the mechanisms of *acquis* enforcement have been modelled on the EU's internal rules and procedures. In the outer rings of lower economic standards, the EU has been more successful in encouraging convergence on its economic norms in countries to which it has extended the prospect of membership. The promise of full integration in the EU has legitimised the EU's external governance through conditionality to steer the course of economic transition in the candidates and potential candidates. In the ENP ring, the EU has excluded the mega-incentive of accession as a member state and this has decreased the possibilities for exerting strong leverage over the ENP partners. The evolving EU economic relationship with the southern and eastern neighbours is less hierarchical in nature and more based on mutual agreement and cooperation. In the outmost ring occupied by Russia, we see the EU reaching the geographical limits of its economic influence. Generally, the EU's gravitational pull is getting weaker in the more distant periphery and the EU instruments are shifting from more traditional methods of hierarchical governance to softer modes of horizontal cooperation.

A further part of the system of external influences bearing upon these states comes with the projection of norms and rules of economic governance by the International Financial Institutions (principally in the present context the IMF, IBRD, WTO and EBRD). In general terms the mix of influence of the EU and the IFIs varies as a function of the strength of the EU integration factor, with the IFIs fading in significance for EU member states, but remaining as important actors in other parts of the European neighbourhood. How best to blend the EU's *acquis* and the *Washington consensus* in the European neighbourhood becomes a major issue for the policy-makers.

Shaping the rules of economic governance in the old EU

The EU's own internal system of economic governance has been analysed in both the economic literature focusing on the substance and economic rationale of EU policies (Gros et al. 2002a; Gros et al. 2004; Gros et al. 2005) and the political economy literature concentrating on the modes of economic policy-making (Linsenmann and Wessels 2002; Collignon 2003). A great number of the economic decisions of EU governments have come to be constrained by the economic competences transferred to the EU level, in particular in trade, competition, monetary and several sectoral policy areas, and commitments made to coordinate other aspects of their economic policies. Yet, regardless of the EU layer of governance, there is substantial discretion left to the national governments to preserve their national economic features that continue to co-exist with the common economic policies. Member states have, for instance, opted for a wide range of policies with respect to the extent of state involvement in the economy that is compatible with EU competition policy, on the speed and extent of privatisation, on the level of social protection and taxation, and the degree of rigidity or flexibility of labour market regulation.

The first feature of the EU's approach to economic governance is encoded in the internal market regime, with regulatory norms and methods adopted in a comprehensive range of EU common policies, such as for technical product standards, indirect taxation, competition policy, transport, environment, energy, etc. The programme to complete the internal market by 1992 required no less than 300 legal acts, which became the heart of the *acquis*, defining the basic rules and standards in the specific sectors. They are tightly linked to the liberal economic logic underpinning the internal market and the 'four freedoms' constituting its core – the free movement of goods, services, capital and labour. The progressive empowerment of the EU institutional structures, considered by many analysts a key factor for achieving progress in market integration, has been at the heart of conceptualisations of the EU economic governance as a supranational system (Bulmer 1997).

A second distinct feature of the EU governance practice is agreement on a limited redistribution function, aiming at strengthening the economic and social cohesion across borders. There is an explicit commitment to 'reducing disparities between the levels of development of the various regions and the backwardness of the least-favoured regions, including rural areas'[1] among the member states. The agreement on substantial regional and structural funds in the common budget is the concrete instrument for promoting cohesion (Lamy 2004). This emerging blend of economic liberalism and social cohesion is a basic reflection of the EU's preferred range of socio-economic models, which while quite wide, can still be contrasted with the more liberal model observed in the United States.

With the launch of EMU, the European Central Bank was empowered to maintain price stability within the eurozone economy. The rules governing decision-making in monetary policy exhibit features of 'traditional' governance with a firm treaty base and institutionalisation at EU level (Wallace and Wallace 2000). The common currency and the single monetary framework are the third feature of the EU economic governance system. The criteria set to ensure the convergence of macroeconomic policies of governments prior to membership in the EMU, known also as the Maastricht criteria (see Box 5.1), constitute the consensus among the member states on the basic principles of macroeconomic governance such as low inflation, sustainable public finances and external accounts, and a transparent and predictable environment for economic agents.

Box 5.1   The Maastricht criteria

Inflation – no more than 1.5% above the average inflation rate of the lowest 3 inflation countries.

Interest rates – the long-term rate should be no more than 2% above the average of the three countries with the lowest inflation rates.

Budget deficit – no more than 3% of GDP.

National debt – no more than 60% of GDP.

Exchange rates – currency within the normal ERM bands with no re-alignments for at least 2 years.

These elements of supranational governance in the economic domain, however, co-exist with softer mechanisms of policy coordination (Heritier 2002). These rely less on hierarchical methods and formal rules and sanctioning procedures, and more on horizontal coordination through common benchmarking, target setting and voluntary implementation. The main elements of real supranational governance, as in the single market *acquis* and the euro currency controlled by the independent European Central Bank, are thus flanked by a complex set of economic policy coordination methods, of varying hardness or softness, and of varying effectiveness too. At the macroeconomic level, the Stability and Growth Pact (SGP) is an attempted example of 'hard' coordination in the area of fiscal policy (Linsenmann and Wessels 2002). It is a framework for regulating the fiscal behaviour of member states by putting limits on government spending and debt levels.[2] It includes a budgetary surveillance mechanism with a legal procedure for penalising governments in breach of the common rules, based on treaty provisions.[3] In contrast, the annual Broad Economic Policy Guidelines (BEPG) and the employment policy present models of 'soft' coordination (Linsenmann and Wessels 2002). They are not legally binding frameworks and work on the basis of policy monitoring and policy recommendation without formal sanctions in the case of non-compliance. At the microeconomic level, the so-called 'Lisbon strategy', launched in 2000, is based on a highly detailed benchmarking of performance indicators, subject to annual review at summit level. It is as an example of the 'open method of coordination', seeking to achieve results through lessons learned and sharing of best practices, and raising the domestic political costs of poor performance, rather than through applying detailed norms at EU level (Eberlein and Kerwer 2004).

The EU economic governance system, therefore, is a mix of modes of governance. EMU, the Single Market regulatory norms, including the social dimension to support the less developed areas, and the 'hard', 'soft' and 'open' coordination mechanisms in other economic areas all form part of the EU economic governance framework. It is a patchwork system of national and supranational elements, of macroeconomic and microeconomic policy components, yet a system with a constantly evolving European dimension that has affected governance structures at national level. Together they form a certain culture of European economic governance that shapes the discourse and expectations of the EU representatives when dealing with the European integration aspirations of neighbouring non-member states.

Exporting the rules of the internal market to the EFTA states

The EU's first important act of export of its economic regime was initiated by Jacques Delors, when the internal market programme was becoming credible, and the EFTA states with their very deep level of trade integration with the EU feared that they could become relatively disadvantaged. Delors for his part wanted to avoid a cascade of new membership applications from these small states, and so offered them a formula for guaranteeing full access to the internal market. The conditions for this were wholesale adoption, with implementation through their domestic legislation, of all the 300 legal acts of the EU to complete the opening of the market. The EU and EFTA states were thus to become joint members of the EEA. It was also agreed that the EEA would be a dynamic jurisdiction, in that the EFTA states accepted an open-ended obligation to adopt further domestic laws to implement subsequent developments of the EU's internal market, which have turned out to be of large importance, especially in the service sectors.

From a political standpoint the EEA involved the highly democratic EFTA states accepting the EU's legally binding specification of their internal economic policies on a grand scale, without any power to join in the policy-shaping process at all (Emerson et al. 2002). This extreme experiment with 'democratic deficit politics' had several results. First attempts were made to give some dignified institutional means for the EFTA state to participate in policy-shaping and legal implementation. Committee structures were set up for consultations over new EU legislation. An EFTA Court was set up in Luxembourg, alongside the European Court of Justice, to rule over legal disputes. This interesting innovation involves judges from EFTA states making binding rulings on the implementation of EU law in their states, a system that could only conceivably work where the officials of the partner states enjoyed the highest trust for their competence and loyalty to the intentions of the EEA. In addition, an EFTA Surveillance Authority watches over the legal transposition of EU directives and publishes twice yearly the Internal Market Scoreboard measuring the success of the EFTA countries in implementing the Internal Market legislation. The results to date show that the EFTA countries have closed down their transposition deficit and have even achieved a better implementation rate than the EU member states (see Figure 5.1).

The EEA experience, while governing only small populations, is nonetheless rich as an extreme experiment in the export and import of economic regimes. It is also an important reference for any analysis of more limited attempts for neighbourhood states to gain 'a stake in the internal market', and for the implications of the import of economic regimes for democratic legitimacy.

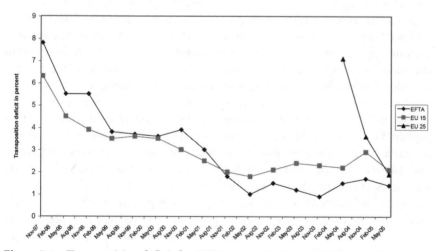

Figure 5.1 **Transposition deficit for EFTA states, EU 15 and EU 25 as of 30 April 2005**

Source: EFTA Surveillance Authority (2005) *Internal Market Scoreboard – EFTA States.* Reprinted with kind permission.

Economic governance and the enlargement into Central and Eastern Europe

The EU enlargement policy towards Central and Eastern Europe has often been cited as a successful example of EU 'external governance by conditionality' (Schimmelfennig and Sedelmeier 2004). The EU conditionality model of offering incentives for EU rule adoption, and disincentives for failure to align with the EU norms, has been credited with the pace of political and economic transformation in the candidate countries in the period preceding their membership in the EU (Grabbe 1999; Kelley 2004a). Given the asymmetry of the EU relationship with future members, and the top-down transfer of EU rules, the candidate states had no choice but to take all elements of the EU governance system described above (Schimmelfennig and Sedelmeier 2004: 675).

The Central and Eastern European countries were relatively open to new ideas about governance methods and practices from the EU because they were in active search of a credible model to replace the collapsed communist system. In the early 1990s, the economies in the region suffered devastating shocks after the breakdown of the centrally planned economic structures. The economic objective of EU enlargement policy was to make sure that the candidate countries had achieved a level of economic stability and acceptance of market principles as the basis for economic management prior to their full exposure to competition within the internal market.

In terms of the mechanisms for bringing about the desired economic change in the candidate countries, the process of rule transfer is clear-cut. The aspiring candidates had no say on the EU Internal Market laws, and the EU was only willing to grant temporary derogations to full alignment with the *acquis* on an exceptional basis. Furthermore, the process of legal approximation is by definition technocratic in nature, driven by officials in Brussels and national capitals and with limited participation of civil society. With regard to the adoption of specific EU directives and regulations, the EU institutional machinery is in a hierarchical relationship above national governments.

Concerning the economic criteria for accession, however, the EU's impact on the governance structures of the candidate countries is not so explicit beyond compliance with EU law. The EU did not and could not prescribe a particular economic model to the transition economies in Central and Eastern Europe. Instead, it formulated two broad economic criteria known as the 'Copenhagen economic criteria' – a functioning marketing economy and capacity to cope with competitive pressures within the single market (see Box 5.2) – and monitored progress towards their fulfilment while giving freedom to the governments to devise their specific reform programmes and adjustment measures.

Box 5.2   The Copenhagen economic criteria and sub-criteria

'Membership requires the existence of a *functioning market economy*, as well as the *capacity to cope* with competitive pressure and market forces within the Union.'

To measure the *closeness* of a country to being a *functioning market economy*, the European Commission applied the following sub-criteria:

• Consensus about economic policy.
• Macroeconomic stability, including price stability, sustainable public finances and external accounts.
• Price and trade liberalisation.
• Free market entry (creation of new firms) and exit (bankruptcy legislation);
• Adequate legal system, including enforcement of property rights.
• Sufficiently developed financial sector.

To determine the *capacity* of a country *to cope with competitive pressures* within the single market, the European Commission employed the following sub-criteria:

• Existence of a functioning market economy.
• Sufficient human and physical capital, including quality of education and infrastructure.
• Public and private stock capital, including FDI levels.
• Progress in enterprise restructuring.
• Sectoral structure of the economy, including sectoral shifts between share of agriculture, industry and services.
• Small and medium enterprise development.
• Limited state interference in the economy.
• Sufficient trade and investment integration with the EU market.

Source: Headings from Regular Reports on Progress towards Accession of candidate countries. Brussels: European Commission.

The Commission did not specify threshold levels that would clearly indicate whether a country has fulfilled a certain sub-criterion or not. The open-ended conditions allow for broad interpretation of what constitutes Copenhagen-compliant economic performance. In the absence of clear benchmarks, the Commission looked at the general progress in the transition process, focusing more on the big picture rather than details. To receive a good score from Brussels, it was sufficient to demonstrate a positive record on the main economic indicators over a period of time and a proven record of structural reforms to demonstrate their sustainability and irreversibility of the general economic trend.[4]

The choices of the candidate countries concerning the precise content of macroeconomic and sectoral policies, however, were constrained by other external sources such as the IFIs, which were keen on providing policy advice and financial resources on condition of their endorsement of the 'Washington consensus' as a platform for economic governance. In essence, there was no contradiction between the European Commission and the IFIs on the broad framework of economic reform. The IMF and the World Bank supported the EU orientation of the countries from Central and Eastern Europe and worked towards their EU membership, and they set the reform priorities in their area of specialisation: macroeconomic policy and structural reform, respectively. The European Commission, in turn, accepted the leadership of the IFIs in their specific fields and complemented their programmes, but put special emphasis on issues that are of particular importance to the EU and are related to the country's relationship with it.

The European Commission directly endorsed the IMF's liberal approach to economic stabilisation and growth and even co-financed it through its macro-financial assistance (MFA) scheme. The major precondition for the provision of such assistance is an agreement between the government of the country and the IMF on a macroeconomic programme, which means that IMF conditionality is built into the EU's macro-financial package. The candidate countries received MFA from the EU mostly in the early days of transition of the 1990s, and strict MFA conditionality was absent from the late stages of substantive accession preparations. There was nonetheless an implicit agreement between the EU and the IMF that the Fund would take the lead on macroeconomic policy, given its expertise in the area and its involvement in the transition economies.

The World Bank in turn added its resources to the incentive of EU membership in order to stimulate structural reform in the transition economies. It anchored its own programmes in the general EU framework, providing additional inducements linked to specific reform conditions in various sectors. Thus, while helping the candidates reach 'EU standards', the World Bank has exercised its own leverage over the reform agenda of the countries. In principle, the World Bank conditionality complemented the EU conditionality. In practice, the World Bank's method of setting concrete and often quantifiable targets went down to a level of detail in the specific policy areas beyond that which the EU reached with its grand approach to accession conditionality.

The EU's own Maastricht criteria, which touch upon issues of macroeconomic governance, played an indirect but important role in making the candidates aware of what the macroeconomic rules of the game were in the eurozone. Although the EU policy is that candidate countries should not join EMU immediately upon accession to EU, and the Maastricht criteria have therefore not been applied in the pre-accession period, the macroeconomic rules of the eurozone were already built into the expectations of the governments of the acceding states, most of whom favoured early joining of EMU (Gros et al. 2002b).

State-building and governance in the Western Balkans

The EU's economic policy in the Western Balkans (i.e. states of the former Yugoslavia not yet accepted as member states, plus Albania), is subordinated to the primary goal of state-building and strengthening the institutional base of the fragile state structures across the region. This is pursued within the political and legal framework of the Stabilisation and Association Process, which represents a preliminary stage to the process of negotiating accession that should follow when the priority political and governance criteria are met. Economic transition is very much on the agenda, but after the outstanding constitutional questions have been settled, notably in the cases of Bosnia and Hercegovina (BiH) and Serbia and Montenegro (SCG), where clear lines of responsibility for economic policy-making remained to be defined between sub-state entities. Post-war reconstruction, state- and institution-building come first. What is similar to the EU approach to Central and Eastern Europe is the conditional offer of membership, which is the strongest incentive the EU can put on the table, even if this may be dulled by the unspecified and distant time horizon. This has set the stage for a strong conditionality policy with concrete demands and rewards for reforms.

Two examples, Bosnia-Hercegovina and Serbia-Montenegro, illustrate these tendencies. The EU has demanded a high level of economic harmonisation between the constituent entities of Bosnia and Hercegovina and between Serbia and Montenegro before the dissolution of their State Union in 2006. Prior to the EU intervention through the SAP, the two entities in BiH in one case, and Serbia and Montenegro in the other, were seeking maximum independence from each other. Bosnia and Hercegovina's progress towards a Stabilisation and Association Agreement (SAA) with the EU was made conditional, among other things, on a reform of the indirect tax system. This has involved the ceding of competences to the state level by the entity governments – most notably, the competence to collect taxes – and has resulted in a more integrated decision-making system for economic policy within the common state. In the case of Serbia and Montenegro, in order to qualify for an SAA, Serbia and Montenegro were initially requested to harmonise their customs tariffs, to coordinate their customs services and to create the conditions for free movement of people, goods, services and capital between the two republics. However, the EU had to relax its requirement of a common external trade regime in 2004 after meeting firm resistance from the governments in Belgrade and Podgorica. Following the referendum on independence in Montenegro in May 2006, the EU had to drop its common state conditionality vis-à-vis Serbia and Montenegro altogether and developed separate relations with the two sovereign states.

Two entities in this region, Montenegro and Kosovo, have adopted the euro as their currency, renouncing both continued membership in the former Yugoslav and now Serbian dinar area, and creation of their own independent currencies. In addition, Bosnia has adopted a currency board monetary regime, with a fixed exchange rate in relation to the DM initially, and subsequently the euro. Such arrangements are a very strong example of regime export, improving weaknesses in the domestic governance of the state concerned. In the two cases of euroisation, Montenegro decided to go ahead unilaterally in spite of discouragement from the EU, while for Kosovo the UN Mission in Kosovo (UNMIK) protectorate authorities agreed only because of the political impossibility of the dinar alternative. For Bosnia the currency board regime was decided by the Dayton powers.

The Western Balkan countries, therefore, are experiencing a special category of external influence over their governance structures through both conditionality and direct imposition by protectorate powers. While the EU's incentive is equivalent to that offered to the candidate countries from Central and Eastern Europe – full membership – the initial state of affairs in the Western Balkans has required a more targeted approach to setting country-specific conditions, penetrating deep into the domestic governance structures of the potential candidates.

The two neighbourhoods: east and south

While the economic objectives of the ENP are comparable to those of the enlargement policy, the initial conditions in the southern and eastern neighbourhoods are quite different. The countries from the former communist bloc, either from Central Europe or the former Soviet Union (FSU), have a similar domestic environment as transition economies coming out of communist regimes, and seeking to modernise and adapt to the market principles governing the capitalist economies. They were all insulated for a long time from international competitive forces due to the restriction of their commercial exchanges within the communist bloc market. Their integration into the international economic system is a major challenge for both the local economic agents driving the process and the public authorities supporting it through creating a favourable regulatory environment. The FSU countries in question – Ukraine, Moldova, Belarus, Georgia, Armenia and Azerbaijan – have a very short history of independence and state consolidation, and their institutional apparatus is still far from fit to manage the enforcement of a regulatory framework necessary for a modern economy. The EU model of economic governance, which has been successful in delivering prosperity to its member states, has a degree of attraction and legitimacy in the eyes of the post-Soviet elites and societies. Yet, there is a wide variation in the openness to and acceptance of EU-inspired economic norms and regulatory rules among the countries from this regional group. Nevertheless, Ukraine, Moldova, Georgia and Armenia all openly express their long-term aspirations for full EU membership, even while this is discouraged by the EU itself, especially after the referendum crisis over the Constitution.

In the southern neighbourhood, however, the EU is confronted with a drastically different institutional and cultural setting. The Arab states are distant from the European core, geographically, politically, culturally and economically. The southern neighbours are consolidated states, mostly with authoritarian regimes, yet with mainly market economies exposed to at least some international competition. Most of the Mediterranean countries have experienced a degree of authoritarian stability in their domestic affairs in the last decades, with little interest in radical change on the scale of the post-communist regime changes. The southern Arab regimes are increasingly under pressure from Islamist political and religious movements. Resistance to EU-promoted ideas and governance methods can be expected to be greater than for the European neighbours, albeit with some countries of the region such as Morocco being more receptive than others to European-style values of political and economic liberalism. Israel is the exception in the region, with a population more interested in re-integration with Europe than with its Arab neighbours.

A comparison of the level of development of the southern and eastern neighbours reveals data that many would consider surprising. The southern Arab neighbours on average enjoy higher income levels than the East European neighbours – see Table 5.1. For example Algeria and Tunisia have significantly higher GDP per capita than the South Caucasus states. Israel stands out in this ranking because its economic prosperity is on a par with that of the EU. These comparisons are confirmed by data on the proportion of population living below the poverty line, with $2 per day taken to be the standard measure. Thus while Ukraine has a poverty ratio of 46% of the population and Moldova even 64%, Egypt records 44%, Morocco 14% and Tunisia 7%.

An interesting outlier is Belarus, with the highest income level among the eastern neighbours, and the lowest poverty ratio of 2%, meaning practically no poverty at all. These relatively positive indicators for Belarus are confirmed in a detailed report recently published by the World Bank (2005). The story is made all the more intriguing when taken together with the data displayed in figures 5.2 and 5.3 on the quality of economic regulatory policy and the rule of law, which are usually fundamental indicators of the quality of economic governance. On these measures Belarus scores outright bottom

Table 5.1   Level of development and poverty rates

	County	GNI per capita (USD) 2004 Atlas (Method)[a]	GNI per capita (USD) 2004 Purchasing Power Parity PPP)[a]	Population 2003 (million)[b]	Poverty headcount ratio at $2 a day (PPP) (% of population)[c]
Eastern neighbourhood countries	Armenia	1120	4270	3.06	49 (1998)
	Azerbaijan	950	3830	8.37	9 (2001)
	Belarus	2120	6900	9.90	2 (2000)
	Georgia	1040	2930	5.13	16 (2001)
	Moldova	710	1930	4.27	64 (2001)
	Ukraine	1260	6250	48.52	46 (1999)
Southern neighbourhood countries	Algeria	2280	6280	31.80	15 (1995)
	Egypt	1310	4120	71.93	44 (1999)
	Israel	17380	23510	6.43	N/A
	Jordan	2140	4640	5.47	7 (1997)
	Lebanon	4980	5380	3.65	N/A
	Libya	4450	NA	5.55	N/A
	Morocco	1520	4100	30.57	14 (1999)
	Syria	1190	3550	17.80	N/A
	Tunisia	2630	7310	9.83	7 (2000)
	WB and Gaza	1120	NA	3.56	N/A

Data Sources: [a] World Development Indicators, World Bank, 2005.
              [b] International Financial Statistics, International Monetary Fund, April 2005.
              [c] World Development Indicators, World Bank, 2005.

place among all neighbourhood states, as it does also in measures of democracy, since its regime is the only remaining first-class dictatorship left in Europe. The explanation for the relatively positive economic data for Belarus is that this country has avoided the typical post-communist economic collapse brought about by sudden regime change, and its state-run economy has continued in particular to supply basic industrial and consumer goods to the Russian market. The World Bank does warn that this relatively positive experience of recent years may be difficult to sustain, as Belarus is not modernising its product lines, and will find international competition increasingly severe, including in the Russian market (World Bank 2005).

The economic objective of the ENP is to help the southern and eastern neighbours develop and modernise by anchoring their economies on the EU model of economic governance. Two measurements from the World Bank's six governance indicators are particularly suited for assessing where the neighbouring countries stand in terms of their capacity to implement effectively the rules governing economic policy-making – the regulatory quality indicator and the rule of law indicator. The former gives an indication of the quality of policies and regulation, whereas the latter measures the respect of existing rules in policy implementation (Kaufmann et al. 2004).

These indicators do not assess convergence on EU regulatory norms and governance practices, but they do give an idea about the difference in the regulatory standards between the developed world and the transition and less developed countries, and their regional groups. A comparison of data for 2004 shows that the Southern Mediterranean neighbours have more advanced regulatory frameworks and institutions on average than the East European neighbour states. Yet the average level of the Southern Mediterranean countries is well below the average for the new EU member states, and further below the standards of OECD countries. The institutional weakness in the FSU countries is particularly striking as most of them score lower than the Mediterranean states on the rule of law. The most authoritarian regimes in both the southern and eastern neighbourhoods – Libya and Belarus – have been disqualified from inclusion in the ENP policy framework on political criteria, and this is illustrated in their bottom rankings in the governance assessments of Figure 5.2.

Has there been any improvement of the governance structures and practices in the neighbourhood in recent years? While the ENP is a new instrument, the EU has maintained relations with the southern and eastern neighbours for about a decade now, in the framework of the Barcelona Process with the Mediterranean countries and in the context of the Partnership and Cooperation Agreements with the Commonwealth of Independent States (CIS) countries. According to World Bank data a comparison of the 1996 and 2004 governance scores of the neighbours shows that

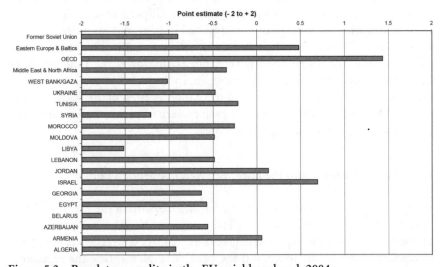

Figure 5.2   Regulatory quality in the EU neighbourhood, 2004
Source: D Kaufmann, A. Kraay, and M. Mastruzzi 2005: Governance Matters IV: Governance Indicators for 1996–2005 (http://www.worldbank.org/ubi/governance/pubs/govmatters4.html).

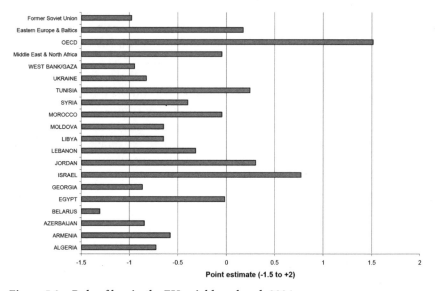

Figure 5.3   Rule of law in the EU neighbourhood, 2004
Source: D Kaufmann, A. Kraay, and M. Mastruzzi 2005: Governance Matters IV: Governance
Indicators for 1996–2005 (http://www.worldbank.org/ubi/governance/pubs/govmatters4.html).

most of them have regressed rather than progressed on both regulatory
quality and rule of law.[5] The three Southern Caucasus countries and Ukraine
have improved their regulatory frameworks, although starting from a very
low level whereas the regulatory regimes in most Mediterranean countries
have deteriorated. With regard to the rule of law, the situation is largely
unchanged in both the southern and eastern neighbourhoods, but with a lot
of room for improvement considering the low ratings of all the neighbours in
comparison with the average of the advanced industrial economies.

The two EU neighbourhoods thus reveal important differences in their
past economic trajectories and governance standards at the time when the
ENP is launched. Intra-regional heterogeneity in terms of level of development and standards of economic governance is present in both regional
groups.[6] It is realistic to foresee an uneven pattern of progress given the initial
conditions in the individual partner states.

Economic governance and the European Neighbourhood Policy

While the ENP is not about preparing for membership of the EU, it is closely
linked to the enlargement process. The primary difference compared to the
accession process is the expected degree of regulatory convergence, the choice
of regulatory norms to adopt and the pace of implementing the regulatory
reforms. While for the candidate countries, it is a 'take-it-or-leave-it'
proposal, where governments have no choice but to harmonise the national

legislation with the whole body of EU law, for the ENP partners full legal harmonisation with the EU *acquis* is not foreseen. The expectation is for partial and progressive alignment with EU legal norms in areas where it makes economic sense, suits the development level and serves the development goals of the neighbours. Moreover, since the Action Plans are the product of joint negotiations between the European Commission and the partner state, there is a further degree of freedom in the choice of reforms that are targeted.

Another difference is in the much greater emphasis in the ENP Action Plans on development objectives. For its future members, the EU did not specify a required GDP or wealth level, as long as the right economic policy mix, largely defined by reference to EU norms, was put in place. The development objective, however, is much more explicit, with references to the country's Poverty Reduction Strategy Paper (PRSP) developed under the auspices of the World Bank. In poorer countries, such as Moldova, welfare improvement is singled out as a target, and the government is asked to take concrete measures to reduce poverty through improving the effectiveness of social assistance and the social safety net in general, including the social protection of children.[7]

The economic sections of the first wave of Action Plans for Jordan, Israel, Palestine, Morocco, Tunisia, Moldova and Ukraine echo in their structure of headings the economic reform agenda from the accession process. The standard agenda has been adapted to an extent in the consultation process with the partner state, to take on board national priorities and government preferences. The reform priorities fall under four thematic areas:

- macroeconomic policies;
- structural reforms;
- social and employment policy, including poverty reduction where appropriate;
- regional development and sustainable development.

Compared to the provisions of the existing Association Agreements with the Mediterranean countries and the Partnership and Cooperation Agreements with the FSU countries, the Action Plans have a higher degree of specificity and go a step further in thematically enriching the economic dialogue with the neighbours. However, the economic reform priorities jointly identified with the national authorities give only broad guidelines about desirable improvements in various domains. They are not of a prescriptive nature nor do they set threshold levels for measuring achievement.

A further difference between the eastern and southern neighbours lies in the balance between the political and economic content of the Action Plans. To the extent that the notion of 'Europe' has a magnetic power of attraction in East European societies, the appeal of the EU's norms of democracy and human rights is especially vivid, as the Georgian and Ukrainian Rose and Orange revolutions showed. In the east, political elites can lean on the European project to legitimise their domestic agenda and thus build a political identity based on *rapprochement* with the Western European democracies. Correspondingly the content of the East European Action Plans is strong on democracy and human rights.

This is in contrast with the southern Arab Mediterranean neighbourhood, which resists the idea of political conditionality and is hardly impressed by the EU's talk about common political values. Instead, for the Arab Mediterranean states, the economic benefits of regulatory convergence with the EU has to be the prime factor to persuade ruling elites to anchor their economic policies in the EU framework. Moreover in the south the EU itself has been hesitant to pursue democratisation policies forcefully, and has emphasised economic reform, counting on a positive spill-over effect from the economic to the political domain (Youngs 2002). Even if this anticipated spill-over from the economic to the political has proved illusory, the Action Plans for the southern neighbourhood reveal a continuation of this trend, with recommended political reforms limited by what is acceptable to the ruling elites. The southern governments could be more responsive to economic arguments and pledges for market access openings where the ENP has the potential to deliver.

A recent World Bank/European Commission study provides the economic rationale that could win the political support of southern governments for regulatory convergence with the internal market, notably in the service sector (Mueller-Jentsch 2004). The study examined the effects of bringing the Mediterranean partner states closer to the EU services market and argues that the potential benefits offered by free trade in goods, which is already programmed in free trade agreements, are rather modest by comparison with what could be achieved by policy reforms and competitive private-sector development in the area of 'backbone services', such as transport, logistics, financial services, telecommunications and electricity, as well as other service sectors that can profit from proximity to the EU market, such as tourism, IT services, business and professional services, and distribution (Mueller-Jentsch 2004). The potential liberalisation of trade in services can constitute a serious offer to southern neighbours by promising to improve the competitiveness of their economies and by giving them a chance to profit from their potential comparative advantage, owing to proximity and cheap labour, in relation to the EU market.

The economic incentives for encouraging such a process are potentially powerful, but need to be worked out on an operational level. The case for doing that in partnership with other external actors, in particular the World Bank, the IMF, the European Investment Bank and the EBRD, is compelling, especially given the successful cooperation between the EU and the IFIs in steering the transition economies from Central and Eastern Europe and the

Balkans (Emerson 2005b). By pooling their financial resources and coordinating their policy advice on macroeconomics and structural reform, the European Commission and the IFIs can build on their existing experience and collectively provide the external anchor for the reform process in both the eastern and the southern neighbourhoods.

Two features of the Action Plan process suggest a less hierarchical mode of EU involvement in the governance structures of the neighbours, firstly the *joint* setting of priorities for action and secondly the *joint* monitoring of reform performance. Partners are free to determine their own 'level of ambition' in how much they want to reform and how far they want to integrate with the European economy. Furthermore, the Action Plans are not legally binding documents and the ENP governments are not obliged to fulfil what they have agreed to. The Action Plans are an expression of the collective will of the EU and the respective government but deviations from the commitments undertaken are not subject to any formal sanctioning procedures. And because the EU has not specified clear incentives for reform, the potential disincentives for non-reform are not credible either. While the incentive-based logic of the conditionality model is not fully endorsed in the ENP, greater emphasis is put on the socialisation of partners who are treated as equals and invited to take on board certain EU norms and practices if those are considered appropriate. Partners are not in a position to determine the EU regulatory rules but they have more freedom to negotiate the import of a sub-set of those rules only. In this sense they are better placed than the accession candidates to define the limits of external influence on their domestic governance structures.

Finally, the process of negotiating the Action Plans and of performance monitoring is predominantly an intergovernmental matter, which gives the central role to national administrations of the partner states. Yet the involvement of civil society actors in the monitoring phase is not precluded – indeed it is explicitly encouraged in the Ukraine Action Plan. In the enlargement context, civil society actors themselves have been keen on making their opinions known to the European Commission as an instrument for putting additional pressure on their governments. Civil society activists from the new democracies in the eastern neighbourhood have also seen an opportunity to influence the reforms in their countries by voicing their concerns and independent views with EU representatives. Some have even been pushing for an official monitoring role of civil society groups in the review procedure of the Action Plans.[8] It remains to be seen how the ENP monitoring process will be conducted, but the possibility for innovation and unconventional approaches is there, suggesting a governance mode different from the traditional state-centred command and control method.

A common economic space with Russia?

In May 2005, the EU and Russia agreed documents on four so-called 'common spaces', one of which is entitled a 'Common European Economic Space' (CEES), the others dealing with education and security questions. This is in principle the outermost ring of the EU's set of economic relationships with its neighbours, but what does it amount to? The concrete trade interdependence is of huge importance, with primary commodities from Russia, especially oil and gas, being exchanged for goods and services on a large scale. But these trade volumes are not informative about the economic policy regimes that govern the EU–Russia relations. The four agreements that were signed in 2005 have been criticised by independent observers from both the EU and Russia for their fuzzy content, and for being the product of bureaucratic processes with little operational and strategic content. The grandiose names reflect their initiation and agreement at summit level by the Presidents of Russia and the EU Commission and Council Presidency (Emerson 2005a; Karaganov et al. 2005).

The exercise in producing the common CEES document involving over two years of work by officials reveals that the outer limits of the EU's economic regime export process has indeed been reached. The CEES document is all about convergence and harmonisation of economic norms, but Russia has insisted on marking its difference. It does not like the ENP either for itself or the eastern neighbours. For itself Russia has insisted on the equal partner principle, rather than accepting an asymmetric and dominant EU role in norm-setting, and is therefore formally excluded from the ENP. For the EU's eastern neighbours, which are also Russia's 'near abroad', the ENP threatens to undermine Russia's own ambitions to re-consolidate the post-Soviet space through initiatives that not surprisingly echo those of the EU. In 2000 Russia created a sub-group of the CIS called the EurAsian Economic Community including Russia, Belarus and three Central Asia republics. After encountering difficulty in giving substance to ambitious programming documents for harmonising and integrating the economic regimes of these states, Russia switched its priority to creating its own 'Single Economic Space' (SES) with a more compact core group, consisting of Russia, Belarus, Ukraine and Kazakhstan, and aiming at deep regulatory convergence and ultimately a customs union. From the beginning Ukraine was wary of accepting more than free trade commitments, recognising that the customs union proposition would be incompatible with free trade or, a fortiori, deeper integration with the EU. Recent years have thus seen implicit competition between two regional hegemons, the EU and Russia, over their overlapping neighbourhoods. In the critical case of Ukraine as the most important piece in the competition, following the Orange Revolution in Kiev at the end of 2004, the Yuschenko regime has more categorically asserted its EU integration ambitions, and distanced itself from the SES initiative for anything going beyond free trade.

Returning to the EU–Russian relations, Russia's insistence on the principle of equal partnership has made the CEES document hugely ambiguous as to how the aims of convergence and harmonisation of products and markets will actually take place. Who will converge on whom? It is inconceivable that the EU will converge on Russian standards, and so the real question is whether the lack of explicit reference to Russian convergence on EU standards is merely a diplomatic discretion masking a process of real convergence, or whether the declared ambition is an empty political paper.

Conclusions

For the time being, the European Neighbourhood Policy stands uneasily located somewhere in the middle ground between political fact and fiction. The export of the EU's economic regime to the EEA, the new member states and accession candidates and those in the Western Balkans that have acknowledged accession perspectives all belong to the world of political, legal and economic facts. The common economic space with Russia, on the other hand, is more of a fiction in policy terms, notwithstanding the importance of the commodity trade between the EU and Russia.

The question of whether the ENP can set in motion a process leading to better governance and improved economic performance in the neighbourhood therefore remains open. The outcome will depend on both the initial conditions in partner states and on the implementation of the ENP. A domestic transformation process equivalent to the economic change that took place in Central and Eastern European countries prior to their accession to the EU is hardly achievable in the ENP states in a similar time frame and without the mega-incentive of full EU membership. Yet there is a set of potential incentives that the EU can put on the table, most of which are in the economic field, and which could form the core of a finely tailored conditionality policy. The EU is not in a position to lead in setting the specific economic conditions in all areas, but it is well placed to coordinate its policies and pool its resources with other key international players such as the IMF, the World Bank, the European Investment Bank, and EBRD. Given the positive experience from Central and Eastern Europe and drawing on the collaborative formulas worked out in the enlargement context, the conditionality component of the ENP could play a central role in stimulating economic change in the neighbourhood.

In general, the economic dimension of the ENP can be seen as an attempt to export the EU norms of economic governance to the neighbourhood. The EU is proposing to partners that they learn from the EU's economic experience and align their rules with the EU's regulatory framework. The EU certainly does not have a recipe for all economic problems of partner states nor can it maintain that it has a model of economic governance that solves all of its own internal problems. It nevertheless offers to partners the opportunity to emulate the path of EU member states and create joint prosperity through economic integration. In essence, this is an extension of the internal economic logic of the EU to its external relations. In line with its internal practice, the EU's external governance methods combine 'hard' and 'soft' mechanisms of promoting convergence towards common economic rules. In the neighbourhood compared to the enlargement context, the EU counts more on partner state initiative for putting in place a regime of governance reflecting the features of the EU's system and taking into consideration the national specificities of individial partner states.

Notes

1 Art. 130a, Treaty Establishing the European Community.
2 See Resolution of the European Council on the Stability and Growth Pact, Amsterdam, 17 June 1997, OJ C 236, 02/08/1997.
3 See Council Regulation No 1467/97 of July 1997 on speeding up and clarifying the implementation of the excessive deficit procedure, OJ L 209, 02/08/1997.
4 Conversations with European Commission officials.
5 See World Bank Governance Indicators, 1996–2004.
6 For analysis of the differences among the CIS countries see Milcher and Slay 2005.
7 See Proposed EU/Moldova Action Plan, 9 December 2004, Brussels: European Commission.
8 Conversations with NGO activists from the Open Society network in the former Soviet republics of the eastern neighbourhood.

$\mathcal{M}$ILADA $\mathcal{A}$NNA $\mathcal{V}$ACHUDOVA[1]

6

Trade and the internal market

The collapse of communism and the disintegration of the Soviet Union between 1989 and 1991 complicated immensely the geopolitical and institutional position of the European Union. The European Neighbourhood Policy (ENP) is part of the EU's response to its complicated new geopolitical surroundings, providing a framework for building closer bilateral relationships with states that surround the enlarged EU, but that are not candidates for EU membership. The ENP seeks to promote prosperity and stability, largely by giving neighbouring states a 'stake' in the internal market in exchange for policy adjustments and reforms that further 'common values'.[2]

The ENP stems from the confluence of two developments during the 1990s. On the one hand, the EU gradually designed tools to enhance and direct its influence on aspiring member states in East Central Europe. The EU's leverage on credible future members within the enlargement process was animated in large part by the economic imperative for neighbouring states of securing full integration into the EU's internal market. This leverage was, in turn, probably the most successful democracy promotion programme ever implemented by an international actor. On the other hand, during the 1990s the EU put foreign and security policy at centre stage, attempting to develop its capabilities and also its credibility as a geopolitical actor in world politics.

Enlargement and foreign policy became closely intertwined as it became clear that the EU's leverage on aspiring members was the EU's most powerful and successful foreign policy tool (Vachudova 2005). Recognising this, EU leaders made the prospect of EU membership the cornerstone of the EU's foreign policy toward the Western Balkans in the EU-led Stability Pact for Southeastern Europe in 1999. It was in this region, after all, that the EU's credibility as a foreign policy actor was most clearly at stake (Vachudova 2002). The Stability Pact raised the EU's official membership queue in 2000 to eighteen candidates and proto-candidates.[3] Meanwhile, the EU's pre-accession process brought potent if uneven conditionality and socialisation to bear on domestic policy-making in the candidate states.[4]

Yet even as the value of the EU's leverage on candidate states was becoming well understood, many EU policy-makers could agree that the EU had reached the limit of how much it could enlarge in just a decade or two. From this situation flow two compatible ways of understanding the ENP. One way is as an attempt by EU leaders to stave off further enlargement from states that can claim to be 'European'. If the EU can reduce some of the costs borne by states that are excluded from the EU, then perhaps it can improve living standards in neighbouring countries while also reducing pressure to take on additional candidates for membership. Another way to understand the ENP is as a strategy to utilise the EU's newfound leverage as widely and intensively as possible as part of the EU's foreign policy. Since the EU has things that neighbouring countries want, short of membership, why not use conditionality to create a potent foreign policy instrument? The ENP is crafted to recreate a weaker form of the influence that the EU has had on domestic policy-making in the candidate states (Kelley 2006).

In this chapter, I will address two key questions that are two sides of the same coin: how can the EU attenuate the costs of exclusion for neighbouring states, thus improving their economic situation while also decreasing the pressure for further enlargement? And what incentives can the EU offer to governments to make policy changes that bring more democracy, better market-oriented economic reforms, and greater stability to the neighbourhood? I argue that these two questions have, in large part, the same answer: access to the EU's internal market. There are other important rewards on offer in the ENP, including foreign aid, visa facilitation agreements, participation in various EU programmes, and enhanced political dialogue. But the promise of greater participation in the internal market will be the catalyst for any reform momentum that develops within the ENP process. Though the EU has taken important steps over the last decade to project influence using police missions, foreign aid, technical assistance, and military instruments, it is the size and prosperity of the internal market that still provides the lion's share of the EU's power.

This brings us to the main puzzle of the ENP: will the incentives offered by the EU be powerful enough to compel neighbouring governments to make the policy changes that the EU seeks in order to democratise, liberalise, and stabilise the neighbourhood? In relation to the internal market, there are two unknowns that, for now, make it difficult to solve this puzzle. First, will the EU offer complete market access, including access for agricultural products, for services, and even for labour? This could make it worthwhile for the EU's neighbours to play the ENP game. But the EU has a rich history of protecting domestic producers, especially in agriculture, and the influx of foreign workers has become very controversial with EU voters.

Second, under what domestic conditions will policy-makers in the ENP countries find the promise of market access credible and compelling enough to deliver progress on the EU's political, economic and security agendas? Full participation in the internal market could bring dramatic economic gains, but ruling elites would have to implement far-reaching reforms that may have significant short-term costs and may even threaten the domestic sources of their political power. As in the candidate states, we can expect compliance when ruling elites consider that a closer relationship with the EU will bolster their popularity, and when the EU's conditions for moving forward are compatible with the ways that they win and hold power at home (Kelley 2004b; Vachudova 2005).

Here we come to the challenge of analysing the ENP at the present time. The European Commission has developed the ENP and the European Council has embraced it: we can study how the ENP draws on the pre-accession process designed by the Commission for candidates from post-communist Europe (Kelley 2006). The Commission has written 'Country Reports' about the ENP participants, and in 2005 it finalised the first Action Plans in cooperation with ENP governments. But it is too early to have any information about how well the ENP participants will make progress toward the goals agreed upon in the Action Plans, whether this progress can be attributed to the ENP, and indeed how richly the EU will reward progress in order to inspire more.

I have divided this chapter into two parts. The first explores the role of the internal market in shaping the EU's leverage on the ENP states. The second explores the potential of the ENP to promote political and economic reform in neighbouring countries. Working from the assumption that the EU will offer very substantial participation in the internal market, I attempt to identify the policy changes that ENP governments would need to implement to take advantage of this opportunity, and the different mechanisms that could create momentum for substantial reforms under the conditions of the EU's diffuse conditionality.

Before continuing, let me clarify the labels that I will use for the various groups of countries discussed in the chapter (and acknowledge that there are geographic or geopolitical faults with all of them). I will use East Central European (ECE) states to refer to the eight post-communist states that joined the EU in 2004 as well as Bulgaria and Romania that joined in 2007. I will use ENP states or ENP participants to refer to all of the states taking part in the ENP process spanning the former Soviet Union (but excluding Russia), the Middle East and North Africa. And I will use the terms Eastern ENP participants and Mediterranean ENP participants to distinguish two groups: the post-communist states on the territory of the former Soviet Union, and the rest of the ENP states surrounding the Mediterranean.

Transforming the EU's leverage through the ENP

Through the ENP the EU seeks to modify the leverage that it has had on the ECE states, putting it to use in a diluted form. I have created the concepts of 'passive' and 'active' leverage to separate theoretically the kinds of influence that the EU can have on states that wish to join it (Vachudova 2005). By passive leverage I mean the attraction of EU membership, excluding any deliberate policies toward prospective members. By active leverage I mean the elaborate conditionality exercised in the EU's pre-accession process. The ENP attempts to preserve both kinds of leverage in a weaker form, while removing the prospect of EU membership from the equation. It seeks to attenuate and transform the EU's passive leverage in order to stave off further enlargement and boost economic prosperity in the neighbourhood. In other words, the ENP substitutes a membership perspective with other benefits, chiefly a 'stake in the internal market' and also foreign aid. The challenge is to accompany the 'no' to EU membership with policies that will prevent a stark economic or political division between the EU and neighbouring states that could undermine the security of entire continent. This is especially true for the Eastern ENP participants, many of whom have consistently voiced their aspirations to join the EU at some point. As Michael Leigh notes, 'the EU's fundamental objective is to "export" stability to neighbouring countries so that its own peaceful development is not hampered by instability in its new hinterland' (Leigh 2005: 9). To export stability, the EU also seeks to create at least some active leverage, substituting the requirements of membership for a more modest 'action plan' that promotes reforms in many areas of domestic policy-making in the pursuit of 'shared values'.

The ENP as an alternative to further enlargement: reducing the costs of exclusion from the internal market
The EU's passive leverage is based on the benefits of membership – and on the costs of exclusion. The costs of exclusion are largely determined by the way that the EU treats non-members, restricting access for goods and also for people. Virtually all European states that have become credible future members of the EU over the last three decades have chosen to apply for membership – and exclusion from the EU's internal market has played a pivotal part. Agricultural products and other goods in 'sensitive sectors' face extensive restrictions, while all other exports to the EU run the ongoing risk of incurring various forms of contingent protection. This takes on unusual importance, especially for the Eastern ENP participants, given the sheer size of the EU market and the poverty of the proximate alternatives, particularly of the post-Soviet market. People are prevented from entering the EU by onerous visa requirements, instilling a sense of rejection by 'Europe' while undercutting economic, educational and cultural opportunities (Jileva 2004; and Chapter 9, this volume).

For states that fail to enter an enlarging EU along with their neighbours, there are other economic consequences besides the loss of export markets: a steady flow of aid, expertise, and foreign direct investment is diverted away from states that are not in the queue to join the EU towards those that are. The costs of exclusion can weigh heavily on relatively rich states as well as poor ones. Walter Mattli has shown that economic integration can cause three kinds of negative externalities for states left outside: trade diversion, investment diversion, and aid diversion. These costs help explain the applications for EU membership of rich West European states as well as relatively backward states from post-communist Europe (Mattli 1999).

The imperative for the Eastern ENP participants of securing access to the internal market is a replay of the situation of the ECE states in the early 1990s: one of their main motivations for seeking EU membership was early vulnerability to EU protectionism. Poland, Hungary and Czechoslovakia were displeased that the EU refused to recognise the Europe Agreements signed in 1991 as a first step toward EU membership, and that it insisted on trade provisions that were much less favourable to them than they had expected given that economic crisis risked undermining their hard-won democratic institutions. While the Europe Agreements provided for a steady liberalisation of trade over a ten-year period, in the 'sensitive sectors' where East European exports would be most competitive – steel, textiles, chemicals and agriculture – the EU demanded long transition periods, extensive anti-dumping safeguards, and, for agriculture, permanent restrictions. The risk of democratic failure and economic collapse in Eastern Europe was one that EU governments seemed willing to take – as opposed to the risk of trumping EU producer lobbies and opening their markets to East European goods. Economists concur that while the welfare benefits of free trade with the EU would have been substantial, the effects on EU producers would have been modest, even making no allowances for the growing Eastern market for West European products (Åslund 2002: 440). Even so, the EU's common foreign policy was still far too weak in the 1990s to command market access as a tool for bolstering stability in the East. After 1999, however, the EU's strengthened foreign policy did deliver valuable trade concessions for Western Balkan states as part of the Stability Pact's strategy to bring stability and economic rejuvenation to this region.[5]

For many of the Eastern ENP participants, exports to the EU market are a *sine qua non* of economic progress. But the EU's effective protection is especially high for agricultural goods, textiles, chemicals, and steel – goods that play a large role in the commodity composition of the exports of the Eastern ENP participants (Milcher and Slay 2005: 9). Trade liberalisation is especially important for the Eastern ENP participants because some industrial products still face tariff protection, in contrast to the Mediterranean ENP participants that have enjoyed free trade with the EU in industrial products for many years (Fantini and Dodini 2005: 74). Moldova's tiny, very backward economy is almost entirely based on agriculture, and its main products, wine and fruit, have been all but blocked from export to the EU market. Thus Moldova, Europe's poorest country, is also probably Europe's greatest victim of the EU's Common Agricultural Policy. Moldova's chances for economic revitalisation are inextricably linked to the lifting of the EU's agricultural protections (Åslund 2003).

The challenge for the ENP now is to diminish visibly the costs of non-membership for all Eastern ENP states. The key to successful external governance is the credible promise of full participation in the internal market: extending the four freedoms – free movement of goods, services, capital and labour – to ENP states. The greatest hurdles will be removing barriers to trade in agricultural goods, and allowing the free movement of labour from the Eastern ENP states. While in the short term the latter seems virtually impossible given the opposition to foreign workers of a majority of EU voters, it may become more realistic in a decade or so when the demographic crisis in EU states deepens. At that time it may be politically quite expedient to import workers from Ukraine or Georgia instead of the Third World.

Trade liberalisation presents itself as an inexpensive way for the EU to counteract poverty and economic backwardness that threaten to undermine progress toward democracy and other 'shared values' in the Eastern ENP participants (Grabbe 2004: 3). Trade concessions would have little impact on the EU's massive trade flows, and would come cheap in comparison with foreign assistance or military intervention. Stronger economies would beget stronger state institutions that could bring the EU real benefits such as improved border controls and capacity to fight international crime and terrorism. Indeed, this is the logic at the heart of the ENP.

So far neither the peaceful civic revolutions in Ukraine and Georgia nor the impoverished and conflict-damaged economies of Moldova, Armenia or Azerbaijan, have been supported by complete access to the EU market for their agricultural and industrial products. Yet by the end of 2005 trade liberalisation was emerging as a priority within the ENP process, especially for the Eastern ENP participants. And the Commission appeared also to be pushing for trade liberalisation, and for mechanisms to help ENP participants meet EU health and food quality requirements that would allow them to boost agricultural exports to the internal market. The Commission's November 2005 progress report notes that among the main priorities expressed by the ENP participants is: 'enhanced cooperation in trade, including liberalization of trade in agricultural, processed agricultural and fishery products; trade agreements for industrial products; liberalization of trade in services; and converging with the sanitary and phyto-sanitary *acquis* to improve public health and to increase agricultural exports' (European Commission 2005a: 4).

The case of Ukraine

The position of Ukraine in 2005 is perhaps the most analogous to the position of the ECE states in 1991. Following on the 'Orange Revolution' in the autumn of 2004, the government of Ukrainian president Viktor Yuschenko promised comprehensive political and market-oriented reform, and sought the prospect of EU membership as an anchor for Ukraine's democratic revolution (Mayhew and Copsey 2005). The EU has refused to recognise Ukraine as a prospective EU member, and has explicitly stated that the Action Plan signed with Ukraine as part of the ENP is *not* a first step toward membership. At the close of 2004, Ukrainian leaders refused to sign a 5–year ENP Action Plan that did not recognise Ukraine as a credible future candidate for EU membership. When the Action Plan was finally signed in February 2005, the time span was consequently reduced to three years.[6]

Given the economic costs alone for Ukraine of being excluded from the internal market, it is not surprising that Ukraine's new Western-oriented leaders would have such an intense preference for EU membership. However, the ENP can be credited for providing an established framework that the European Commission could use to respond immediately to Ukraine's aspirations for closer relations after the October 2004 Orange Revolution. The ENP gave the EU a way to pledge political and economic support for Ukraine, without forcing the EU to respond with a 'yes' or a 'no' to Ukraine's membership bid at a time when EU governments were in no mood to take on a new candidate. Indeed, with a little imagination the ENP can be understood as a way for the Commission to help Ukraine begin the long and laborious preparations for EU membership on the gamble that once it is (more) fit to enter, EU leaders will find it impossible to reject it.

Even without membership, there are tremendous economic incentives for Ukraine to earn unfettered access to the internal market. As much as two-thirds of Ukraine's potential exports of industrial and agricultural products to the EU market are in the 'sensitive sectors', and therefore subject to tight protections. Of course, Ukrainian and other Eastern ENP leaders made it easy for the EU to shut them out of the internal market by showing much less determination than ECE leaders to push through difficult economic and political reforms. For this reason the aftermath of Ukraine's Orange Revolution is important: if the Ukrainian government successfully implements economic reforms that include shoring up the rule of law, combating corruption, improving the state administration, and dismantling regulations that discriminate against foreign investors, how will the EU respond? The reforms included in the Action Plan are very extensive and ambitious, as are the measures adopted by Ukraine's Cabinet of Ministers to make them happen.[7]

There were signs in 2005 that the EU is laying the groundwork for responding to Ukrainian reforms with greater access to the internal market – even as the ability of the new Ukrainian government to complete ambitious reforms was looking more and more doubtful. Agreements in 2005 regulating Ukrainian steel and textile exports to the EU improved somewhat the terms of trade in Ukraine's favour. The Commission concluded that Ukraine had finally met the technical criteria for the granting of Market Economy Status (MES), though this is largely symbolic, having few direct economic consequences. More important, the EU declares that it is committed to negotiating the establishment of a free trade area as part of an enhanced ENP agreement, once Ukraine has joined the WTO.[8] After a summit of EU and Ukrainian leaders in December 2005, the joint statement included the following on trade: 'EU leaders reconfirmed the goal of promoting deep economic integration between the EU and Ukraine and, in order to achieve this, looked forward to an early start of negotiations of a Free Trade Area once Ukraine has joined the WTO. EU leaders noted good progress made on the feasibility study on a Free Trade Area between the EU and Ukraine. EU leaders underlined strong support for Ukraine's early accession to the WTO, and stressed their commitment to continue to offer assistance in meeting the necessary requirements.'[9] In another parallel with the enlargement process, how much an Eastern ENP partner gets out of the ENP may depend, in part, on how much the government pushes the EU to deliver – and so far the new Ukrainian government has been the most persistent.

Future EU policy
The question is how far traditionally protectionist member states will be willing to override the interests of some of their producers and open their markets to non-EU members whose exports are concentrated in the 'sensitive sectors'. Whether or not the EU will eventually offer 'full' participation in the EU market has been deliberately kept vague in Commission documents with phrases such as 'a stake in the internal market'. The fact that in the mid-1990s it seemed easier for EU leaders to accept ECE states as candidates than to grant their goods access to the internal market is indicative of the tough road ahead for the ENP (see Mayhew 1998: 164). The irony is that France, the state most interested in stalling EU enlargement in the early 1990s to prevent 'widening' from undermining 'deepening', was also the state that hardened the resolve of ECE governments to attain full EU membership by insisting on the highest levels of protection from ECE imports.[10]

This sequence of events could repeat itself in the EU's relationship with the Eastern ENP participants. The member state governments most keen to open EU markets and scrap the trade-distorting Common Agricultural Policy, including the United Kingdom and Denmark, are also the governments that have traditionally been the most amenable to taking on new candidate states (though their publics have become less amenable) (see Sissenich 2004; Vachudova 2007). But the member states most reluctant to continue enlarging the EU, including France and Belgium, are also the states most likely to insist on continuing high levels of protection for agricultural and other 'sensitive' goods from Ukraine, Moldova and the South Caucasus.

The ENP will have little success in promoting economic prosperity or using conditionality to improve democratic standards if complete market access – including free trade in agricultural products – is not forthcoming. Here the logic of using the ENP to forestall further enlargement may yet be for the greater good: if EU politicians see trade liberalisation as a way to avoid further enlargement, this may trump domestic interests and open markets. If they do not, they will severely undermine not just the ENP as an alternative to EU membership, but also the ENP as an effective foreign policy instrument.

The ENP as a foreign policy instrument: participation in the internal market as an incentive for compliance

As it stands, the ENP is a much more complex and ambitious tool of external governance than an exchange of market access for diminished enlargement pressure and better economic performance in the periphery. For ENP countries, gaining full access to the EU's internal market will require substantial approximation of EU legislation and convergence with EU standards. These in turn demand broader market-oriented economic reforms and substantial improvements in the competence of the state administration. And the EU has not stopped there, seeking to obtain much more than economic reform for a 'stake in the internal market': it is asking for political reforms that include strengthening democratic standards, the rule of law, minority rights, women's rights, labour rights, media freedom, and social justice (see Sasse 2004; Chapter 3, this volume). The EU thus wants to extend its leverage on domestic policy-making well beyond exporting the rules of the internal market and creating domestic institutions that can enforce them. Can the EU expect that the ENP participants will do all of this without the incentive of EU membership?

While the language of the ENP documents and Action Plans tends to portray the project as consensual cooperation between equal participants, the reality is that there is obviously a profound asymmetry of economic power between the EU and its neighbours. The key to understanding why an ENP partner *might* go along with the far-reaching ENP economic *and* political agenda is the relationship of asymmetric interdependence between it and the EU. Robert Keohane and Joseph Nye (1977) have shown that power in an interdependent relationship flows from asymmetry: the one who gains more from the relationship is the more dependent.

Eastern ENP participants that seek to modernise their economy and bolster prosperity have a great deal to gain from a very close relationship with the EU – through trade liberalisation, as a source of foreign direct investment, and also as a catalyst for structural and macroeconomic reforms. For the EU, building an economic relationship with such a tiny economy is unimportant, yet as we discussed above, the EU still takes care to limit or block market access for goods that Eastern ENP countries would like to export. In other words, when it comes to market access, the EU still has a lot to give the Eastern ENP participants in exchange for democracy, human rights and economic reform.

The relationship of asymmetric interdependence between the ECE states and the EU in the early 1990s was similar to the relationship in the 2000s between some of the ENP states and the EU. The EU had significant bargaining power – and it showed no compunction in using it to shape the content of the Europe Agreements, to impose vast requirements for membership, and to force ECE states to accept a phase-in of some of the benefits of membership upon accession (Moravcsik and Vachudova 2003). As Andrew Moravcsik has argued (1991, 1998), such patterns of 'asymmetrical interdependence' have determined relations between the EU and candidate states in the past – and also among EU member states during major treaty negotiations. The underlying logic is that more 'interdependent' countries tend to benefit more from liberalising markets, and are thus willing to make concessions to reach agreements. The ECE states reacted to their position by treating trade and integration with the EU as a matter of economic survival. By taking on EU standards and attempting a wholesale reorientation of their trade to EU markets, ECE elites adopted what amounted to a strategy of maximising their dependence on the EU (Vachudova 2005: 63–92). Between 1991 and 2002, their trade with the EU increased tremendously; the best way to decrease their vulnerability to the EU was to maximise it – and then become members. The Eastern ENP participants could follow suit, taking a gamble that at least full participation in the internal market will be forthcoming – and, by earnestly playing the ENP game, make that outcome all the more likely.

Why take such a gamble? The greatest expectation for the ENP is that it will allow the EU's neighbours to benefit from a weaker version of the surge in economic growth experienced by economically less developed countries when they join the EU (see Chapter 5). Marco Fantini and Michaela Dodini argue (2005: 75) that 'If the ENP is successful in fostering growth through integration with the Internal Market, structural reforms and better macroeconomic management, it seems reasonable to expect some replication of the catching process which has been witnessed in the EU after successive enlargements. The strength of these effects will clearly depend on whether a "critical mass" of internal market regulations and macroeconomic reforms are implemented by the ENP participants in a satisfactory manner. If the ENP process can be likened, in qualitative terms, to a weaker form of membership of the EU economy and economic model, it seems logical to assume that the economic effects of the ENP will be analogous, although less pronounced, to those witnessed by accession countries during previous EU enlargements.'

The ENP's influence is more likely to founder with the Mediterranean ENP participants with whom the relationship is less asymmetric: for example, if the EU depends on them for energy supplies, or to keep extreme Islamic fundamentalists out of politics by eschewing democracy. Moreover, the EU has already given the Mediterranean states greater trade concessions, and its long relationship with them that has thus far not elicited reform (Emerson and Noutcheva 2005; Kelley 2006).

Still, some Mediterranean ENP participants are very dependent on trade with the EU. In 2004, for example, 71 per cent of Moroccan exports went to the EU (while 58 per cent of Moroccan imports came from the EU). A substantial part of its exports are agricultural products, which are still subject to tariff barriers. The Commission has stated that it will open negotiations on liberalising trade in agricultural, processed agricultural and fishery products with worthy Mediterranean ENP participants (European Commission 2005c: 13). For a Mediterranean ENP partner with an export profile like Morocco, agricultural trade liberalisation could prove a strong incentive to comply with the EU's political demands. However, some Mediterranean ENP participants, such as Jordan, either trade relatively little with the EU, or, as with Tunisia, trade primarily in industrial products and textiles that have already been liberalised. The EU's leverage on these states by way of the internal market will necessarily be lower, although the need for EU foreign aid and tourism could help make up the difference. In the case of Algeria, the EU depends on oil imports to such an extent that Algeria is the EU's sixth largest source of energy. Thus the EU may find itself with very little leverage once the ENP process begins moving with Algeria.[11]

Whether or not the EU will be able to translate its economic power into direct leverage on structural and macroeconomic reforms by the ENP participants will ultimately depend on the scale and the credibility of the benefits that are on offer. For now, the benefits of playing the ENP game are not well-specified, especially 'participation' in the internal market and liberalisation of agricultural products. Policy-makers in the ENP participants will be more likely to go forward with costly reforms if they are convinced that substantial economic rewards are guaranteed and will come on their watch. In any case they will face less domestic pressure to reform: even if full participation in the internal market is guaranteed, the ENP will not engage the interest of citizens and domestic groups in the same way as joining the EU. Nevertheless, my argument here is simply that because of its economic power and also its past miserliness, in this relationship of asymmetric interdependence the EU has much to give many, though not all, ENP participants: should the EU offer complete participation in the internal market, this could indeed be a powerful incentive for some governments to deliver on their side of the ENP ledger.

The ENP as an engine for economic reform

Whether or not the ENP is successful in individual ENP states will depend not only on the richness of the economic incentives, but also on the nature of the politicians holding power. The extent to which a state engages in EU-mentored reforms in exchange for economic and other benefits will depend critically on the nature of the domestic power base of the ruling elites (Kelley 2004b; Vachudova 2005). For some ruling elites, the thrust of the democratic reforms demanded by the EU as part of the Action Plans may be at logger-heads with the way that they win and hold political power. For others, the reforms that are a condition of increased participation in the internal market could threaten the interests of elites with close ties to the government. Belarus is an extreme example of incompatibility between the ENP's goals and the comportment of ruling elites. For now, Belarus has kept itself out of the process, and the EU has excluded it.

For the rest that have cast their lot in with the ENP, it will be fascinating to see whether the EU will manage to coax real improvements in democratic standards, human rights and economic governance through the ENP. In the first part of this section I sketch the economic challenges ahead for the ENP states if they are to take full advantage of participation in the internal market (see also Chapter 5). In the second part I identify ways that the ENP could create momentum for these economic reforms and also political reforms, possibly even reaching those ENP states that expect to keep the EU and it's 'common values' at arm's length.

The challenge of macroeconomic stability and regulatory reform
Let us assume that full participation in the internal market is a benefit that ENP participants could expect to enjoy after a decade or so of being a star pupil within the ENP. What will the ENP states have to do in order to convert this opportunity into economic prosperity? The first challenge for ENP governments will be to deliver the sustainable fiscal and monetary policies envisioned by the Action Plans. Without macroeconomic stability, the full benefits of integrating into the internal market cannot be realised. The second challenge will be improving their regulatory environment by adopting the legislation, the standards, and the state institutions that are necessary in order to gain unfettered access to the internal market. The EU insists that neighbouring states adopt *and enforce* EU product standards. They must also take on board rules that limit state subsidies, protect competition, care for the environment, modernise the customs service and make state institutions more transparent and more accountable (Fantini and Dodini 2005).

Given the weakness of state institutions in many of the ENP participants, progress in both areas will be very difficult. Kataryna Wolczuk sketches the stumbling blocks: 'Ukraine's young and still evolving state will struggle to enact and implement such an extensive legislative program. Entrenched business interests will oppose the greater openness and transparency that would come with these changes. The inefficient and often corrupt bureaucracy will not be up to the job of implementing EU rules' (Wolczuk 2004: 5). And some of the EU's complex rules and regulations will not only be cumbersome and costly, but may also be unsuitable for the lower levels of economic development in the ENP participants.

Building EU-compatible regulatory frameworks and administrative capacity will take years, if not decades, and require the large-scale unilateral adoption of EU rules with no local input (see Kelley 2006). The EU's new members still lag well behind the older members after some ten years of preparations (Cameron 2003). And the post-Soviet states, including the Eastern ENP participants, have fallen dramatically behind the ECE states in regulatory reform since the early 1990s (Cameron 2001). Yet for the ENP participants, as for the EU's new members, becoming locked into the EU's legal and regulatory frameworks promises to facilitate fuller insertion into the EU economy – thereby bringing substantial opportunities for higher growth and higher returns to the national budget in the long run.

The sources of momentum for domestic reform

I now turn to three mechanisms observed in the ECE states through which the ENP process could create momentum for domestic reform: by providing a focal point for domestic groups that support reform; by servings as a credible commitment device for domestic and international economic actors; and by socialising local elites. These mechanisms could work even in the context of the more diffuse conditionality and the absence of a membership perspective within the ENP as compared to the EU's pre-accession process. All of them draw on the experience of the ECE states whose reform efforts revealed the central importance of domestic groups that are motivated to craft and implement fundamental reform, and use external pressure to make their case (Vachudova 2005: 139–94; see also Schimmelfennig and Sedelmeier 2005a). However, for these mechanisms to work in the ENP context, monitoring and hard-hitting progress reports by the Commission seem essential.

Strengthening certain domestic groups. For those domestic groups that support economic reform and also liberal democracy, the ENP could serve as a focal point for cooperation. They could organise themselves around the goal of moving the country forward in the ENP process, and use the absence of progress as a way to put pressure on the government. This dynamic was central to breaking the hold on politics of illiberal elites in several of the EU's candidate states. If a government forsakes clearly specified trade opportunities and financial assistance by not complying with its ENP commitments, then this should open it up to domestic criticism. In two of the Eastern ENP states, Ukraine and Georgia, civil society groups have already had a critical role in mobilising citizens to demand a more accountable and more democratic political leadership (Forbrig and Demeš 2007).

For the ENP to strengthen the hand of reform-oriented political forces, close monitoring, tough reporting and clear benchmarking on the part of the European Commission, akin to the EU's pre-accession process, would be indispensable (see also Chapter 7). These are largely absent now, in favour of more consensual arrangements. The principle of 'joint ownership' means that the priorities set out in the Action Plans have to be agreed jointly by the 'participants'. But the Action Plans could still develop in this direction if domestic factions that win power in key ENP states see the process as a way to lock in domestic reforms. Also, the European Commission will eventually be writing its own unilateral progress reports on the ENP participants that could be used by domestic groups.[12] The case of Turkey demonstrates that states may go very far to satisfy the EU's membership requirements, even when the prospect of actually getting membership is far from certain. Part of the explanation is that in Turkey important groups of elites used EU conditionality to help push through reforms that they wanted in any case.

So far there are also no well-defined benchmarks tied to clear economic rewards that could cause the ENP states to compete with one another and feel domestic pressure to 'keep up'. But the first year of the ENP did bring one very encouraging sign: several of the eligible ENP states did not want to fall behind in developing an Action Plan with the EU even though they were 'at first disinclined to become involved because of the ENP's strong accent on human rights, the rule of law and good governance' (Leigh, this volume).

Establishing economic reform credentials. The second source of momentum for economic reform will come from foreign investors *if* the ENP delivers on the promise of trade liberalisation. Geographic proximity to the EU combined with reliable access to the EU market is likely to attract greater foreign direct investment to ENP countries. Studies indicate that because of raised investor confidence FDI inflows have been concentrated in those post-communist states that were at the front of the queue to join the EU: if the internal market promise is truly robust within the ENP, then FDI could now flow to the countries that are its best pupils. Foreign direct investment brings capital, technology and management skills. It has been an effective driver of market reform under many different kinds of domestic regimes (Malesky 2005; Milcher and Slay 2005: 5).

Ultimately, however, domestic economic actors as well as foreign investors are sensitive to risk: political risk connected with violent conflict or unpredictable regime change; and economic risk connected to a volatile business environment. The ENP does address the political risks (a little) by institutionalising more intensive dialogue in the areas of conflict prevention, crisis management, regional security, and international criminal activity. But it remains to be seen whether it will bring greater involvement by EU leaders in conflicts in the South Caucasus. Several of the EU's key member states, including France, German and Italy, have in 2005 and 2006 proved very reluctant to criticise or oppose Putin's de-democratising Russia. For now, it is therefore difficult to imagine, for example, a European Union Police Mission deployed in the South Caucasus. This stands in contrast to the EU's ECE members whose regional stability seemed assured by 1995 and was solidified by NATO membership. It also stands in contrast to the Western Balkans where ongoing EU and NATO engagement is guaranteed. Still, the new 'European Neighbourhood Policy Instrument' could funnel substantial funding after 2007 to conflict resolution in the Eastern ENP states.

The ENP is better suited to address the economic risk associated with an unpredictable business environment. For ECE candidates, entering and making progress in the EU's pre-accession process served as a credible commitment to economic reform (Vachudova 2005). For domestic and foreign economic actors, especially investors, progress in the EU's pre-accession process served as a guarantee of a stable business environment and sustained economic reforms as well as access to the EU market. Economic actors had every reason after 1989 to question how far post-communist states would go in implementing liberalising reforms. But once a candidate was well on the way to joining the EU, the costs of reversing course became prohibitive for any government, especially since even a small reversal would be highlighted in the EU's monitoring reports and could cause the country's credit and risk ratings to be changed. The strictures of the EU's pre-accession process thus assured economic actors that the commitment to liberal economic reforms would be protected from economic downturns and from government turnover.

Through monitoring and reporting, the EU could make the ENP into an important way for the ENP states to establish their economic reform credentials vis-à-vis domestic and international economic actors. The Commission has made close cooperation with the international financial institutions (the World Bank and the International Monetary Fund) a priority of the ENP programme (Kelley 2006). Indeed, the Commission reports that the 'international financial institutions (IFIs) are beginning to take the ENP Action Plans as the basis of the strategic agenda for their operations with partner countries and to "screen" proposals for their fit with participants' ENP priorities' (European Commission 2005a: 4). This could in turn give the EU far more leverage on political reforms. A government that had already made substantial progress in structural reforms to access the EU market and satisfy foreign investors might be loathe to slide back in the queue for full market access due to failures in the area of minority rights or media freedom.

Socialisation of national elites. The ENP could also become an important proving ground for the impact of socialisation on domestic elites (see Checkel 2005). Part of the ENP's strategy is clearly to involve elites from neighbouring countries in extensive dialogue and expose them to the EU's institutions and practices. During the enlargement process, the EU used socialisation to promote domestic debate and elite learning aimed at changing the norms and values of the societies entering the EU. The material incentives of adopting a political agenda compatible with European integration attracted many elites and put them in a position to be receptive to socialisation: they knew it was in their interest to adapt to the expectations of international actors (Vachudova 2005). Socialisation was widely used in the pre-accession process, although for significant policy changes to take place it had to be coupled with political conditionality (Kelley 2004b; 2006). But Rachel Epstein (2006) finds that as international organisations export policies (or try to) they simultaneously export social relations. Thus, through the ENP, the EU may promote certain economic institutions and policies. And whether these are adopted or not, it may at the same time export beliefs about what constitutes a legitimate claim about distributional politics – beliefs that are ultimately more durable than any effects of conditionality.

Conclusion

There are two main reasons for the EU to improve the access of ENP states to the internal market. The first reason is to promote economic prosperity along its borders in order to reduce the likelihood of instability, to strengthen state institutions that fight international crime and terrorism, and to reduce immigration. In order to benefit from greater market access, ENP states would have to adopt the EU *acquis* relevant to any exports to the EU market, and also reform state institutions that certify these products or interact with the EU in other ways.

However, the ENP is much more ambitious than this as it also seeks to change the political environment. Thus the second reason to open markets is to use a 'stake in the internal market' as an incentive for ENP governments to implement political reforms ranging from free and fair elections to improved human and women's rights. This raises two questions about the ENP that have yet to be answered. In this chapter I have offered theoretical insights and empirical analyses to begin answering them.

First, how much of a 'stake in the internal market' bundled with other benefits will the EU credibly offer to a star pupil in the ENP process? For the Eastern ENP states, complete market access for industrial products, already granted to the Mediterranean states, seems a likely outcome over time, and recent developments with Ukraine point in this direction. The difficult areas will be labour mobility and also agriculture: most Eastern and the Mediterranean states stand to gain substantially from agricultural trade liberalisation, yet here EU protectionism has been the fiercest.

Second, will the ENP bundle of benefits (falling well short of full membership) be enough to motivate substantial economic and political reforms by successive governments? The answer to this question obviously depends on the answer to the previous one. Generally, however, it appears that for all of the Eastern ENP states and some of the Mediterranean ones, the condition of asymmetric interdependence caused chiefly by the imperative of trading with the EU does open the door to significant EU leverage – as long as the EU's reform priorities are not at loggerheads with the ruling parties' sources of domestic support. Thus the ENP appears to have substantial traction today on Ukraine, some on Moldova, but none on Belarus. For the Eastern ENP states, however, it will be difficult to know whether any EU-induced reform momentum is not also a product of lingering aspirations to win full membership in the EU.

The ENP also poses a potential danger to democracy promotion: the EU may use it as an excuse not to open its markets to agricultural goods from ENP states that fall short – even though this is the single best step it could take to alleviate poverty. More generally, it may hinder the trade that promises to build a middle class and extensive 'linkages' (Levitsky and Way 2006) with democratic states for those states that need it most – the ones that are the most anti-democratic and repressive, such as Belarus.

Notes

1 I would like to thank Judith Kelley as well as the editors of this volume for their excellent comments on my chapter. I am also indebted to conversations with Pavol Demeš, Wade Jacoby, Michael Leigh and Gergana Noutcheva.
2 On the ENP's genesis and the structure, see Leigh 2005; Kelley 2006; and Chapter 2, this volume.
3 Poland, Hungary, Slovenia, Slovakia, the Czech Republic, Estonia, Latvia, Lithuania, Cyprus and Malta joined the EU in May 2004, leaving Bulgaria, Romania, Turkey, Croatia, Macedonia, Albania, Serbia-Montenegro and Bosnia-Hercegovina at various points in the membership queue.
4 Recent books include Jacoby 2004; Kelley 2004b; Pridham 2005; Vachudova 2005; Grabbe 2006. See also the contributions to the volumes edited by Kubicek 2003; Dimitrova 2004; and Schimmelfennig and Sedelmeier 2005a.
5 Even here, some restrictions on agricultural imports remain in place. Western Balkan producers are frequently unable to certify that their products meet EU health standards because of the lack of competence of local regulators, but it is not clear that the EU has offered sufficient help to remove this important barrier to trade.
6 Interview with an official of the European Commission, Brussels, December 2004.
7 See 'Measures to Implement EU-Ukraine Action Plan in 2005', The Cabinet of Ministers of Ukraine, Decision #117, 22 April 2005.
8 'Commission Ferraro-Waldner to Visit Ukraine 2–3 March', Press Release, European Commission, IP/06/255, Brussels, 2 March 2005. See also the Commission's external trade website for Ukraine at: http://europa.eu.int/comm/trade/issues/bilateral/countries/ukraine/index_en.htm.
9 'EU-Ukraine Summit' Press Release, Presidency, PRES/05/337, Kiev, 1 December 2005.
10 On the EU's decision to enlarge, see Torreblanca 2001; Schimmelfennig 2003a; and Sedelmeier 2005.
11 All trade statistics are from the Commission's bilateral external trade website at: http://europa.eu.int/comm/trade/issues/bilateral/countries/index_en.htm.
12 It is difficult to predict how hard-hitting these assessments will be for governments that serve one or more of the EU's pressing strategic interests, such as containing Islamic fundamentalism or delivering energy.

JOHN D. OCCHIPINTI

7

Justice and Home Affairs: immigration and policing

This chapter makes two main arguments regarding Justice and Home Affairs (JHA) in the ENP. The first is that the effectiveness of the ENP on JHA will be shaped by 'logrolling' and the EU's ability to enhance the internal security capabilities of ENP participants. To a lesser degree, the United States and Russia will also impact the success of the ENP. The chapter also argues that the ENP has resulted from the enlargement of the EU, its desire to address the external dimensions of its internal security, the TACIS and MEDA programmes, the example of Ukraine, and the nature of border management and transnational crime. In supporting these points, the chapter also employs case studies of Morocco and Ukraine to help analyse the main operational components of the ENP regarding JHA, namely country reports, action plans and the European Neighbourhood Policy Instrument (ENPI).

Influences on effectiveness

The effectiveness of the ENP on JHA matters will ultimately be determined by how well the EU and ENP participants can cooperate, especially regarding compliance to agreements embodied in the country-specific action plans. One potential source of compliance is mutually shared norms, such as those referenced in the Commission's 2004 Strategy Paper: 'The ambition and pace of development of the EU's relationship with each partner country will depend on its degree of commitment to common values, as well as its will and capacity to implement agreed priorities' (European Commission 2004a: 8). Although the Commission has been the policy initiator, ENP participants can be expected to accept many of the JHA goals expressed in the Action Plans. After all, by taking aim at organised crime and terrorism, many objectives endeavour to strengthen state control, which is accepted as legitimate by the

ENP participants. Thus, in these areas, a relatively high level of compliance can be expected, provided governmental corruption can be avoided.

However, this will not be case for initiatives directed at the EU's particular internal security problems or issues related to human rights. While ENP participants may share some norms with the EU on these issues (see Chapter 3), they may not value them as highly as norms buttressing state sovereignty. For example, the partners may accept the norm that non-nationals who come to their country as migrants, refugees, or victims of trafficking are entitled to certain human rights, but this might not rank as highly as the norm that obligates their government to maintain internal security. Likewise, ENP participants may accept that reaching a re-admission agreement with the EU is an 'appropriate' goal (normatively speaking), but not at the expense of violating other norms, such as those related to security or economic prosperity. For its part, the EU may accept visa-facilitation with ENP participants (i.e. easing of rules or costs for entry in the EU) as an appropriate goal but not to the detriment of its own security or economic well-being.

In the absence of sufficient normative convergence on JHA, cooperation in the ENP must be facilitated by logrolling. Some European Commission officials interviewed for this book argued that success linkages will be more likely *within* policy domains areas, such as JHA, rather than across policy areas (Interviews, DG Justice, Freedom and Security (JLS)). However, some ENP participants will certainly attempt to trade their cooperation on JHA matters that are dear to the EU for greater assistance on economic development. Indeed, even when there is normative agreement on an issue, either side may pursue logrolling if only because the opportunity to do so exists. In addition, the EU enjoys a bit more leverage over Ukraine and Moldova, which hold out some hope for future membership in the EU, compared to the other ENP participants, which do not have this perspective (Interviews, DG External Relations (RELEX)).

However, sufficient normative motivations or instrumental rationality may not guarantee compliance to JHA objectives by ENP participants simply because they lack the capability to do so (Interviews, DGs JLS and RELEX). For instance, in the fight against illegal immigration or drug trafficking, a partner may have inadequate equipment, infrastructure, criminal intelligence, or knowledge of 'best practices' to combat a sophisticated and well-financed transnational criminal organisation. This can be thought of as a form of transactions cost that can result in involuntary defections.

Drawing on the experience of the TACIS and MEDA programmes, the ENP anticipates such inadequacies and entails programmes funded by the ENPI aimed at mitigating these. In Chapter 1, Smith and Weber argue that when parties require special investment in training and equipment to solve a collective action problem, then there is a 'greater desire for bindingness' to reduce transaction costs. This is borne out by the case of JHA in the ENP, which demonstrates the willingness of the EU and its partners both to manage borders and fight cross-border crime, as well as to provide/utilise programmes funded by the ENPI – just as in the past via the TACIS and MEDA programmes.

In addition to factors impacting compliance, the effectiveness of the ENP will also be influenced by the actions of the United States and Russia. The US and the EU share a common interest in fighting threats to internal security from common terrorist groups or criminal organisations. On both sides of the Atlantic, the promotion of democracy and economic development in Eastern Europe and the 'broader Middle East' are viewed as important for addressing the underlying sources of crime and terrorism, as well as improving countries' capacity to deal with these. Specifically, US initiatives to promote trade, rule of law, and the fight against corruption in some of the ENP participants can complement EU efforts also intended to tackle challenges related to JHA. A good example of this is American assistance to the reform-minded governments of Ukraine and Georgia. So far, however, US development programmes in the 'greater Middle East' have focused on the Gulf states, rather than the ENP participants in the Mediterranean region (see Yacoubian 2004; Fried 2006).

Russia will also have an impact on the ENP's success on JHA. From the beginning, issues related to 'Freedom, Security and Justice' have comprised one of the so-called 'common spaces' in the emerging EU–Russian partnership. Indeed, many of the specific objectives noted in the 2005 'roadmap' detailing areas of JHA cooperation between the EU and Russia are identical to those regarding the ENP participants. Given the east to west flow of criminal organisations and their trafficking networks, the EU's success in helping Russia deal more effectively with its internal security can only enhance the ability of ENP participants in Eastern Europe and the Caucasus to do the same. Moreover, the recent Russian–EU agreement on visa-facilitation and the re-admission of illegal agreements will likely increase pressure for the same to be accomplished with ENP participants, whose relationship with the EU on JHA matters has been developing since the end of the Cold War.

Enlargement and externalisation

Since the late 1990s, concern over the relatively weak internal security apparatus of most new and future member states has caused the EU to expedite its own progress on JHA and encourage reforms in this area in the accession countries. In particular, the expectation that new EU members will one day join the Schengen free-travel zone has contributed to a degree of urgency concerning the nature and pace of such reforms (see Occhipinti 2004a). A variety of topics emerged as standard points of discussion in the EU's negotiations with its accession partners, and these same issues can now be found in ENP country reports and action plans to be discussed below (Interviews, DG JLS).

Enlargement has also meant that the EU's external borders have moved eastward, and managing these borders thus requires a new way of dealing with ENP participants in Eastern Europe. Moreover, the expected accession of Romania and Bulgaria to the EU will create an even longer border with Ukraine, a new EU frontier with Moldova, and a lengthy Black Sea coast that will tempt smugglers and traffickers. In turn, this may increase organised crime problems in the Southern Caucasus, particularly in Georgia, located at the other end of the Black Sea.

The JHA-related impact of EU enlargement is much less dramatic regarding the ENP participants in the Southern Mediterranean. Even before the accession of Malta and Cyprus, the long coastlines and many islands of Greece, Italy, France and Spain served as inviting access points for those trying to move illicit cargoes into the EU. In various ways, the ENP anticipates that the eventual inclusion of Malta and Cyprus in the Schengen free-travel zone will only add to the challenge of managing JHA in the Mediterranean.

Along with the impact of enlargement, the EU's increasing desire to address its internal security goals with external action also helps explain the nature of JHA in the ENP (see Occhipinti 2004b: 192–3; Lavenex 2005). 'Stronger external action' was a major component of the EU's 'milestones' for progress on JHA, as approved by the historic Tampere European Council of October 1999. Since then, as echoed in the EU's current Hague Programme on JHA, more specific objectives on border management, organised crime and terrorism have called for enhancing relations with non-EU states. This approach has also encompassed multilateral instruments, including international conventions on criminal justice sponsored by the UN, the Council of Europe, or the OECD.

Regional templates

Over time, the TACIS and MEDA programmes developed into funding sources for JHA projects, which allowed these programmes to serve as templates for the ENP. When TACIS was created, it excluded funding for JHA, but this was because the EU's third pillar was still on the drawing board. The full impact of struggling economies and weak criminal justice systems on organized crime in the Central and Eastern European countries (CEECs) would not be evident until the mid-1990s. Subsequently, internal security reforms in these new democracies became a priority. By then, the evolutionary direction of the third pillar had also been established via the Amsterdam Treaty's provisions for an 'area of freedom security and justice'. These influences contributed to the inclusion of JHA in the TACIS regulation of December 1999, which took effect for the period 2000–6.

Crime fighting is mentioned in several of the TACIS strategy papers under the heading of 'institutional and legal reform'. In addition, this task and the full range of JHA matters are covered in the complementary programmes for regional cooperation and cross-border cooperation. The latter have been aimed especially at enhancing integrated border management and migration and asylum administration, as well as anti-corruption measures. TACIS funding has also targeted organised crime, with an emphasis on the trafficking of human beings, illicit drugs, and stolen cars, and, to a lesser extent, terrorism. Finally, as with the other policy areas, the Partnership and Cooperation Agreements (PCAs) forged with the TACIS states (see Chapter 2) were intended to impart a sense of shared ownership over JHA projects and help foster the belief that effective border management and the fight against organised crime were mutual interests and not merely bricks in an emerging 'fortress Europe' (see Lavenex 2004b, 2005). Ukraine's PCA eventually led to an action plan on JHA that subsequently served as a model for handling this policy domain with other ENP participants (see below).

In contrast to the TACIS programme, JHA was included in the Barcelona Process from the beginning. Although emphasised much less than other policy areas, JHA issues were addressed in three different parts of the Barcelona Declaration. Its 'Political and Security' chapter, for example, refers to the need to strengthen cooperation in preventing and combating terrorism, organised crime, and 'the drugs problem in all its aspects'. Meanwhile, the 'Social, Cultural and Human' chapter of the declaration highlights the need for closer cooperation on illegal immigration, re-admission agreements, and the fight against terrorism, drug trafficking, international crime, and corruption. The Work Programme annexed to the Barcelona Declaration also deals with JHA, but curiously lumps all of the measures in this area under the main heading of Social, Cultural and Human Affairs and the sub-heading of 'Migration'. These measures call for international meetings on migration flows, terrorism, organised crime and illegal immigration.

Over time, the development of the EU's own *acquis* in the area of JHA helped to strengthen the attention to this in the Barcelona Process's Association Agreements and regional programmes. Although terrorism is not mentioned in many of the Association Agreements, all call for dialogue on migration issues in some fashion, and many express the need for talks on money laundering and drug trafficking. Such discussions on JHA subsequently occurred within the Association Councils and their specialised committees, sub-committees, and working groups. As with the TACIS states, this was intended to provide the Euro-Med partners with an opportunity to share in the ownership of the goals and programmes established in the framework of ENP and thus give them a greater stake in insuring their success.

Meanwhile, the regional dimension of JHA in the Barcelona Process has also grown, especially after the implementation of the Valencia Action Plan approved by the Euro-Med foreign ministers in April 2002. Coming soon after the terrorist attacks of September 11, this communicated the view of all parties that 'the Barcelona Process cannot remain indifferent to terrorism'.

The Valencia conference also endorsed a framework document on JHA and approved a regional cooperation programme aimed at improving 'good governance' and 'the rule of law' and more specific objectives on organised crime, terrorism and migration. The EU allocated €6 million in MEDA funds for these initiatives for 2002–4, targeting the training of magistrates, the creation of an information system to analyse migration flows, and police training managed by the European Police College (CEPOL) – the EU's virtual police academy. A second regional MEDA programme on JHA enjoyed a budget of €15 million for 2005–6. At the Euro-Med summit of November 2005, the partners could not agree how 'terrorism' should be defined, but they did approve a 'code of conduct' to combat terrorism, as well as a five-year work programme that makes the related issues of illegal immigration and economic development in Africa top priorities.

Crime and crises

It is possible to miss the fundamental point that JHA is a significant facet of the ENP because transnational organised crime and border management are issues that the EU has difficulty handling alone. Crime control and border management are essentially collective action problems that necessitate cooperation for optimal outcomes to be achieved. The trafficking of illicit goods, terrorism, and various forms of immigration pose particular challenges.

Two basic criminal variations of illegal immigration can be identified (Europol 2004b). 'People smuggling' is when a would-be migrant pays for illegal travel documents or clandestine passage, such as being hidden in a shipping container on a freighter. In contrast, 'human trafficking' is when victims, frequently women or children, are coerced or tricked into servitude and shipped as virtual commodities, often for the purpose of prostitution or pornography.

Asylum policy, refugee issues, and visas are important non-criminal matters dealt with through border management. Regarding these, EU policy in these areas typically strikes some kind of 'balance' between competing concerns for internal security and human rights. Human rights concerns can also arise in criminal matters, such as the protection of human trafficking's victims. Similarly, human rights concerns have been expressed regarding 're-admission agreements', which facilitate the speedy return of illegal immigrants or unsuccessful asylum applicants to the state from which they came, no matter what their nationality.

In recent years, the EU's desire to manage its borders has been fuelled by a series of illegal immigration crises, involving the suffering or even deaths of would-be immigrants. Recent incidents have involved boatloads of desperate illegal immigrants overwhelming border authorities at Sicily, the Italian island of Lambedusa, Malta, and the Canary Islands – or dying en route. Not surprisingly, illegal immigration has been a hot topic in many EU member states, especially around the time of elections. In some cases, this has caused political leaders to look to the EU for solutions. In the summer of 2006, for example, Spain, Italy and Malta received assistance in the form of EU-sponsored land, sea and air border patrols, coordinated by Frontex, the European Union's new external borders agency.

Along with the challenges of border management, there are also a wide variety of transnational organised crimes that impact the EU and its ENP participants. Fuelled by globalisation, these include the smuggling of tax free cigarettes and the trafficking of stolen automobiles, small arms and nuclear substances, or other illicit cargo. Drug trafficking remains the most serious form of cross-border crime in Europe. Finally, there is the problem of money laundering, which is related to nearly all forms of organised crime, including the financing of terrorism.

Terrorism can be conceptualised as a variant of transnational organised crime, distinguished by its political aims, rather than profit motives. Unlike other types of organised crime, terrorism is not fuelled by a 'demand' within the EU or the ENP participants, though governmental policies can influence terrorists' goals and choice of means. However, terrorism is similar to other forms of transnational organised crime regarding how networks are organised, operate across international boundaries, and obtain financial resources to carry out their activities. As with illegal immigration, periodic crises have influenced the inclusion of strategies for terrorism in the ENP. For example, several ENP participants have experienced terrorist attacks on their territory, including Israel (numerous occasions), Tunisia (suicide bombing of a Djerba synagogue in 2002), and Egypt (attacks on tourists at Cairo and Luxor in 1996–97 and Sinai resorts in 2004–6). The recent terrorist attacks in the US, Spain and UK (successful and foiled) have had a similar impact in the EU, with the latter contributing to an ongoing debate on how to better integrate 'immigrant' populations into European communities and prevent the radicalism of Muslim youth.

Country reports and shared challenges

Aside from that of the Palestinian Authority, each of the ENP country reports contains a section on JHA. An analysis of these reports reveals several common themes and priorities, which have their roots in both the enlargement process and the experience of Ukraine (Interviews, DGs JLS and RELEX). In a few instances, topics are included for which the EU has an interest in the protection of human rights. However, most JHA matters stem from the EU's desire to address its own internal security problems related to cross-border crime and border management.

Each report also highlights particular internal security issues in each country and related ongoing or necessary domestic reforms. For example, each indicates whether an ENP partner has signed, ratified, and fully implemented relevant international conventions, such as those of the UN or Council of Europe. The reports also describe whether the partner is an important source or transit state for particular forms of cross-border crime.

Concerning the intersection of human rights and JHA, the country reports highlight the treatment of migrant workers, refugees, and asylum seekers *in the ENP participants*. Egypt and Jordan, for example, must deal with thousands of migrant workers. In addition, several ENP participants, particularly in the Caucasus, are challenged by internally displaced persons or refugees fleeing regional conflicts. Each country's report also indicates whether it has signed and ratified the 1951 Geneva Convention on the status of refugees and its related protocols.[1]

The EU is concerned not only with refugees who hope to reach the EU, but also those who make their asylum claims in ENP participants. This includes, for example, persons fleeing from sub-Saharan Africa or Iraq, seeking asylum in places such as Tunisia, Morocco or Egypt. Israel's country report describes a rising number of asylum seekers from Africa and, to a lesser extent, Eastern Europe and the Balkans.

Overall, the challenge of 'migration' among the ENP participants is unique, not only because of its prominence in the country reports, but also because it encompasses both legal and illegal immigration. Visa arrangements for legal entry in the ENP participants are mentioned, though the reports do not deal with legal entry into the EU. Meanwhile, illegal immigration is addressed in the paragraphs on the need for re-admission agreements with the EU. The reports note whether any bilateral re-admission agreements are in force between EU member states (e.g. Lebanon with Cyprus; Armenia with Lithuania; and Moldova with Poland, Hungary and, soon, Lithuania and Italy) or whether this aim is at least included in the country's association or partnership and cooperation agreements (e.g. Georgia and Jordan, no, and Lebanon, yes). The country report for Tunisia is especially interesting because it clearly reveals the 'logrolling' inherent in the ENP, noting that 'the Tunisian authorities have stated a willingness to discuss an EU re-admission agreement on the condition that this issue is addressed in discussion within the wider Association Agreement framework, as a corollary of discussion on socio-economic development'. In other words, for the EU to achieve one of its JHA goals in ENP, it will have to help its partners address their priorities in other areas.

The country reports do not deal specifically with the problem of people-smuggling. Indeed, a recent Europol report on this subject indicates that the source countries currently of most concern to the EU are Iraq, Turkey, Russia, Afghanistan, India, Pakistan, China, and countries in Sub-Saharan Africa (Europol 2004c). However, illegal immigrants from these countries bound for the EU use transit points in the Balkans, Eastern Europe and

Northern Africa, including nearly every ENP partner, at least to some extent (Europol 2005: 2). Azerbaijan's country report highlights this problem with regard to illegal migration from several countries bound for the EU. Moreover, the problem of illegal immigration related to North and West Africa had grown especially acute in 2005–6 (see, e.g., Harding 2005 and Spongenberg 2006).

In contrast to people-smuggling, the disturbing crime of human trafficking is prominently mentioned in many ENP country reports. Georgia is both a source and transit country for this crime. According to Europol's analysis, the key 'pull' factor here is the demand for these victims in Western Europe (Europol 2004c). Although this appears to be a significant problem, it is not addressed in the ENP. The ENP country reports for Israel and Lebanon mention their status as *destinations* for trafficked human beings for domestic servitude or sexual exploitation. The 'push factors' identified in the source countries are also noteworthy. These include high unemployment, discrimination, a desire to escape human rights abuses and the perception of increased opportunities in the EU (Europol 2004c).

Many of the ENP country reports also address the problem of drug trafficking and efforts to combat this. Egypt's report, for example, notes increasing drug addiction and the spread of opium cultivation in the Sinai and upper Egypt. Meanwhile, cannabis and poppy are also grown illegally in southern Azerbaijan, according to its ENP country report.

Beyond a few cases of production, the ENP participants are mainly notable as transit states for illicit drugs, especially narcotics. Jordan is described as being a trafficking nexus for heroin moving from or through Asia and Turkey headed to elsewhere in the Middle East, including Israel. Azerbaijan's report notes its emergence as a narcotics transit route after conflict in the Balkans disrupted trafficking there. Along with Georgia, Azerbaijan now serves as a transit-state for heroin from Afghanistan or northern Iran bound for the EU or Russia. The country report for Armenia is noteworthy for a different reason, indicating that its poor infrastructure actually inhibits its use by drug traffickers. This implies that economic development and improvements in its transportation networks could actually exacerbate this crime problem.

In addition to immigration issues and organised crime, the JHA sections of several of the country reports also discuss the nature and capabilities of border control agencies, police organisations, and judicial authorities. Elsewhere in the country reports, the issues of administrative capacity, rule of law and corruption are also discussed. Within the section on JHA, the particular issue of police reform is noted as a priority for the three states of the Southern Caucasus.

Regarding money laundering, the country reports indicate that the partners in the Southern Caucasus are particularly vulnerable because they still have cash-based economies. In most cases, the majority of laundered funds stems from the trafficking of narcotics. In general, each country report focuses on whether the OECD's Financial Action Task Force (FATF) has deemed that ENP partner to be 'cooperative' on investigating money laundering and whether it is following its recommendations.[2] Finally, the country reports mention any new legislation or 'financial intelligence units' that are in the works to tackle the problem of money laundering.

Terrorism is covered in the country reports in the paragraphs on money laundering found in the JHA sections, as well as in the sections on regional and global stability. The money laundering paragraphs of each report mention how the financing of terrorism is being addressed, including the implementation of the UN Convention for the Suppression of the Financing of Terrorism. The sections on regional and global stability ask whether states are supportive of and in compliance with various international measures on terrorism, including UN Security Council Resolutions 1373/01 (on denying financial support and other assistance to terrorists) and 1267/99 (on the Taliban and Osama bin Laden). As noted above, some ENP participants have direct experience with terrorism, and some of these incidents are also mentioned in the country reports.

In sum, ENP participants face a variety of JHA-related challenges as pointed out in the country reports. Overall, the countries in Eastern Europe and the Southern Caucasus suffer from generally weak criminal justice systems, requiring reforms in their police, judicial, and border agencies. Almost all of these states find themselves on drug trafficking transit routes, and a few have serious problems with human trafficking. Many of the countries of the Southern Mediterranean are undeveloped economically and are transit states for drug trafficking. Some are drug producers. Several states in this region are also extremely troublesome for the EU regarding people-smuggling.

Morocco

The case of Morocco illustrates many of the key JHA problems faced by ENP participants in the Southern Mediterranean. Moreover, Morocco's proximity to Spain makes its problems especially troublesome for the EU. As with the other Southern Mediterranean partners, Morocco is undeveloped economically. This not only contributes to organised crime and migration, but also hinders its capacity to deal with these problems (Interviews, DG RELEX). For example, Morocco is a key transit state for drug trafficking, similar to other states in the region. Morocco is somewhat unique because it is also a drug producer, specifically of cannabis, much of which is sold in the EU (Europol 2004a). In general, drug trafficking is a sensitive issue for Morocco and has only recently been included in its discussion with the EU (Interviews, DG RELEX).

Its problems with illicit drugs notwithstanding, Morocco's biggest JHA challenge is illegal immigration. The significance of the Moroccan migration route to Spain was highlighted in the autumn of 2005 by the deaths of dozens of would-be African immigrants who were attempting to enter the Spanish enclaves of Ceuta and Melilla on the Moroccan coast (BBC News, 6 October 2005). The complexity of the task at hand was evident in February 2006 when Moroccan authorities arrested several local members of a criminal organisation based in India and Pakistan that had been smuggling Indians into Togo, Burkina Faso and Senegal. The migrants were then assembled in Mali, moved to Morocco by road via Algeria and eventually sent into the EU (*Agence France Press,* 6 February 2006). Similar Mediterranean routes pass through Tunisia and Libya, while Balkan networks have hubs in Sarajevo and Belgrade (Europol 2005: 3).

Morocco is also challenged by asylum seekers, which has raised human rights concerns in the EU and among NGOs. Tunisia and Egypt are burdened with the same problem regarding refugees from sub-Saharan Africa or Iraq seeking protection in North Africa or, ultimately the EU. Finally, Morocco, like its neighbours, has not been immune to terrorism, notably the simultaneous suicide bombings in Casablanca of May 2003.

Morocco reflects many of the transnational organised crimes common to the region but also some of the typical limitations for dealing with these. Its ENP country report notes that it lacks specific domestic criminal legislation on money laundering, which inhibits crime fighting in many different areas. However, the report also indicates that Morocco's domestic anti-terrorism laws have been enhanced and utilised in the wake of terrorist attacks on its soil – just as in Egypt and Tunisia.

Ukraine
Ukraine's case is illustrative of many of the problems and challenges that confront the EU's TACIS partners. As with Morocco, Ukraine's geographic location is also significant, especially in light of the recent and planned enlargement of the EU. The emergence and planed lengthening of Ukraine's direct border with the EU exacerbates many problems of transnational organised crime.

Foremost among these problems is human trafficking. Along with Moldova, Ukraine is at the top of Europol's recent list of the 'main sources' of victims who are trafficked into the EU for sexual exploitation (Europol 2004c: 2). Moreover, Europol has specifically mentioned Kiev as one of the most common assembly or departure points for illegal immigration of all kinds into the EU (along with Moscow and Istanbul).

Ukraine's internal security problems are certainly not limited to illegal immigration. Its ENP country report connects the threat of terrorism to the need to prevent arms proliferation regarding weapons of mass destruction and its stockpile of conventional munitions, which includes millions of anti-personnel land mines. The EU has offered to help destroy these.

Ukraine's significance regarding the EU's internal security was recognised relatively early on, leading to its 'Action Plan on Justice and Home Affairs'. This was agreed upon with the EU in December 2001 and contains a list of mutual goals that were developed through Ukraine's PCA, which had been signed in June 1994 and entered into force in 1998 (see also Lavenex 2004b). Work on JHA matters was handled by a sub-committee, whose efforts contributed to the agreement on the JHA Action Plan. This plan identifies common challenges and strategic aims, the legal/historical 'framework' of collaboration, areas of cooperation, and instruments and means to implement points of action. The Action Plan called for the creation of a 'scoreboard' that has since been used effectively by the EU and Ukraine for monitoring implementation, policy evaluation, and the definition of annual priorities (Interviews, DGs JLS and RELEX).

Seven general areas of cooperation are covered in the EU–Ukraine action plan on JHA, each encompassing seven to fourteen more particular objectives:

1   Migration and Asylum.
2   Border Management and Visas.
3   Organised Crime.
4   Terrorism.
5   Judicial Cooperation.
6   Law Enforcement Cooperation.
7   Strengthening the Judiciary, the Rule of Law and Good Governance.

The first version of the Ukraine–EU JHA scoreboard was published on 19 June 2002 and was structured according to these areas. For each action to be taken, the scoreboard indicates the actors responsible (e.g. Ukraine, the Commission, the Association Council and/or the EU member states), the timeframe for action, and the state of progress. Monitoring of progress is entrusted to the JHA sub-committee, which meets at least annually under the auspices of Ukraine's PCA.

In sum, Ukraine's experience not only reflects many of the internal security problems found among other MEDA and TACIS states, but its action plan has served as a model for the handling of JHA in ENP. The model provided by the Ukraine Action Plan thus helps to explain the uniformity in the way various JHA issues are handled in the other partners' Action Plans. Meanwhile Ukraine's own ENP Action Plan simply refers to its own Action Plan on JHA, rather than containing a fully developed section on this topic.

Taking action on JHA

As with the country reports, the ENP Action Plans (with the exception of that of the Palestinian Authority) contain sections devoted to JHA . Unlike the country reports, however, the Action Plans are organised according to a common structure. The seven Action Plans published by the Commission in December 2004 are similar but hardly identical. Each plan specifies several objectives or actions, including many identified in both Ukraine's JHA Action Plan and the ENP country reports. The differences among the Action Plans reflect country-specific challenges or interests vis-à-vis the EU, as well as contending levels of political sensitivity on some matters, such as terrorism.

Table 7.1   Main areas of JHA cooperation in the ENP Action Plans of 2004

Headings used in JHA sections	Examples of topics covered in each section	Examples of related objectives under each topic
Migration	• Asylum and refugee issues	• Implement principles of the 1951 Geneva Convention and its 1967 protocols • Training for officials
	• Migration flows	• Information exchange • Information campaigns in the partners on the risks of legal immigration • Information campaigns in the EU on the benefits of legal migration
	• Transit migration (via the partner) • Illegal migration to and via the ENP participant	• EU assistance with third parties (source countries) • Supporting measures in partners • Active cooperation (operations)
	• Re-admission of illegal immigrants found in the EU	• Conclude and implement agreement with the EU
	• Dialogue on visas with the EU	• Improve travel document security • Facilitate visas for travel and work
Border management	• Border control and surveillance	• Improve infrastructure and equipment • Improve institutional capacity (e.g. through training)
	• Cross-border cooperation	• Multi-national cooperation among law enforcement agencies in border areas

Headings used in JHA sections	Examples of topics covered in each section	Examples of related objectives under each topic
Combating organised crime	• International instruments	• Sign and implement UN Convention of 2000 Against Transnational Organized Crime and its related protocols
	• Trafficking of human beings	• Improve data collection and sharing • Training programmes • Improve support for victims
	• Counter-terrorism	• Specialised training (e.g. on the financing of terrorism)
Drugs	• Drug trafficking	• Specialized training for law enforcement • Reduce demand for drugs in the EU • Reduce the supply/production of drugs in the ENP participant, including using economic development • Implement UN conventions on drugs (e.g. 1988)
	• Drug addiction	• Prevention and rehabilitation programmes
Money laundering, economic and financial crimes	• Money laundering	• Implement Financial Action Task Force (FATF) recommendations • Implement new legislation
	• Corruption	• Establish national monitoring agency
Judicial and police cooperation	• Cooperation between judicial authorities	• Explore cooperation with Eurojust • Sign and implement international conventions • Resolve disputes on family law
	• Cooperation among law enforcement officials	• Explore cooperation agreements with Europol • Increase contact points and information-sharing with law enforcement in the member states

Table 7.1   Continued

Headings used in JHA sections	Examples of topics covered in each section	Examples of related objectives under each topic
	• Strengthen judicial and police authorities in the ENP participants	• Training (by European Police College (CEPOL))

Several of the objectives contained in the Action Plans refer to changes needed in the ENP participants, aimed at enhancing their ability to deal with the JHA-related problems and challenges covered in the country reports. In some cases, the required action is legislative change, including the signing or ratification of international conventions or the drafting of new domestic criminal law. Other points of action indicate improvements in the partner country through assistance from the EU, potentially funded by the ENPI or provided by existing EU institutions or funding programmes. This includes, for example, new equipment or infrastructure for border management, as well as training programmes conducted by the EU for judicial or law enforcement officials, which could take place in the EU or in the partner country. Such initiatives could potentially be funded as stand-alone programmes supported by the ENPI (see below), or they could be financed by CEPOL or the EU's JHA funding initiatives, including the 'Agis programme' for law enforcement officers and the 'Argo programme' for border control officials.

Additional objectives covered in the Action Plans are directed at strengthening cooperation between the ENP partner country and the EU or its member states to tackle problems associated with transnational organised crime and border management. In just about every area of cooperation, the Action Plans refer to the need for greater information sharing. Some objectives, such as those related to illegal immigration or border management, mention the need for greater operational collaboration, while others call for the ENP participants to forge cooperation agreements with the EU's evolving crime-fighting institutions, namely Europol (for police officials) and Eurojust (for judicial authorities and prosecutors).[3]

Still other objectives covered in the JHA sections of the Action Plans identify particular areas of interest for either the EU or the ENP participant. In several instances, there is an obvious quid pro quo or 'logrolling' rationale at work. For example, the EU wants to forge re-admission agreements with each partner to ease its ability to return illegal immigrants, while the ENP participants want EU assistance in promoting socio-economic development to reduce the incentive to emigrate (see Chapter 5). Some ENP participants would also like the EU to use its influence on third countries (e.g. Russia or 'ACP' states – countries of sub-Saharan Africa, the Caribbean and the Pacific) to help them prevent their territory from being used as a transit or destination point for illegal immigrants from these states. At the same time, the ENP participants would also like to open up dialogue with the EU on its common visa regime for the Schengen zone to make it easier for their citizens to travel legally to the EU for business, education, tourism, or to find temporary employment. The EU wants these countries' assistance in creating more secure travel documents. Likewise, the EU wants to engage its partners in combating drug trafficking, while these states want assistance from the EU to fight drug abuse among their citizens or to promote economic development in drug-producing areas.

Along with all of this, JHA is also included in two other areas of the Action Plans. These are the introductory sections of each Action Plan under the heading of 'Priorities for Action' and the sections on 'Political Dialogue and Reform', which is the first policy area covered in the Action Plans' sections on 'Actions'. The sections on political dialogue and reform also cover the issue of terrorism.

Each of the seven Action Plans of December 2004 identifies a number of areas deserving of 'particular attention' from among the many policy domains covered. There are six areas impinging on JHA that show up at least twice as priority areas in these Action Plans. These are summarised in Table 7.2. Given the prominence of migration issues in the Action Plans, it is no surprise to find issues related to this among the priorities for several of the ENP participants.

As noted above, the Action Plans deal with terrorism in their sections on JHA and political dialogue and reform. All seven of the Action Plans are very similar in this regard. For example, all call for a general strengthening of cooperation with the EU on terrorism and point toward more specific measures contained in the JHA section of the document. In addition, all of the Action Plans address the need to implement fully the relevant UN Security

Table 7.2   Priorities for action in ENP Action Plans of 2004

JHA topics mentioned as priorities	Action Plans including this topic
Managing migration flows	Ukraine, Moldova, Jordan, Tunisia
Improving judicial capacity	Ukraine, Moldova, Jordan, Palestinian Authority
Forging re-admission agreements	Ukraine, Moldova, Morocco, Tunisia
Facilitating visas	Ukraine, Jordan, Morocco, Tunisia
Fighting terrorism	Israel, Tunisia
Fighting organised crime	Israel, Moldova

Council resolutions. Regarding the fight against the financing of terrorism, the Action Plans specify some combination of the implementation of the UN Convention for the Suppression of the Financing of Terrorism, FATF recommendations on terrorism, or new domestic legislation. All of the actions also address the need to respect human rights in the fight against terrorism. Interestingly, Israel's Action Plan follows this with a reference to the need to protect the rights of those targeted by terrorism. In addition, the section on terrorism in Israel's ENP Action Plan adds the objectives of sharing information and best practices with the EU, as well as with third countries, in the fight against terrorism.

Pressing issues for Morocco and Ukraine

In a communication to the Commission of 22 November 2005, Benita Ferrero-Waldner laid out her immediate and longer terms plans for implementing ENP. Among the 'priorities and expectations' listed are several dealing with JHA. Here, cooperation on border management and the fight against various forms of organised crime are specifically linked to enhancements for partners' citizens regarding legal immigration, including visa facilitation and managed economic migration.

Commissioner Ferrero-Waldner's communication also noted several policy-specific priorities to be addressed before the end of 2006 for each of seven ENP participants with published Action Plans. For Morocco, the fight against organised crime and terrorism was highlighted, as was the need to 'intensify a comprehensive and balanced dialogue and cooperation on migration with the EU and neighbouring countries'. The report was published soon after the episodes at Ceuta and Mililla, which had prompted Spain to use a dormant bilateral re-admission agreement forged with Morocco in 1992 to return some of the illegal immigrants involved in the incidents. In this context, it is not surprising that Ferrero-Waldner's communication also expressed hope for a rapid conclusion of ongoing negotiations for an EU-Moroccan re-admission agreement. However, the issue of returning non-Moroccan nationals to Morocco, among other matters, endured as a point of contention, pushing talks beyond the summer of 2006.

The impact of the deadly events at Spanish enclaves, as well as other crises throughout the Mediterranean, contributed to the European Council's decision in December 2005 to focus more attention and resources on illegal immigration into the Euro-Med region. Along with Algeria and Libya, Morocco was identified as a priority country for the earmarking of up to three percent of the ENP's eventual funding (roughly €400 million) for actions in the region, such as joint patrols and a feasibility study for a coastal patrol network. The European Council also emphasised the need to address the deeper sources of the migration problem in sub-Saharan Africa and endorsed a programme with Tanzania to provide regional protection for asylum seekers (*European Report*, 21 December 2005). In July 2006, as the crisis of illegal immigration from Africa to Europe worsened, delegates from 58 countries and several NGOs met in Rabat, Morocco for the first-ever Euro-African Ministerial Conference on Migration and Development. The conference's final declaration prioritised European assistance for African economic development but also included several areas of border management cooperation, such as joint monitoring of sea and border routes.

Regarding Ukraine, Ferrero-Waldner's communication listed as priorities the fight against the trafficking of human beings and the linked issues of visa facilitation and a re-admission agreement. Negotiations on the latter had been ongoing since March 2002, but talks on simplifying Ukrainians' visa needs for travel to the EU did not begin until 21 November 2005. Since the break-up of the Soviet Union, the EU has hoped to facilitate the return of illegal immigrants who enter its member states via Ukraine. At the same time, policy-makers in Ukraine have been pushing for a visa-free regime with Brussels. In May 2005, Ukraine unilaterally suspended visa requirements for EU citizens for short-term visits, and, by the end of October 2006, a deal on the issues of re-admission and visa facilitation was finally reached.

In addition, the EU has established a monitoring mission along the Ukrainian–Moldovan border in the disputed Transnistria region. This was created on 30 November 2005 as a €7 million project for two years, consisting of over fifty customs and border officials seconded from EU member states. Their task is to monitor, guide, and train their Moldovan and Ukrainian counterparts in the fight against trafficking crimes and customs fraud. The EU hopes that resolving these issues will contribute to a long-term resolution of the territorial dispute and bring peace and stability to the region (*European Report*, 8 October 2005).

The ENPI and JHA

Similar to other policy domains encompassed by the ENP, there are only a few direct references to JHA in the ENPI regulation proposed by the Commission in 2004. For example, JHA is mentioned in its preamble, as well as in Title I ('Objectives and Principles'), Article 2 ('Scope'). Specifically, the scope of the ENPI entails 'ensuring efficient and secure border management' (point n), as well as 'promoting cooperation in the field of justice and home affairs, including on issues such as asylum and migration and the fight against and prevention of terrorism and organized crime, including its financing, money laundering and tax fraud' (point o). 'Refugees' and displaced persons are mentioned in the same article under the topic of support for post-crisis situations regarding conflicts and natural disasters (point w). The fight against terrorism is not mentioned at all in the regulation, but the legal basis for its inclusion can be found in Article 2, point y, which refers to 'addressing common thematic challenges in fields of mutual concern and any other objectives consistent with the scope of this Regulation'.

Most of the ENPI regulation deals with how funding can be spent, and this presents several options for ENP projects on JHA. For example, the country-specific or multi-country programmes could entail training programmes on border management or counter-terrorism provided by EU member states for officials in the ENP participants. There might also be specialised training for prosecutors or judges on financial crime related to money laundering. Funding of this type could also be used to help pay for modern equipment, such as computer hardware needed to create data bases for information exchanges regarding crime control or border management. A trilateral agreement among Moldova, Ukraine and Romania is already in place to fight organised crime, and some of its projects could be funded by this type of ENPI assistance.

Likewise, the thematic programmes funded via the ENPI could be directed at specific forms of organised crime, such as human trafficking and drug trafficking. Funding for cross-border projects under the ENPI might include initiatives on border management or organised crime for regions of Ukraine adjacent to Poland or Hungary, such as programmes sponsored by the so called 'Northern Dimension' group of countries or the 'Söderköping Process.' This kind of ENPI funding might also benefit illegal immigration projects in the Euro-Med region or programmes on the trafficking of drugs or human beings developed by the newly established 'Black Sea Forum'.

Conclusion

This chapter has explained the origins of the ENP in terms of the EU's enlargement, its external efforts regarding JHA, the templates provided by the TACIS and MEDA programmes, the example of Ukraine, and the challenges posed by border management and transnational crime. The chapter began by arguing that the effectiveness of the ENP on JHA will be determined by compliance to the agreements contained in the Action Plans for this policy area. One reason for optimism is the increased focus that the ENP brings to issues long since addressed by the TACIS and MEDA programmes. In the end, however, ENP participants must either embrace the norms embodied in the EU's emerging JHA *acquis* or find it in their interest to comply with agreements contained in their Action Plans (Interviews, DGs JLS and RELEX). At this stage, one can only speculate about this, because it is not clear that ENP participants will adopt reforms promoted by the EU without the prospect of membership. Accession to the EU was, after all, the main incentive for new and future member states to adopt the JHA *acquis*. This is where logrolling can prove useful, especially concerning issues such as visa facilitation and re-admission agreements.

Of course, it remains to be seen whether the ENP will be more effective than its regional predecessors at helping the EU and its ENP participants reach their mutual goals. The increased political and budgetary focus on JHA in the EU and ENP are reasons to be hopeful. At the same time, however, the problems of border management, transnational organised crime, and terrorism in Europe's new neighbourhood seem to be greater than ever before.

Notes

1   All but Jordan, Lebanon, and the Palestinian Authority have done so.
2   All of the TACIS ENP participants are Council of Europe members (aside from Belarus), but they do not belong to the OECD or its FATF. Instead, they are among the twenty-seven countries forming the Council of Europe's MONEYVAL group, which is connected to the work of the FATF. None of the Mediterranean partners belong to these NGOs.
3   Europol, or the European Police Office, facilitates police cooperation through a liaison network, computer data base, and analytical staff. Eurojust entails a liaison network of criminal prosecutors designed to facilitate information sharing.

SANDRA LAVENEX AND ADAM N. STULBERG

8

Connecting the neighbourhood: energy and environment

The ENP lies at the intersection of the European Union's domestic and foreign policies. Though short of offering full EU accession, it is intended for eastern and southern neighbours to 'share the benefits' of enlargement and 'strengthen stability, security and well-being for all concerned' via a 'privileged relationship' on critical policy issues (European Commission 2004a: 3). The ENP is also part of a strategy for exerting 'soft power', involving the 'securitisation' of internal policies to mitigate vulnerabilities and extend the normative standards of the EU's *acquis communautaire* (Lavenex 2004a). In short, the ENP constitutes more than benign international cooperation; it is a form of external governance for advancing EU values and interests along its new periphery.

The prospects for realising these twin ambitions vary. The EU's historical relationships and asymmetric concerns vis-à-vis prospective partners impose obstacles to replicating the 'conditionality' principle of enlargement strategies through a patchwork of alternative ENP institutions (Kelley 2006). This is epitomised by early developments on energy and environmental security that have been uniformly inserted into the ENP as technical issues for 'connecting the neighbourhood' and facilitating 'convergence' towards EU standards. Yet Brussels has developed robust institutional and policy mechanisms for managing environmental issues, while retaining only limited capacity to contain supply disruption or to influence transit in the oil and gas sectors. How do we explain these mixed results?

Combining insights from theories of public goods and governance, we argue that the attributes of energy and environmental goods circumscribe the forms and effectiveness of the ENP. The distribution of bargaining power to manage collective action derives from different institutional parameters, shadows of the future, market standing, and allocation of internal property rights across respective policy fields. Accordingly, we find that the quasi-public and private goods issues presented by the oil and natural gas trade, respectively, can explain why the institutionalised energy dialogue has been orchestrated primarily between member states and critical suppliers, such as Russia and Algeria, often at the expense of prospective ENP participants, with the EU confined to harmonising pan-European market objectives and coordinating damage limiting and crisis management regulatory policies with neighbouring supplier and transit states. Collective action challenges and attendant bargaining weakness restrict the credibility and effectiveness of the ENP in compelling new neighbours to accept the EU's preferred pipeline routes, gas distribution, internal pricing, and regulatory transparency and investment policies. This contrasts with the depth of institutionalisation and variety of strategies developed under the ENP to contend with essentially common pool environmental problems. On these issues there has been significant transnational policy transfer between Brussels, EU member states, and private actors (at local, regional, national, community and international levels). The objectives defined by the EU's robust and technical environmental *aquis*, and reinforced by broader international conventions, provide the foundation for extending 'good governance' and mobilising support from local political and civil authorities to promote adaptation along the new periphery.

This chapter has four parts. The first section analyses the main objectives of ENP energy and environment policies, mapping underlying EU perceptions of interdependence and securitisation. Second, we outline alternative forms of governance and bargaining factors that condition the effectiveness of strategies for managing collective action. The third part traces the consequences for Brussels' limited capacity to direct energy policies in the eastern neighbourhood, on the one hand; and multidimensional capacity to deliver favourable ENP initiatives on environmental issues, on the other. The conclusion reviews strategic and regional policy implications associated with these alternative forms of external governance.

The EU strategy for 'neighbourhood' energy and environmental cooperation

Energy

Although the level of dependence varies across sectors, maturation of indigenous reserves and enlargement ensure that the aggregate EU energy balance will be dominated for the foreseeable future by rising demand for fossil fuels, subject to international production and pricing beyond Brussels' direct control (European Commission 2001e: 2). Harbouring no illusions that energy security can be attained through self-sufficiency, expanding alternative (renewable and sustainable) energy resources, or managing internal consumption alone, the EU has placed priorities on managing the diversification of external supply and market stability in Europe.

Relations with Russia and new ENP partners figure prominently for managing the EU's structural vulnerability and long-term energy security. From 1999–2003, imports from Russia constituted approximately 18–21 and 41–44 per cent of European member state supply of oil and natural gas, respectively. This is forecast to grow with EU enlargement, as new members are expected to rely on Russia for nearly 90 and 94 per cent of gas and oil supply, respectively, until 2030.[1] Accordingly, reliable access to the European market for established and emerging suppliers and transit states lies at the crux of ENP Action Plans for advancing the gradual convergence of infrastructure and regulatory mechanisms towards the EU. The ENP envisions that this not only will arrest impulses for geostrategic competition, but will provide 'mutual business opportunities and also contribute to socio-economic development and improvement to the environment' (European Commission 2004h: 17). This will become especially important as energy markets begin to tighten in response to the expected swelling demand from developing countries – especially China, India and Latin America – over the coming decades.

Each fuel sector presents different strategic concerns for the EU. The combination of limited indigenous reserves and growing appeal of 'clean' fuels has elevated natural gas in the EU's overall energy balance. This threatens to intensify dependence on Russian imports, exacerbating the EU's vulnerability to future external supply bottlenecks and disruptions, as displayed during the winter 2006 Russia–Ukraine 'gas war' that precipitated temporary delivery shortfalls of one-quarter to one-half of planned volumes of Russian gas to several member states. Accordingly, successive EU Commission reports and Parliamentary 'joint resolutions' call for a comprehensive plan to develop renewable fuels, boost energy efficiency, diversify liquefied natural gas (LNG) options and regulate sole sourcing, as well as to strengthen ENP relations with emerging supplier and transit states in the NIS and Southern Mediterranean (European Commission 2001e: 74; European Parliament 2006). However, due to the limited impact that alternative suppliers will have on covering Russian supply gaps, Brussels also places a premium on integrating the internal market and harmonising Russian and NIS market and regulatory structures with EU standards. Conversely, oil reserves in Russia and the NIS offer potential alternatives for reducing the risks of supply disruption for EU member states. Declining internal production, rising demand, and persistent dependency on oil imports from the Persian Gulf in the period to 2020 raise the stakes for developing Russian fields (and to a lesser extent the Caspian Basin), as well as pipelines and transit facilities spread across the new neighbourhood (especially in Ukraine and Georgia). In sum, the EU looks to the East as both a reflection of structural dependence and a solution for long-term energy supply stability.

The EU's 'eastern vocation' for energy security stands out among other dimensions of the ENP. It constitutes a rare set of issues of rough parity between Brussels and ENP partners, as there are mutual vulnerabilities and complementary interests in preserving stable demand in the European market. Given the character of international oil and gas markets, the EU's long-term interaction with its new neighbours is heavily dependent on the behaviour of regional (Azerbaijan) and extra-regional suppliers (especially Russia and OPEC), and transit states (Belarus, Georgia, Turkey and Ukraine), as well as on the economic and strategic disposition of other large consumers, including the US, China, Turkey and Japan. To realise mutual benefits in a stable long-term European market will require that each eschews competition that can result in less secure markets and supply for all. Thus, the success of the ENP at maintaining the EU's energy supply and market access turns on managing asymmetrical interests and visions among strategic suppliers, consumers, and transit states operating in both the near and far abroad.

Environment

Issues related to environmental security are less politically divisive among member states, more indirectly affected by geostrategic concerns, and generally less salient during economic downturns than with energy (Lenschow 2005). Nevertheless, environmental issues figure prominently in the ENP for three reasons. First, anxiety persists over the potential negative externalities associated with perpetuation of traditional environmental practices among neighbouring states. Priority problems typically include 'centres of great industrial pollution', such as inefficient heat generation and distribution systems; exhaust from road transport; poor surface and ground water quality; underdeveloped municipal environmental infrastructure; and inefficient use of natural resources (European Commission 2003a: 6). The centralised command system, heavy industrialisation, urbanisation, and the traditional low priority accorded to public awareness and conservation, created dangerous ecological legacies, as well as rendering national laws primarily declarative and marred by unrealistic and weak implementing norms and guidance (ERM 2003; European Environmental Agency 2003). Given the transnational characteristics of environmental hazards, many of these problems affect the enlarged Union, particularly at the regional level. This pertains especially to 'hot spots' in the water sector that put at risk residential communities and commercial operators along major European rivers, as well as fragile marine environments in the Baltic, Barents and Black Seas. Accordingly, the EU has become the main sponsor of regional cooperation initiatives, such as the Northern Dimension Initiative (NDI) and the DABLAS-initiative on the protection of water and related ecosystems of the tributaries of the Danube and Black Sea Region.

Second, the priority accorded to environmental issues within the ENP stems from the EU's general commitments to sustainable development

(Article 2 of the EC Treaty) and leadership in multilateral regimes, such as the Kyoto Protocol or the Biodiversity Convention. The EU has encouraged prospective partners to ratify relevant regional and global environmental agreements. At the forefront of this environmental 'Ostpolitik' has been support for Russian and Ukrainian accession to the Kyoto Protocol and implementation of the UN Framework Convention on Climate Change.

Third, the ENP is directly linked to the EU's commitment to widening the scope of the single market and external trade. This is formally acknowledged in respective Partnership and Cooperation Agreements concluded with the Eastern ENP partners. These documents state not only that 'an important condition for strengthening the economic links' with the Community is 'the approximation of legislation', but that 'cooperation shall take place particularly through ... improvement of laws towards Community standards' (See Articles 55 and 69 of the EU–Russia PCA and the corresponding articles in the PCAs with Ukraine and Moldova). According to the 2003 Report on the Environment for Europe process, the goal of the European Commission is 'improvement of laws, towards EU standards, both for the environmental benefits this will bring and in order to facilitate trade and investment' (European Commission, 2003e: 7).

Notwithstanding these impulses, the transfer of EU standards is very costly, and presupposes large-scale monetary and technical investment in the post-Communist countries. As evidenced in the pre-accession process, the extension of EU standards requires that target states possess significant administrative capacity at different levels of government and civil society (Carius et al. 2000; Ecotec et al. 2000, 2001; Carmin and Vandeveer 2004; Vandeveer and Carmin 2004). Yet deficiencies in both areas constrain the application of EU norms and practices among Eastern ENP partners.

Collective goods and external governance

Public goods theory specifies parameters for international energy and resource security. Typically, two criteria classify goods: excludability and rivalry of consumption (Olson 1965; Cornes and Sandler 1996; Ostrom 2003). Specific combinations determine an actor's incentives to provide or secure the flow of the common good, as well as the conditions for international monitoring and enforcement to contain respective free-riding and transaction costs. As depicted in Figure 8.1, this formulation yields four ideal types of goods and corresponding requirements for international institutions (Barkin and Shambaugh 1999: 4–6).

Though the intrinsic characteristics of goods can condition outcomes for joint provision, the extant literature on collective action and external governance generally do not address each other. The former typically overlooks that foreign actors tend to assign different existential or consumptive values

		Consumption	
		Rival	Non-rival
Excludability	High	**Private Goods** Minimal institutional requirements for cooperation or coordination to protect property rights; reliance on market mechanism	**Club Goods** Institutional requirement to safeguard exclusion of non-members
	Low	**Common pool resources** Strong institutions and enforcement mechanisms to discourage harmful free-riding given weak incentives for cooperation	**Pure public goods** Institutions to ensure the provision of the good despite weak incentives; once established, cooperation is self-enforcing

Figure 8.1   Types of goods and institutional requirements for collective action

to joint solutions, as well as possess different bargaining strengths at over-coming collective action problems (Barkin and Shambaugh 1999; Mitchell 1999). They also neglect the institutional context for bargaining among 'multilevel' international actors, such as the EU, where competencies vary across issues areas. Conversely, the literature on governance and statecraft short-shrifts the constraints imposed by different collective action problems. Conditions for effective pre-emption, coercion, or crisis management are narrowly linked to the structural, institutional, or political endowments of interacting parties. Thus, to comprehend the variance of external governance on energy and environmental security within the ENP, we must examine the constraints imposed on collective action and bargaining by the specific attributes of goods.

From this rational-institutional perspective, several factors are critical to overcoming collective action problems and establishing effective external governance. The first pertains to the balance of time horizons. Actors that possess a shorter shadow of the future for a resource and are less sensitive to the long-term costs of over-consumption (relative to the present benefits of consumption), are in a stronger position to coerce concessions from a rival. Because they place a higher value on present gains and losses, they can credibly threaten to delay or impede the long-term benefits of collective action. This affords greater bargaining power to secure favourable terms of cooperation or to pre-empt the preferred alternative to a common aversion. In either case, the party with the longer time horizon is at a disadvantage, as any settlement within reach (that minimises damage or defers to a rival's preferred outcome) is more acceptable than eschewing joint action altogether (Barkin and Shambaugh 1999: 12–14).

A second bargaining advantage goes to actors that wield market power. In scenarios involving dilemmas of common interests for tradable goods where small decreases in the value of the good produce large increases in demand, there are strong incentives for unilateral exploitation. With market power to alter the future value of a resource or lower the elasticity of demand, an actor (supplier or consumer) should be well positioned to shape favourable cooperation. Conversely, an actor that lacks market power must defer to the terms set by others for redressing common interests, despite possible distributional losses short of the costs incurred by non-provision. The capacity to mitigate these losses derives from either limiting the negative externalities of collaboration or containing the damages of coordinating a minimally acceptable outcome (Stein 1990: 41–2). In the case of non-tradable goods, such as environmental protection, market power can indirectly affect the costs versus benefits of cooperative solutions, generating external incentives for compliance.

Third, an actor's institutional capacity can shape its international bargaining power. Many actors lack legitimate authority to exercise, transfer, exclude, or regulate resources in a policy field. If an actor retains only partial bundles of rights to national resources or does not realise the full costs or benefits of exercising these rights, then it will have neither sole authority to exploit or contribute to the common good, nor political capacity to uphold international commitments. This can prevent it from credibly threatening to reduce the future availability of the good, or from effectively constraining furtive cheating by domestic agents. The weaker the internal control of an international actor over implementation of policies aimed at realising common interests or aversions, the more its bargaining strength depends on tailoring diplomatic initiatives to concentrated agency interests or appealing to swing groups among the foreign target's constituency (Putnam 1988; Moravcsik 1993: 27–30).

Collective action and ENP energy and environmental security

Oil and gas policies

In today's integrated market, oil displays characteristics of a 'quasi-public' good where the benefits of supply are not excludable and incentives for rival consumption are modified by the price mechanism. The release of new oil anywhere increases pressure to lower prices everywhere, but because supply is finite consumption by one state diminishes the amount available to others over both the very short and long terms. This encourages under-supply and over-consumption, as there are disincentives to pay the full costs for greater access if benefits cannot be denied, as well as generating strong incentives to hoard scarce resources against rival consumers (Barkin and Shambaugh 1999: 6–8).[2] However, the price mechanism tempers typical common pool problems. Scarcity propels innovation and raises the economies of extracting poor mineral grades, improving recovery of developed fields, tapping new reserves, and pursuing alternative fuels. Conversely, very low price levels can delay investments to create future supply squeezes, and discourage diversification of suppliers or fuel type (Claes 2001: 35–93; Victor and Victor 2003: 51–4; Clingendael Institute 2004: 39). This creates common interests in securing cost-effective access to even marginal quantities of new stocks, extending productive horizons and ensuring competitive but stable prices. Though consumer states can free-ride, they cannot prevent short-run supply disruptions, costly price fluctuation, or long-run depletion without institutionalising joint action or coordinating unilateral adjustment (i.e. exploration, conservation and strategic reserves).

Natural gas more closely resembles a 'private' good that can be purchased and consumed exclusively by the contracting parties. Prices and pipelines are tailored to specific gas markets, with little incentive to hoard against oneself (Barkin and Shambaugh 1999: 3–6).[3] Rapid depletion must be avoided, however, generating mutual interests in coordinating consumption. This drives consumers to coordinate, as they can bear both the direct costs and benefits of their efforts to a greater extent than with traditional common pool problems.

Similarly, supplier states that possess abundant reserves and depend heavily on energy revenues have strong incentives to reduce the volatility of global energy markets and exposure to downward price shocks. Given the relatively low price elasticity of demand, the persistence of high prices induces new suppliers to enter energy markets to boost output, reducing revenues for traditional producers. Alternatively, sustained low prices provoke intense competition among rival suppliers that drives higher cost producers to exit the market or default on debts. Given price links between energy markets, the persistence of low oil prices also can sap investments in gas exploration, extraction and production. Concerns for 'demand security', therefore, encourage energy exporting nations to solicit long-term commercial relations with large customers. Barring extreme cases where states or firms can corner global energy markets, both producers and consumers benefit from stable energy supply, demand and prices.

These collective action challenges generate mixed motives for energy security in Europe, subjecting the ENP to significant constraints imposed by foreign markets and Russia. The quasi-public goods problem in the oil sector reinforces incentives for the EU to stabilise deliveries from Russia and prospective NIS suppliers. Unlocking Eurasian reserves offers modest relief from Europe's own concentrated dependency on the Persian Gulf, while presenting an opportunity to relax Moscow's energy stranglehold over the

NIS. In the long run, oil from Russia and the Caspian Basin can moderate a potential global crisis that could reverberate from Asia's vulnerability to supply disruption. Accordingly, the EU maintains strong interests in bolstering regulatory transparency and protecting private and non-discriminatory exploration, production and export of Russian and NIS oil. In the gas sector, EU member states not only seek to diversify supply and ease transit across the eastern neighbourhood, but share interests in boosting Russian production and exports to cover an expected deficit due to structural limits on rival suppliers from North Africa, the Middle East and Central Asia (Gotz 2005). Brussels seeks to encourage Moscow to deregulate the market, raising domestic prices above loss-making levels, and to relax territorial restriction clauses on imports that undermine creation of a unified, liberalised EU gas market (Johnson 2003; Lynch 2003b).

Yet the EU bargains from relative weakness. Concerns about supply security are expected to become acute by 2020–30 with depletion of North Sea reserves and rising consumption among old and new members (European Commission 2001e). The EU also lacks market power in both sectors, despite consuming more than 20 and 16 per cent of world oil and gas production, respectively. This is due to the integrated oil market and structural rigidity of the current gas market that prevent European consumers from turning away from Russia, as well as the faster growing demand for fossil fuels by China, India, Latin America and the US (European Commission 2001e). It is compounded by the institutional weakness of the EU that has historically lacked competency to impose common prices, supply and regulatory practices, or to transcend rival national prerogatives to implement market or state-based mechanisms among member states (Luciani 2002).[4]

Simultaneously, Russia's dependence on energy revenues binds it to Europe. Between 2002–04, energy trade with EU member states comprised nearly 53 per cent and 36 per cent of Russian oil and gas exports, respectively, and constituted 64–70 per cent of the Russian gas industry's hard currency receipts (Piper 2004; Cleutinx 2005). With 'excessive concentration' on the EU market, both the Russian government – motivated to maintain formal control over offshore resources and influence in the 'near abroad' – and Russian oil firms – primed to acquire stakes in international consortia and to compete against rival development projects – share interests in guiding the pace and direction of Caspian oil development and export (Ministry of Economic Development and Trade 2004; Stulberg 2004).[5] As envisioned by the Russian government, economic growth will become more sensitive to the dramatic contraction of oil prices below $26/bbl, but less affected by oil price increases above $30–32/bbl until 2015. Accordingly, Moscow's main interest in closer cooperation with the EU lies with attracting large-scale investment in Russia's oil development and export infrastructure, as well as with participating in NIS prospecting and transport projects to stabilise international prices (Ministry of Economic Development and Trade 2004).[6]

Similarly, Russia must rationalise long-term natural gas production and exports. Russia relies on its dominant position in Europe to generate critical state revenues, contain global competitors, capitalise on comparative and legacy advantages of delivering gas to new member states, attract foreign investment to modernise field development and diversify export options, and demonstrate its credentials as a reliable supplier to new markets (Lynch 2003b; Hill 2004). Russia also stands to benefit from coordinating with Caspian suppliers to stabilise incremental competition in liberalised European markets, and to meet growing demand at home and in emerging Asian markets that will outstrip the capacity of the Russian industry to service on its own. Though Russian gas suppliers are loath to jeopardise standing in Europe and access to cheap Central Asian imports, they could gain roughly $600 billion in loans and capital by coordinating deliveries and reassuring potential European investors in domestic development projects (Adams 2002: 20; International Energy Agency 2002). Coordinating long-term gas supply with the EU also is integral to the Kremlin's strategy for integrating into the global economy, modernising the national infrastructure, and insulating the domestic economy from adverse pressures of liberalised EU markets (Ministry of Economic Development and Trade 2004; Olcott 2005).

Moscow's capacity to realise preferred energy outcomes, however, varies. In the oil sector, it too is a relatively weak player. Though time horizons are noticeably shorter than those of EU consumers – owing to the projected slow-down in output growth by 2007 and depletion of highly accessible reserves by 2010 – the country's vast reserves and rising international demand mitigate immediate burdens imposed by bottlenecks or gluts on the domestic market (Hill 2004; Ministry of Economic Development and Trade 2004; Dienes 2005). While Russia produced nearly 10 per cent of the world's crude by 2001, it holds less than 5 per cent of global reserves and pales in comparison to Saudi Arabia as a swing producer. The decentralised and opaque structure of the national oil sector also hampers Moscow's bargaining leverage. Though Putin streamlined national 'stewardship' over the largely privatised sector (capped by the forced sell-off of Russian oil company YuKOS's assets in 2004–5), the state owns only one major oil company and retains minority stakes in others (Olcott 2005).[7] The inefficient and predatory pipeline monopoly, as well as persistent confusion over mineral rights, production-sharing legislation, pricing policies, volume-based taxes, and export regulation collectively threaten to shut-in production and render Russia a net petroleum importer as early as 2010 (Sagers 2001; Ministry of Economic Development and Trade 2004; Milov and Selivakhin 2005).

On gas issues, however, Russia is poised to become a spoiler for the ENP, as it controls over 32 per cent of the world's proven supply and 50 per cent of global exports. The industry giant, Gazprom, wields a virtual monopoly over ownership, production, processing, and transportation of Russian and NIS gas (International Energy Agency 2002). Though it cannot legally impose commercial decisions on corporate ownership, the federal government possesses a critical 38 per cent stake in the company, and can set domestic prices and levy taxes to manipulate the cost-effectiveness of the firm's domestic and foreign business (Stulberg 2004). Moscow also benefits from relatively short time horizons, as industrial and household consumers are virtually kept afloat by huge gas subsidies. Yet the debt-ridden gas monopoly cannot afford to incur additional non-payments or to finance much-needed construction of new pipelines or exploration of new fields to meet the ballooning demand (Hill 2004; Milov and Selivakhin 2005).

Finally, the collective goods problems in the oil and gas sectors colour motives for cooperation among eastern supplier, consumer, and transit states. There are fundamental common interests in forging closer relations with the EU to ease vulnerability to Russian, Kazakh, Turkmen, and Middle Eastern suppliers. In the oil sector, this features cooperation to stabilise global prices and reduce inefficiencies of domestic consumption. The primary concern on gas issues rests with coordinating policies with the EU to stabilise long-term throughput and prices for Russian gas, while attracting investment to modernise indigenous storage and production capacity and to connect isolated transmission networks. For transit states (i.e. Ukraine, Belarus and Georgia) this is reinforced by motives to collect payments for the use of national pipeline segments. Because NIS producers (Azerbaijan and to a lesser extent Ukraine) seek to land gas in Western Europe, they share interests coordinating policies with the EU to secure third party access to long-distance pipelines in the region (Saprykin 2002; Balmaceda 2003; Gatev 2004). Yet each of the eastern neighbours seeks to extract premium rents from preferred pipeline routes for Russian gas. Due to their indebtedness to Moscow and deep penetration of Russian capital in respective national energy sectors, nearly all of the NIS are reticent about embracing relations with the EU at the expense of antagonising Russia or Gazprom.

Due to the structural dependency and politicisation of energy security, eastern customers, suppliers and transit states generally wield only modest bargaining power vis-à-vis the EU or Russia. These debt-stricken and cash-strapped regimes can ill-afford to disrupt even disadvantageous barter arrangements with Russia; nor do they have the capacity to stave off short-term social costs of curbing national energy subsidies. None of the NIS suppliers possess significant market power in respective sectors, and transit states must compete against each other as well as extra-regional states to woo expanded deliveries or new pipelines. Moreover, the institutional weakness – derived from murky ownership and control of large energy companies, equity stakes controlled by Russian firms, opaque energy markets, and political rents earned by dependency on Russia – saps the capacity of NIS governments to adapt to EU standards (Balmaceda 2004).[8]

This constellation of mixed motives and bargaining power ultimately circumscribes the credibility and effectiveness of the ENP. To date, the EU has succeeded in setting targets for the convergence of regulatory standards, internal pricing, and import diversification in Action Plans for Ukraine and Moldova. This was complemented by negotiations to bolster transparency in the management of oil revenues and transit in the future Action Plan with Azerbaijan and Georgia. Since October 2000, an ongoing bilateral dialogue with Russia (outside of the ENP) was regularised to 'improve energy relations, while ensuring that the policies of opening and integrating markets are pursued'. Through this channel, the EU pursued access to the Russian energy transport system, as well as pressured Moscow to improve fiscal stability, protect foreign investment, and accelerate liberalisation of the energy sector compatible with EU standards. Yet both the perfunctory energy reform and convergence proposals embodied by respective Action Plans, as well as lingering disagreements and concessions regarding pipelines, supply contracts, and internal reform in the EU–Russia Dialogue reflect Brussels' weak bargaining position and limits to the ENP. President Putin, for example, flatly rejected Pascal Lamy's 'six-point gas ultimatum' for liberalising domestic prices, reducing internal and foreign tariffs, easing third party access to Russian pipelines, constructing private pipelines, and abolishing Gazprom's monopoly over exports (*Izvestiya* 2004). Though committed to preserving a delicate balance of demand and supply security, Putin reminded his European partners that 'arm-twisting' was futile. He stated boldly that there should be 'no illusions' about Moscow's determination to preserve unified control over the export infrastructure and stewardship over energy 'offspring' located beyond Russia's borders (*Izvestiya* 2003).

Due the character of the sector and the EU's relative weakness, the success of ENP gas initiatives is virtually held hostage to Russia, as evidenced by concessions on key regulatory issues:

Pricing. Though Moscow considered raising domestic prices within the WTO framework, it maintained that low prices reflect the abundant supply of gas in the home market, not an artificial deflation of prices. The EU also gradually relaxed demand for the liberalisation of Russian prices, and sought to avert a dumping crisis by coordinating prices and 'requesting' that Russia charge domestic industrial users prices at least above loss-making levels. Furthermore, Brussels has been stymied by Gazprom's assertion that it is the EU's responsibility to slash internal distribution costs and to optimise taxation, passing cost savings on to European consumers (*Interfax* 2004).

Contracting. The persistence of long-term supply contracts for Russian gas. Many of these contain territorial restriction clauses, permitting Gazprom to sell to different EU members at different prices that are inconsistent with the EU's single market rule and rush to improve internal competition and liberalisation. Gazprom also retains favourable contracting arrangements by exploiting the EU's limited competency and cultivating direct ties with key member states. Specifically, Gazprom secured long-term contracts and mounting equity stakes in the German distribution system by accepting a series of joint ventures, feasibility studies for new pipelines, and favourable terms for German investment in Russian gas exploration (Socor 2005a). Ruhrgas also obtained rights to re-sell gas within the internal market at a price premium exceeding the costs of direct purchases from Gazprom (*Financegates.com* 2005; *RIA-Novosti* 2005).[9] Though Gazprom granted rights to the Austrian oil and gas company OMV to re-sell Russian gas to any point in the internal market, it did so by circumventing the EU and requiring Vienna to increase long-term deliveries until 2012 (*Kommersant* 2004).[10] The EU also was unable to discourage Georgia from signing a 25–year agreement with Gazprom for supply and infrastructure development.

Transport. Russia has not ratified the Energy Charter Treaty (ECT). Gazprom refused to secure 'third party' access to Russian pipelines, arguing that it would cost an annual $5 billion in domestic revenues and $10 billion in export earnings. Brussels' endorsement of new pipelines (Yamal, Northern Europe and Blue Stream) without pushing for corresponding increases in Russian production not only undercut the EU's supply diversification strategy but threatened transit interests in Ukraine, Poland and the Baltic states (Socor 2005b). By conceding to the Yamal and North European pipelines the EU neither upheld principles of 'non-discrimination' embodied by the ECT, nor coordinated with Ukraine to compensate for prospective lost transit rents. This is interpreted in Kiev as consistent with the EU's bargaining weakness and preference for negotiating directly with Moscow over the heads of transit states within the eastern neighbourhood (Saprykin 2002; Balmaceda 2004).[11]

Similarly, the EU has not been able to pre-empt or contain the prospective negative effects for the ENP of Russia's preferred gas policies. Though the EU effectively coordinated commitments among member states to free prices for industrial goods by 2004 and for household goods by 2007, destination clauses on Russian imports have compromised the EU-wide gas market. EU price liberalisation also has reduced the cost-effectiveness of piping gas from alternative Caspian suppliers, such as Kazakhstan and Turkmenistan. Because of the price premium on distance and volumes of pipelines (and lack of LNG infrastructure), the very success of the EU Gas Directive complicates the diversification of external supply via the ENP (Joseph 1998; Stauffer 2000).

The prospects for the ENP are slightly different on oil issues. As with gas, the EU's direct pressure on Russia and NIS transit states has failed to secure favourable outcomes on key ENP-related oil concerns. Brussels has been unable to compel regulatory transparency, as Moscow has remained committed to state ownership, arbitrary licensing rules, and raising export pipelines and production tariffs, as well as to protecting government guidance and competitive advantages of upstream assets via strengthening the production footprint of the state-owned oil firm (*Interfax* 2004; Olcott 2005).[12] Furthermore, though the EU endorsed alternative oil pipelines to enhance supply diversity for member states, the specific routes will either bypass or stoke competition among NIS transit states, alleviating neither their mounting energy arrears nor structural dependency on Russia (Gatev 2004).[13]

Because of the mutual weaknesses and common interests in the oil sector, Brussels has managed to pre-empt and contain negative spillovers for the ENP. This has been evidenced by the indirect success at both reassuring European investors and co-opting potential ENP participants vis-à-vis:

• Establishment of an 'arbiter award' with a non-commercial guarantee mechanism. Though not intended to involve directly EU monies or management, it is aimed at creating a compensatory fund to facilitate international arbitration of contract disputes (*Nezavisimaya gazeta* 2004).
• Exploration of an EU-Russian oil reserve to insulate member states from future price shocks.
• Improvement of the safety and security of the Eastern transit system. The Commission is exploring the use of EU resources via the International Maritime Organization to support a joint EU–Russian assessment of the investments required to improve efficiency and protection of the existing pipeline network. This includes the creation of a joint accident prevention and satellite surveillance monitoring system that integrates the Russian and European navigation systems, GLONAS and GALILEO.
• Formation of a joint oil market monitoring service, staffed by European and Russian experts, aimed at improving transparency and predictability of global market trends.
• Creation of the EU–Russia Energy Technology Centre to exchange information on advanced energy designs and encourage partnership among European and Russian firms. The Centre will target new technologies to exploit 'hard to recover' oil reserves and improve efficient oil consumption. It will also identify sources for international investment for designated projects.
• Arrangement of a regular forum and working groups comprised of European and Russian energy executives.

Environmental policies
Unlike with oil and gas, the lion's share of environmental issues constitute common pool problems for the ENP. Cooperation centres on the provision of global goods (e.g. climate change, biodiversity) or regional goods (e.g. transboundary rivers, common seas, crossborder air pollution). The benefits of preventing global warming or water pollution are shared by everybody and do not diminish with additional beneficiaries. In contrast to non-rival 'pure'

public goods, the benefits are reduced as soon as one actor over-consumes or emits damaging pollution. At the same time, no single actor can independently provide the good. Environmental problems are usually characterised by long time horizons, as symptoms become apparent considerably after the causation. The establishment of common rules is imperative to prevent environmentally harmful behaviour (or free-riding), and to safeguard cross-border common pool resources. The need for strong institutions, therefore, raises the stakes for effective ENP governance.

Environmental protection outcomes may generate externalities for regional peace and security, national public goods (e.g. health and safety), or private goods (economic activities). In the Black Sea region, for instance, water protection is a central element of the regional stabilisation strategy. With the 2001 DABLAS initiative, the Commission concluded that cooperation 'will be a key element for the development of broad cooperation among the countries and the peace and stability of the Danube–Black Sea region' (European Commission 2001f: 4). Though a safe environment and regional stability are mutually reinforcing, the relationship between environmental protection and private economic goods is more complex. At least over the short and medium term, measures to protect the climate (i.e. saving carbon energy) or limit nitrogen and phosphorous discharges in rivers and ground waters from municipal, industrial or agricultural polluters will entail significant economic costs. Therefore, external environmental governance must not only prevent free-riding, but facilitate cooperation amid potentially strong economic disincentives. Accordingly, the EU may attempt to exploit its superior market power to facilitate trade in exchange for environmental cooperation. An additional complication for collective action results from the number and variety of states involved in managing environmental problems. The DABLAS initiative, for example, involved not only old and new EU member states, but candidate countries for EU membership as well as prospective ENP partners.

The complex geography of environmental issues and attendant common pool problems pose specific challenges for external governance. Traditional theories of collective action suggest that strong enforcement mechanisms are a prerequisite for managing common pool problems. As applied to the ENP, this consists of detailed rules and procedures for cooperation, and binding obligations and intrusive review requirements tantamount to the EU's environmental *acquis*.

While such an approach may prove effective among homogeneous partners with shared interests in environmental protection, it is problematic for countries that confront significant economic and political constraints. Reduced emissions in the air and water hold high costs for East European economies that are heavily based on energy-intensive industries, with outdated technology and infrastructure (Kotov 2004).[14] Strong economic disincentives may run counter to a mode of cooperation based on specified targets and 'hard' enforcement mechanisms. This could lead to considerable implementation gaps and long-term inefficiencies, as suggested by problems encountered with exporting the EU's environmental *acquis* to new eastern and southern member states in the course of the respective enlargements (Carius, Homeyer and von Bär 2000). These problems are accentuated by the lack of environmental expertise and administrative capacity of public institutions, as well as the dearth of credible environmental NGOs.

Yet the EU's institutional capacity to act on environmental matters is appreciably stronger than with energy. With the dynamic evolution of European environmental legislation since the 1980s, the EU gained external competence on environmental policies. This authority was specified by the EU's Sixth Environmental Action Programme that ceded Brussels' competence on foreign environmental policy through instruments such as TACIS, LIFE or INTERREG. Throughout the enlargement process and related international environmental negotiations, the EU's Directorate General for the Environment expanded its role, and made strides towards international leadership on environmental matters.

The push for strong external governance has been reflected in the ENP. As stated in a 2003 report by the Commission on the pan-European Environment for Europe process, 'EU legislation will become the principal and most effective means of international law making for most countries of the region', with the EU becoming 'increasingly the principal driving force in the normative field for environmental improvement and sustainable development in Europe' (European Commission 2003e: 14f.). Whereas the aim of approximating EU standards was included in the PCAs of the 1990s, the wording of the ENP Action Plans adopted with Ukraine and Moldova in 2004 cautiously included:

- **Improvement** of environmental governance, including administrative capacity, information dissemination and civil society participation.
- **Strengthening** of legislation and other measures on environmental protection.
- **Enhancement** of regional and multilateral environmental cooperation.

Although environmental cooperation is not a main priority of the ENP, it is a dynamic field of cooperation with the Eastern ENP partners. With Ukraine, a special working group was created on climate change within the Subcommittee on Transport, Energy, Civil and Nuclear Cooperation, Environment, Science, Education and Technology established under the PCA that supports the country's implementation of the Kyoto protocol.[15] Yet the bulk of environmental cooperation is decentralised and occurs in specific regional settings.

The experience with Eastern enlargement demonstrated the limits to exporting the EU's sophisticated environmental *acquis*. Both the economic costs associated with adaptation and weak administrative capacity imposed severe limits to effective implementation for prospective partner states. This persists despite the fact that Ukraine ruled that all environmental legislation should comply with EU law as part of the PCA (European Communities 2003: 13).

The DG Environment devised a number of a indirect strategies to enhance environmental standards in neighbouring countries. The emerging external governance structure responds to the requirement for strong intervention via four partially overlapping strategies that:

- Place emphasis on shaping the conditions for good environmental governance;
- Promote inclusive and non-hierarchical 'soft' modes of governance to enhance environmental policy;
- Embed rule-export to a multilevel structure of cooperation which links Community Policy to overarching international conventions and sub-national governance;
- Spearhead regional cooperation frameworks.

The emphasis on capacity building is embodied in ENP Action Plans with Ukraine and Moldova. These plans link broader requirements for 'good governance' to access to improved information, public participation and legal remedies. Rather than defining requirements in terms of the EU environmental *acquis*, the Action Plans focus on implementing an overarching international agreement: the 1998 UNECE Convention on Access to Information, Public Participation and Decision-Making and Access to Justice in Environmental Matters (Aarhus Convention). By promoting political transformation more broadly, these plans raise public awareness and create more effective structures at implementing environmental legislation among new Eastern partners. This approach to capacity-building carries broad implications for developing democracy and civil participation that required profound institutional change by new partners (Zaharchenko and Goldenman 2004).

The context-oriented approach of the Aarhus Convention is emblematic of the use of 'soft' instruments that are key to the EU's internal environmental policy. These information-based instruments are intended to raise awareness and precipitate learning, without imposing binding legislation (Lenschow 2005: 319ff.). The focus is placed on procedural aspects of environmental policy and less on the prescription of substantive outputs. This features participation of municipal public and private actors that share responsibility and ownership in policy-making. These 'soft' instruments empower designated actors involved with flexibility to adapt respective activities to specific political, administrative and economic fora at the regional, national, and local levels. This is especially important in the case of third countries that would otherwise have to embrace costly legislation without the opportunity to participate in the formulation of such regulations.

Another factor that bolsters identification with EU environmental policies derives from international treaties that enjoy broad adherence among states and NGOs. Such links increase the sense of ownership and the legitimacy of convergence procedures. The Aarhus Convention grew out of the Environment for Europe process started in 1991 among Environment Ministers from thirty-four West and East European countries, the United States, Brazil, Japan, various UN bodies, governmental organisations and NGOs. The EU is a major source of funding for the Environment for Europe process, and co-chairs, with an NIS environmental minister, the Task Force responsible for the implementation of the Environmental Action Plan (EAP). This effectively unites policy-makers from Central Europe, Eastern Europe, Caucasus and Central Asia (EECCA) and donor countries, as well as international institutions active in the region. Parliamentarians and social partners – the business sector, trade unions, environmental citizens' organisations and Regional Environmental Centres (RECs) – also are directly engaged in Task Force activities. Since 1998, RECs have been established in Moscow, Kiev, Chisinau, Tbilisi and Almaty. These are non-profit organisations created with TACIS funding to promote trust and cooperation at a regional level, support stakeholders within civil society, and build capacity among NGOs, the private sector, and national governments. The approach of the EAP Task Force mirrors 'soft governance' developed first in the framework of the OECD and then adopted by the EU to address issues where domestic sensitivities or lack of formal competence inhibit legislative intervention. The Task Force seeks to enhance environmental standards by:

- Promoting analysis and exchange of experience among countries on key environmental policy and institutional reforms, as well as developing guidelines and best practices for environmental policy and institutional reforms based on experience in EECCA, CEECs and OECD countries.
- Identifying ways in which environmental policy reform can be integrated into the broader process of economic and political reform.
- Working with donors to strengthen capacity building to implement demonstration projects that can serve as models for environmental reform, and to remove obstacles to investments in the environmental sector.
- Forging cooperation between governmental and non-governmental sectors and the RECs to build public and political support for environmental protection.

Still another characteristic feature of ENP environmental governance lies with the regional focus. The DABLAS regional multilateral framework was set up in 2001 as a response to an EC Communication that highlighted priority actions for improving environmental conditions in the region. It serves as a framework for implementing the international Danube River Protection Convention of 1994 and the Memorandum of Understanding on Common Strategic Goals between the International Commission for Protection of the Danube River (ICPDR) and the Black Sea Commission. The leading role of DG Environment in these processes is assured through overlapping structures; it not only assumes the secretariat of the DABLAS Task Force, but, in 2004, headed the ICPDR. This overlap also provides a springboard for expanding EU environmental governance, as implementation of the EU Water Framework Directive of 2000 has become integral to Black Sea cooperation. A special working group was established in the Commission on the Protection of the Black Sea to monitor implementation of the directive – although to date the Commission does not include an EU member state (its members are Bulgaria, Georgia, Romania, Russian Federation, Turkey and Ukraine).

Conclusion

A cursory review of the main ENP documents and Action Plans suggests that energy and environmental policies are viewed mainly as 'technical' instruments for 'connecting the neighbourhood'. Yet both the form and effectiveness of ENP partnership policies vary significantly. Our analysis shows that the EU faces significant constraints on engagement in oil and gas sectors bounded by both the nature of the collective action problem and its relatively weak bargaining position. Brussels lacks effective tools to coerce or induce preferred outcomes for cooperation or coordination. To the extent that it wields appreciable soft power influence, it is in the oil sector where the EU interacts with equally weak Russian and ENP partners. Here the EU can exercise modest influence via strategies of pre-emption and damage limitation to co-opt allies both among member states and among Russia and Eastern transit and supplier states.

There are costly externalities to deferring to Russia on gas issues and to international majors and Middle Eastern suppliers in the oil sector. The EU threatens Eastern transit state interests by negotiating independent pipeline deals with Gazprom. The liberalisation of internal policies complicates the diversification of supply by raising the costs of long-distance deliveries, displacing potential extra-regional suppliers, such as Turkmenistan and Kazakhstan. In the oil sector, the remedial effects of insurance and security policies cannot offset the pull of global markets, contain Washington's disproportionate geostrategic influence concerning the viability of alternative Caspian pipeline routes, or fundamentally alter dependence on Middle East suppliers.[16]

Notwithstanding the problems associated with the EU's Eastern fossil fuel vocation, there are potential opportunities for deepening cooperation and influence. In the gas sector, the EU may be better positioned to apply modest investment resources to explore projects and transit options in East Asia. Both the EU and Russia share interests in boosting production and transit to this region to avert the potential disruptive impact that the expected ballooning demand may have on established markets. NIS transit states also may have a stake in such efforts, as long as new pipelines are complemented by increased Russian production so that current volumes are not sacrificed. Accordingly, the ENP may be best served by avoiding direct intervention into specific gas disputes between Russian and ENP participants while exploring residual alternatives, thus compelling the parties to confront sharp market costs for violating delivery contracts to EU member states and stalling respective domestic energy reform.[17]

In the oil sector, the EU maintains a strong interest in encouraging the liberalisation of pricing and regulatory policies. The best bet for arresting future supply concerns lies with combining internal conservation and exploration of alternative fuels, with ENP policies aimed at allowing the market to enter the different neighbours. The latter, in particular, will help to raise the costs of predatory and opaque ownership and control, freeing up the flow of investment and oil to meet rising demand.

The situation is quite different concerning environmental security, where the EU assumes a leading role in external governance towards its eastern neighbours. The common pool attributes of environmental goods and the relatively strong institutional legacy fortify ENP initiatives. The Commission has developed a sophisticated network of administrative forms to mobilise not only different levels of governance (international, Union, regional, national, sub-national) but a host of private and public actors with shared objectives. Whereas emphasis is put on 'soft' policy instruments and capacity building through bottom-up coordination, EU environmental legislation serves as the template within the network.

One consequence of this decentralisation is that EU influence may be stronger at local and regional levels than at the national level. The DABLAS initiative and creation of RECs focus on capacity building from the bottom up. Moreover, the Black Sea cooperation reveals explicitly that the designation of ENP partners, EU candidates, possible candidates (Turkey) or others (Russia) makes little sense. There also are significantly less rivalries or situations of asymmetric dependence in this policy area than on hydrocarbon issues traditionally dominated by extra-neighbourhood factors.

What will be the likely significance of the ENP in the energy and environmental sectors? For environmental cooperation, the polycentric structure and regional focus of most initiatives suggest that action on the ground is only loosely coupled to the overarching ENP. Most transgovernmental and transnational contacts do not take place in designated subcommittees but in respective issue-networks.[18] More than enhancing inner-sectoral synergies, however, we expect the ENP to yield enhanced cross-sectoral coordination, especially between energy and environmental policies. A particular advantage in this regard may be that issues concerning both sectors are treated within common subcommittees to facilitate transparency and communication between the actors in each field. The capacity to internalise the costs of parallel sectoral evolution would indeed be a major step forward for developing a web of pan-European relations, and shifting current international cooperation towards a more integrated system of wider European governance.

In sum, a comparison of two presumably 'technical' aspects of the ENP reveals more differences than similarities. The relatively neutral language of diplomatic documents obscures the significant collective action problems at play in the energy sector. Analysis of both sectors disclosed the panoply of pan-European and EU–Russian cooperation arrangements beyond the framework of the ENP. Taken together this reveals the complexity of the emerging web of EU neighbourhood relations, as well as different strategies for managing collective action on these critical issues.

Note

1   Russia's contribution to the expected increase in EU oil imports by 2020 will likely decline from 30% to 27% (dropping from 80% to 50% of Russia's total oil exports) owing to the Russian government's planned growth of exports to the CIS, US and China. Though the volume of Russian gas exports to the EU is expected to grow, it is forecast to cover less than 30% of the EU demand by 2020 due to Moscow's expected reorientation towards Far Eastern and American markets (Gotz 2005).

2   There are caveats to this discussion. First, we draw distinction between collective arrangements concerning the 'provision' of oil as a commodity (such as inputs that go into the 'creation, maintenance, and improvement of the environment within which the good is located'), and the 'appropriation' or 'flow' of oil to customers via market mechanisms (Barkin and Shambaugh 1999: 6–8). Second, we assume that a state's collective interests in stable supply are distinct from the strictly private benefits derived by energy firms in developing new oil fields.

3   For the foreseeable future, gas markets will remain distinctly regional and rigid due to technical difficulties of switching between fuels and storing natural gas, capital-intensive exploration, limited commercially viability of LNG sources and re-gasification terminals, and cost-effectiveness of long-distance pipelines.

4   The EU's institutional weakness persists despite growing European public support for enhancing EU-level decision-making at the expense of national prerogatives (European Commission 2006).

5   EU demand for Russian oil (which constitutes nearly 98% of present demand for Russian oil exports) is projected to increase by no more than 1–2% per year until 2015. This concentration on the EU costs Russia $5–8 billion annually in price discounts, and because of technical requirements that restrict the processing of crude quality for rapidly growing American and Asian markets, threatens to 'stagnate Russian exports until 2020' (Ministry of Economic Development and Trade 2004). Moreover, Russian exporters stand to earn a net bonus of $800 million per year on average by delivering an additional 50 tons of Siberian light crude to the North American market: a bonus they would not receive by shipping the same volume of

Urals blend to the European market. Moreover, with 50% of export earnings, 30% of revenues, 25% of GDP, 0.6–0.8% of GDP growth, and the fate of the balanced budget linked to expanded oil and gas exports, Moscow shares strategic interests with the EU in averting potential disruptions in global supply.

6 According to economic growth scenarios projected by the Russian government, the economy will be positively affected less by oil price increases above $30–32/bbl over the medium to long term, than by the adverse consequences of a dramatic short-term drop in prices below $26/bbl (Ministry of Economic Development and Trade 2004).

7 However, the Russian state's share of oil production jumped from 10% to 30% from 2004–6.

8 During the 2005–6 Russia–Ukraine 'gas war', for example, Ukrainian officials were presented with the challenge of crafting a delicate balance between rival domestic interests and Russia, while remaining sensitive that neighboring EU countries were 'watching quietly' as the crisis unfolded and more concerned about moderating their dependence on Russia and Ukraine than with defending Kiev's interests (Kovtun 2006).

9 On the comparative disadvantages of disrupting long-term supply contracts for new member states, such as Poland, see especially Balmaceda (2003).

10 Prior to the deal, Austria depended on Russia for 63% of its gas supply.

11 The Yamal pipeline is slated to bypass Ukraine via a Polish–Slovak corridor to Europe; the North European Pipeline is expected to pass from Russia's Vologda and Leningrad regions, along the Baltic Sea floor, to Sweden, and then across Germany and the Netherlands, along the North Sea floor to the UK.

12 The opacity of the regulatory process was on full display in 2004–5, as the government forced the sell-off of prized YuKOS assets to Rosneft and arrested the company's CEO Mikhail Khordokovsky. Though the latter was officially justified on grounds of tax evasion, Moscow failed to dispel anxiety concerning the protection of Western investment and respect for transparent corporate governance. Since 1999, Moscow also has refused to submit production sharing agreements (PSAs) to independent international arbitration, raise domestic prices to world standards, or relax ceilings on the proportion of oil fields available for future PSAs.

13 Specifically, the EU endorsed the connection of the Druzhba oil transmission system, through Belarus and Ukraine, with the Adria network. It also supported the construction and opening of the Baku-Ceyhan pipeline from the Azerbaijan to Turkey, as well as the transit of North Caspian oil from Kazakhstan through newly built Russian pipelines and the future Burgas-Alexandroupolis pipeline.

14 The politics surrounding Russia's ratification of the Kyoto Treaty demonstrate that neither the environmental goals of the Treaty nor the potential benefits derived from emissions trading were as decisive as the EU's support for Moscow's entry into the WTO.

15 The other subcommittees established under the PCA include Trade and Investment; Finance, Economy and Statistics; Customs and Cross-border Cooperation; and Combating Illegal Migration, Money Laundering and Illicit Drugs.

16 Georgian policy insiders generally agree that the success of EU gestures at wooing Iran as a Caspian energy hub are contingent upon US policy, as the latter is critical for protecting Tbilisi's geostrategic interests and more lucrative projects involving the transit of Kazakh and Azerbaijani oil and gas (*Tbilisi Rezonansi* 2005).

17 In the 2005–6 Russian–Ukrainian 'gas war', the EU resisted the lure of intervention by both parties, forcing Russia to risk future contracts with EU member states by perpetuating the crisis and compelling Kiev to shoulder the burden of reliance on 'arbitrary' Russian gas subsidies (Guillet 2006).

18 Notable exceptions include cooperation on climate change and the security of nuclear plants.

MICHELLE PACE[1]

9

People-to-people: education and culture

Following the May 2004 enlargement, the European Union's image as a global actor in world politics has re-emerged as an important debate in academic, policy, and NGO circles. After the French and Dutch 'nos' to the ratification of the EU's constitution, and with a weakening image among European citizens, the EU has been seeking to re-emphasise its attempts to govern its own institutions in accordance with shared principles (of openness, participation, inclusiveness, accountability, fairness, effectiveness, coherence and legitimacy) and through the application of these principles to its global responsibilities.

Furthermore, driven by a moral objective of securing a peaceful, stable and united world – the very same principles which brought about the creation of the EU itself – EU foreign policy spokesman Javier Solana clearly expressed the EU's global role in the European Security Strategy in 2003. Through a shared respect for common values – the rule of law, good governance and democracy – the EU aims to contribute to global peace and better global governance through assistance programmes, targeted trade measures, conditionality, support for political and social reform and the protection of human rights.

With its European Neighbourhood Policy, the EU focuses once again on its core values as the *raison d'être* for its actions to prevent the emergence of new dividing lines between the enlarged EU and its (new) neighbours. With this new policy, the EU seeks to offer neighbouring states opportunities to participate in various EU activities, through greater political, security, economic and cultural co-operation. Under the last mentioned domain, as part of the ENP, the Commission's New Neighbouring Instrument (NNI) aims to promote local, 'people-to-people' actions between its neighbours and EU member states.

Accordingly, this chapter seeks to understand what motivates the EU's approach in two action fields (education and cultural policy), how this approach has evolved over time, which power resources the EU uses to encourage development in these fields, and the overall prospects for the effectiveness of educational and cultural programmes. To help answer these questions, the chapter focuses on two case studies: EU–former Soviet Union (FSU) relations[2] and EU–Israel relations. The focus on education and culture and on these two cases attempts to yield important insights into the motives, logic and constraints that drive the EU to seek enhanced relations with historically difficult neighbours like the FSU and with neighbours involved in often violent border conflicts with their own neighbours, like Israel. Overall the chapter endeavours to show how, in the ENP context, education and culture are aimed as tools for external governance. As will be highlighted in the chapter, this strategy involves political controversies both within the EU as well as within and among ENP participating states. The chapter will also draw attention to the extent to which this domain affects other ENP domains, in both positive and negative ways.

Overview of EU cultural and educational programmes

Culture first became an active concern of the European Community when in 1992,[3] through the Maastricht Treaty, the EU committed itself formally to make a contribution to education and training of quality and 'to the flowering of the cultures of the Member States, while respecting their national and regional diversity and at the same time bringing the common cultural heritage to the fore'.[4] Moreover, by instituting a European Union, the Maastricht Treaty marked a new step in the process of creating an 'ever-closer union among the peoples of Europe'. Thus, in the view from Brussels, educational programmes serve as power resources to develop understanding between EU member states and cultural programmes as instrumental resources to promote exchanges of shared experiences: these programmes are also flagged as models of cooperation for non-EU members to emulate.[5] Hence, a central principle of 'unity in diversity' emerged. In the Amsterdam Treaty (1997), Article 151, the Community undertakes a commitment to take cultural aspects into account in its action under other provisions of the treaty and to promote cultural diversity. Thus, when developing policies, culture must be taken into consideration, for example, in the fields of education policy, economic and social cohesion policy, job creation and the elimination of social exclusion. The spill-over effects of this area are thus, presumably, positive. In its resolution of 5 September 2001 on cultural cooperation in Europe, the European Parliament underlined its resolution to encourage the formation of a 'European cultural area'.[6] However, in reality EU members often compete with each other when it comes to promoting their own national culture(s) as a 'brand'. Sources of disagreement and internal EU conflicts regarding this aspect of the ENP include the easing of visas for cross-border cooperation between artistic organisations which results in member states voluntarily defecting from the ideal of a cross-border cultural space.[7] Despite these internal confrontations, there remains a window of opportunity for the EU's good governance capabilities to demonstrate the added value of EU activities fostering international cultural cooperation not just between the EU-25 but also including the EU's neighbouring states. The example of the Bologna Process could be a valuable model in outlining the important steps towards the creation of a European Cultural Area (more below). However I will also argue here that the value-added of the ENP over existing programmes in this area do not always represent steps forward with regards to cultural contacts.

An overview of other EU multilateral cultural projects reveals that in none of these is the promotion of a European dimension of culture explicit as a funding category in its own right. More acceptable objectives and criteria for selection of these programmes' funding emphasise the potential of economic benefits of cultural activities and business-related outputs. The INTERREG III initiative is a case in point which concentrates on cooperation between states, regions and across border areas and finances a programme of cooperation between costal states of the Baltic that includes a cultural dimension. The advantage, at least in theory, is that these funds are administered at the regional level which allows cultural operators the opportunity to solicit their projects vis-à-vis regional development planners.[8]

Following the momentous political changes in Eastern Europe in 1989, the EU developed the PHARE and the TACIS programmes to fund 'hard sector' investments and administrative reforms with some measures to support the cultural sector. Another strand of the programmes supports cultural exchange projects and includes cross-border projects focusing on forging lasting relationships between border regions. For instance, the organisation of exchanges for young people, art and folk events are supported through these programmes. The strengthening of cultural infrastructure and tourism development (to a limited extent) can also be supported through the TACIS programme. Other EU cooperation mechanisms such as CARDS or MEDA with neighbouring countries do not explicitly include a cultural chapter in their mandate. Rather than a strategic objective, financing culture under these programmes is more of a by-product – for example, to enhance regional cooperation.

The development of ongoing EU policies like the ENP will shape the future of the European integration project. They will help to determine the legitimacy of the EU and to answer the question: 'What sort of Europe?'. The interdependence of integration and governance suggests that EU governance is shaped by the emerging properties of the EU polity and has an impact on system formation at the national as well as the European level (Kohler-Koch 2005). The ENP, like other policies, continues along lines which were initially drawn by early EU policies. Aspects of the ENP now extend into domains which, until recently, were largely – if not entirely – the province of the member states. These policies, together with examples of possible topics, include the following:

- Education, for example EC competence and policies in the field of education, the Bologna process, the relation of EC education law to the General Agreement on Trade in Services.
- Culture, for example the protection of cultural property, law and EU cultural policies (cinema, arts and other).

Thus, with the inclusion of 10 new countries in May 2004, new zones of interest have been created and new mechanisms of cooperation have been defined, aiming at new and meaningful means to secure a democratic Europe open to its direct neighbours and the rest of the world. But why would the EU include education and cultural programmes as one of these zones of interest?

Cultural inclusiveness within the ENP context: why culture and education?

Through the ENP, the EU seeks to export its own model of how culture and education can build a more stable surrounding area. The EU's model of reconciliation and a lasting balance of interests among European nations is thus superimposed on its new neighbours through the ENP. The EU also seeks to export the civic dimensions of European integration, that is, the social and cultural cohesion among EU citizens. The EU's educational mobility programmes, namely, ERASMUS, TEMPUS, LEONARDO DA VINCI and others were important milestones, and were programmes related to exchanges of Europe's cultural diversity, for example, formerly KALEIDOSCOPE, ARIANE, RAPHAEL and currently CULTURE 2000. Together with national governments and cultural organisations, the EU contributed to an enhanced appreciation of a culturally defined 'Europeanness'. But the gap between rhetoric, capabilities and expectations remains. Only about 0.1 per cent of the total EU budget power resources are devoted to cultural programmes per se – relatively weak resources when compared to the ambitious objectives laid out in EU documents on cultural cooperation.[9]

So how did culture find its way into the ENP's policy-making processes? With the challenge of its largest enlargement wave and its weak image among European citizens, the EU has been seeking to re-emphasise its attempts to govern its own institutions in accordance with shared principles and to apply these principles in its global responsibilities. Following 1 May 2004, the EU's global responsibilities stretch out to its new neighbouring countries to the east and south. In its broadest sense, culture is a medium through which the EU can project a sense of shared ownership and belonging to its own citizens as well as the citizens of its neighbouring countries: culture is thus projected as the bridge of wider Europe's social relations. Culture is framed as a space within which EU and neighbouring countries' citizens share and negotiate common values, views and visions as well as differences. In line with the ENP's objective to enhance co-operation across the EU's external borders, the EU's addition of culture in the ENP framework is a signal for moving away from discourses of nation-state identities (which were sources of destruction in the first half of the twentieth century) to exploring the areas that unite the wider European continent. Thus, following the 2004 enlargement, the EU carves out an opportunity to replicate its model of cultural convergence to reach out to its neighbours and expand to an enlarged, secure and stable space through cultural and educational linkages across borders.

But are the values of the EU interpreted through a common language in EU member countries and in neighbouring countries? What does it mean for a neighbouring country to pursue EU values? What do such policies look like and what criteria can be used to assess arguments about the importance of shared values in particular cases like the FSU and Israel? These latter cases show that discrepancies remain in the dialogic encounters between these neighbouring states and the EU. Another major problem lies in the fact that culture and education are de-linked from political and economic aspects of the ENP. An inherent contradiction emerges within the people-to-people theme of ENP Action Plans which seeks to enhance mutual knowledge among the peoples of the European–Neighbourhood space by purely intergovernmental methods, without giving any say to the people affected: the place of civil society so far has been neglected in that action plans have been negotiated with governments but without any consultation with civil society. Before turning to these cases, the chapter examines EU power resources, their implementation and effectiveness in the areas of education and culture.

EU governance in neighbouring areas

The ENP's people-to-people programmes seek to support transnational cultural and educational cooperation with and between countries to the south, south-east and east of the enlarged EU. From a policy implications perspective, it is important that the EU systematically seeks complementary measures and greater coherence in the implementation phases of educational, cultural and social activities in these regions provided by not only European, but also national, regional, local and private sources.

Socialisation processes through the domains of education and culture enrich EU–neighbouring parties' relations and help to de-securitise discourses on security threats, fears, confrontations, etc. over the long term. Moreover EU member states have the opportunity to learn more about neighbouring countries and likewise, neighbours can benefit from enriching their knowledge of the EU and its member states. In terms of the likely coordination between the cultural/educational and security aspects of the ENP, the logic followed in Brussels is that through the development of more understanding between ENP participants, combined with more economic development in the neighbouring states, there should be less fear of potential threats and hence more security.[10] But when Russia's stand-off with Ukraine over gas prices in early January 2006 disrupted and challenged secure supplies to Europe, energy security divided European opinion: in fact, the EU did not take any action following Russia's bill on greater state control over non-governmental organisations (see also Chapter 8, this volume, and the *Guardian*, 29 December 2005).

People-to-people cultural and educational exchanges are constrained by other factors. The key to lively and significant international cultural and educational exchanges and cross-fertilisation is mobility. Existing obstacles to increased mobility across the new EU boundaries, namely rigid visa regulations, should be ultimately removed or at least eased in the short to medium term (see Chapter 7). The current visa regulations to enter the Schengen zone provide huge bureaucratic hurdles to the free flow of ideas and intellectual and artistic stimulation. The actual process of acquiring a visa is not just cumbersome and time-consuming but also very discouraging, not just for an artist but also for an inviting institution. The latter is faced with some considerable challenges: an invitation letter to an artist from a neighbouring country has to include a written guarantee of being solely responsible for the invitee's personal and medical needs during the stay in the Schengen zone, and also for his or her return journey after the expiry of the visa. These stipulations can have a deterring effect, particularly for smaller cultural institutions within the EU that have no prior experience in inviting guests from non-EU countries: such procedures thus prevent cultural exchange and intellectual mobility. ENP Action Plans should move beyond rhetorical action and include provisions that extend current and future EU mobility programmes and instruments to the new neighbouring countries. In terms of EU governance, this is not a question of whether rigorous visa regimes to protect EU countries against illegal immigration are justified or not: the issue is how the EU can find appropriate ways of avoiding unintended effects of such rules and avoid conflicting policies. If the objective is to promote more mobility with neighbouring countries then surely one cannot inhibit participants from entering the EU through rigid entry requirements. The idea of a special multi-entry visa for cultural operators has already been flagged and could help avoid cumbersome procedures. The EU could also establish a liability fund for inviting organisations that works like an insurance and covers the financial damage in very rare cases where problems may arise. Such mechanisms could significantly reinforce the ENP's stated objectives of cross-border mobility and cultural exchanges.

The linkage between cultural and educational programmes on the one hand and support of social and economic development in the neighbouring countries on the other hand cannot be underestimated. Current EU programmes in support of the latter do not explicitly include culture as a programme objective. ENP Action Plans need to clearly define the terms under which culture and education can be funded as part of social and economic development programmes.[11] This would help clarify Community policies with regards to these two important sectors (culture and education) and help monitor the actual level of EU investment into international cultural and educational cooperation. The vague rhetoric so far in ENP documents shows no sign of any will in Brussels to come up with specific devices for such cooperation. In fact, in this area, the ENP lacks coherent and strong instruments required for beneficial ways forward for neighbouring states.

Moreover, duplication of limited funds for culture and education must be avoided and the allocation of funds carefully considered – the need for improved cross-border collaboration must be clearly identified and priorities established. The promised 'sequencing' in the rhetoric of ENP officials promises such clarifications. For instance, large amounts for prestigious projects have to be considered in opposition to smaller amounts for more diverse, spontaneous activities. The information capacity of the cultural and educational sectors can be strengthened through a common European platform – this could also serve as an interface of communication and consultation with long-term challenging neighbours like the FSU and neighbours facing conflict situations like Israel. The chapter will now turn to these two specific case studies.

EU–FSU relations

Artists and promoters of culture in Central and Eastern Europe have been struggling against a daunting set of challenges: the hardships of the intermittent economic transformation have hit the FSU in a very severe way and have often incapacitated support for culture. The overall political climate has not been conducive to energetic cultural manifestations: the lack of respect for principles of democratic governance, rule of law, etc. were some of the barriers for cultural expressions. Censorship has been common in the past and critical voices have often been silenced and not backed through public support. Opportunities for cultural exchange and cooperation between Central and Eastern neighbours and EU member states are still, however, very limited and people are often unaware of the possible options.[12] The exception is the FSU with whom the EU has had a strategic partnership/PCA since 1997.[13] The EU also laid down its basic approach to relations with the FSU in a 'Common Strategy' of 1999 (which expired in June 2004). The role of culture and education in cross-border collaboration is vital in bridging the mental gaps that presently separate the EU's neighbours from the EU-25. From the EU's perspective, cultivating good neighbourly relations is important mainly to address its own concerns related to migration, human and drug trafficking and overall security concerns. ENP people-to-people programmes are thus aimed at constructive and non-confrontational encounters with the FSU, at the same time projecting principles of freedom of expression, tolerance and civil liberties.

In light of the development of the ENP, the EU has been keen to step up cooperation with the FSU (Russia in the Southern Caucasus and the Western NIS). Overall, the EU's main interests are to encourage political and economic stability in the FSU indirectly through the 'soft' issue areas of cultural and educational cooperation.

At the St Petersburg Summit in May 2003, the EU and the FSU confirmed their commitment to further strengthen their strategic partnership. They agreed to reinforce co-operation with a view to creating four EU/FSU common spaces, in the long term and within the framework of the existing PCA, on the basis of common values and shared interests. These common spaces cover economic issues and the environment; issues of freedom, security and justice; external security, including crisis management and non-proliferation; as well as research and education, including cultural aspects.[14] In the context of work to create the common space of freedom, security and justice, the Commission emphasises the common values on which EU/FSU relations are built, namely democracy, rule of law and human rights. In this context, negotiations on visa facilitation as a first step to enhance people-to-people contacts have been put forward.[15]

At the Summit in Rome, in November 2003, the concept of the common European economic space was endorsed. The renewal of the Science and Technology Cooperation Agreement was another important decision of the Summit, as well as the FSU's participation in the Bologna process, which provides for the mutual recognition of diplomas. The dynamics of the EU–FSU partnership requires building adequate capacity in a wide range of expertise. European Studies, for example, is a relatively new field of study in the FSU and the need for its development has been confirmed by an Agreement of the 14th summit in The Hague on 25 November 2005 to establish a European Studies Institute in Moscow.[16] The development of European Studies (as one example) in the FSU has the potential to create a stronger base of knowledge and understanding, if FSU citizens and institutions are to make the most of these developments, following the 1 May 2004 enlargement and the launching of the ENP. Such a programme would meet the needs of the FSU as well as feed into the declared policy goals of the EU with regard to the development of much stronger and closer cooperation with the FSU. The commercial sector strongly supports such initiatives. A European Studies focus also contributes directly to the goals of the Bologna Process.[17] Such a programme would support the development of the FSU's regional educational capacity. The European 'Higher Education Area' (that defines the goals of the Bologna Process) allows for unrestricted mobility of students and faculty, transferability of academic degrees and a common understanding of quality standards. The European 'inclusiveness' is indeed something to celebrate of this process: from its beginning, it was designed to embrace member and non-member states of the EU as long as they commit themselves to the common objectives and agree to certain measures of accountability regarding these objectives.

For both sides, it is a huge imperative to engage in closer relations – in the political, economic, social and cultural spheres. From the FSU side, this imperative is recognised at the federal and regional level, by business and increasingly the younger generation. Both seek full advantage of the expanding opportunities for employment mobility in the new Europe. Thus, young people in the FSU are particularly keen on educational and cultural exchanges across Europe.

Since 1996, when the Cross Border Cooperation (CBC) programmes were introduced, there has been an increasing demand for information from beneficiary institutions on funding possibilities. An indirect impact of these programmes is an increase in the need for capacity building within public administrations. The EC has responded to these through increased CBC activities and increased funding. TACIS CBC Action Programme 2004 directly reflects the policy objective of the Commission Communications on Wider Europe and on the New Neighbourhood Instrument. Based on these policy orientations, each Neighbourhood Programme, including the TACIS CBC programme, aims at addressing issues related to common challenges arising from proximity, such as economic and social development of the border areas, environment and communicable diseases, illegal immigration, trafficking and people-to-people contacts.[18] In this context, education and culture act as instrumental tools of EU foreign policy through their spill-over effects into other issue areas. The CBC programme covers all those FSU regions (Russia as well as Belarus, Ukraine and Moldova) which border or will border the EU and the accession and candidate countries. In the Commission's own view, 'the "proximity benefits" include shorter transport costs and cultural linkages, which will certainly promote cooperation between border regions. Cross-border cooperation contributes to the creation of greater opportunities for people in the border regions and enhanced regional cooperation can contribute to economic development and integration at the grass roots level as well as better mutual understanding and confidence building across the borders.'[19] Such cooperation will also presumably have positive effects on stability and security in and around the EU.

The ENP marks some lessons learnt from past EC Assistance programmes. In the case of cross-border programmes, for example, the Court of Auditors (CoA) issued a critical report in 2001. Many of the CoA recommendations were incorporated into the design and implementation of the CBC programme, including the enhancement of the CBC Small Project Facility (SPF) which operates through a call for proposals, allowing TACIS to support small-scale local initiatives and to foster cooperation between local and regional authorities in the western border regions of Belarus, Moldova, Russia and Ukraine. It is a 'grass roots' programme, directly benefiting the border region population. The TACIS CBC SPF will be succeeded by the Neighbourhood Project Facility (NPF). The Neighbourhood Programmes represent another substantial step forward with an increased allocation in CBC assistance programmes. As one Commission official put it: 'the ENP offers more money than any other previous programmes in this area'.[20]

In terms of governance, efforts have been made to ensure that projects under the CBC programme are coordinated properly with other funding sources, such as the INTERREG Community Initiative and PHARE. The Commission services[21] have taken a number of measures to improve coordination and communication between the three funding instruments to eventually increase the number of joint TACIS-INTERREG/PHARE projects. However, in this respect, concrete achievements have been limited due to the different regulations governing the various Community instruments.[22] In the case of Euregion Karelia, for example, officially inaugurated in 2000 and which comprises the Republic of Karelia and the Finnish provinces of North Ostrobothnia, Kainuu and North Karelia, 'the goal of the project is the stimulation of transboundary subregional cooperation in various spheres, the priority areas being the economy, the environment, tourism and culture'.[23] According to one author, however, the institutional structure of the European Commission poses problems for the Euroregio Karelia project, since regional development and external relations are handled by different Commission DGs and the coordination of these activities is often problematic due to bureaucratic hurdles (Cronberg 2000).

To address these constraints, the Commission has established internal guidelines on harmonisation of these instruments. Within the context of the ENP, the objectives and scope of the individual Neighbourhood Programmes (NPs) are to be defined *jointly* by the participating countries. Thus the implementation procedures of these programmes will involve the joint programming of measures, the adoption of a single application process, a single call for proposals on both sides of the border and a joint selection process for projects. Each NP involving countries on the external borders of the enlarged EU[24] will define its specific eligible areas from within a specific list of regions. In the case of the FSU, the Murmansk oblasts, the Republic of Karelia, St Petersburg City and Leningrad, Pskov and the Kaliningrad oblasts are eligible for cross-border programmes. Assistance is provided based on conditionality, in particular respect of democratic principles and human rights. There is a danger however that the concept of differentiation embedded within the ENP logic turns into 'self-differentiation': following his welcome into the G8 after promising to turn his country into a democracy, Putin played a clever hand in dividing Western opinion and using energy as a strategic asset. The price of international silence on the FSU's authoritarian turn and consolidation of power at the centre is high in the sense that the ENP's conditionality does not carry much weight (*Guardian*, 29 December 2005). This leaves the FSU with much leeway for selective democratic tactics.

Thus, although Community institutions are projected as open and transparent for others to emulate, this representation does not work in the case of the FSU. While ENP programmes should, in theory, open opportunities for societal groups in neighbouring partner countries that so far have been either excluded or silenced, these groups may find it very difficult to get organised on the European level when they face severe domestic constraints (as in the case of the FSU). Thus far, only in a few cases in some FSU regions, thanks to EU power resources, have regions been able to bypass national governments and have access to additional resources (see Chapter 1). Thus through the ENP, EU member states need to be more forceful in emphasising a possible European meaning of democracy.[25] As with the case of the FSU, the interpretations of what is constitutive for a well-functioning democracy vary considerably. If the EU aims to encourage the FSU to endorse its principled beliefs through their strategic partnership, it needs to transpose a shared understanding of democracy to the multi-level, non-state system of the EU. Equally important is how these principled beliefs relate to mass public opinion on central democratic values in the FSU and their relevance for European governance. It follows that through people-to-people linkages, the EU has an opportunity to link civil society in partner countries to its multi-level governance structures and institutions. As mentioned earlier, however, this is not the case in the FSU. Even though cultural/educational cooperation is considered as a 'soft' issue area relative to some other areas of the ENP (such as border security or immigration), potential sources of conflict/politicisation arise – as the case of the FSU shows. Since the FSU perceives the EU as interfering in its sphere of influence, the EU is constrained in prioritising what is in the best interest of its member states (in this case energy security rather than democracy or cultural and education cooperation). This in turn may impact the EU's power resources and the overall effectiveness of the ENP. In the end cultural and educational cooperation is subsumed well below other EU foreign policy concerns and will not be 'sacrificed' for other objectives. Controversies and internal EU conflicts on these matters remain especially between the view from the EP, the Commission and the Council.

Thus, in reality, the EU's real power sources of leverage in this area are very limited: apart from programme funding, policy bargaining, imitation of best practices (mainly EU practices – for neighbours to emulate), development funding and market access, negative conditionality – in the past – has never been used.

These challenges facing ENP people-to-people programmes lead us to EU relations with another challenging partner, Israel.

EU–Israel relations

The first diplomatic relations between Israel and the European Community were established in 1959. A first cooperation agreement was signed in 1975. An EU–Israel association agreement, which forms the legal basis of EU–Israel relations, entered into force in June 2000: it enables continuous dialogue and cooperation between Israel and the EU in a wide variety of fields and is thus more than a free trade agreement (see Chapter 4). Following the agreement, two main bodies were established: the EU–Israel Association Council, held at ministerial level, and the EU–Israel Association Committee, held at senior officials' level. Discussions at these meetings which are held at regular intervals usually focus on political and economic issues. However, the Agreement includes provisions on cooperation on social matters, supplemented by cultural cooperation.

Israel has been a member of the Euro-Mediterranean Partnership (EMP) since its establishment in November 1995. However, it does not benefit from bilateral financial support under MEDA, due to its relatively high level of economic development (Pace 2006). Nevertheless, Israel is eligible for MEDA funds earmarked for regional cooperation and initially participated in a number of projects, notably in the fields of audiovisual issues (EURO-MED AUDIOVISUAL), cultural heritage (EURO-MED HERITAGE), economic and industrial networks and environment.[26] This marks a main disadvantage of the ENP over the EMP: the principle of *regionality* was inherent in the Barcelona Process while the ENP is based on the principle of *differentiated bilateralism*. The ENP's bilateral, individual approach may compromise the EU's role as an even-handed broker in the Middle East Peace Process (MEPP). As EU–Israeli relations develop and with Israel's eventual integration into the EU's internal market, the future of EU–Mediterranean bilateral relations at large are most likely to be *disconnected* from the fate of Middle East peace-making – unless the EU seeks other tracks for its involvement in the MEPP.

Israel participates in other EMP programmes such as the EURO-MED YOUTH, so far the most successful third basket programme of this policy (Pace 2005a). This programme promotes people-to-people contacts, as well as cooperation between civil society actors, including associations and NGOs in the youth field. With regards to higher education, Israel is eligible for participation in the Community programmes ERASMUS MUNDUS and on a self-financing basis, TEMPUS.

In terms of Research and Development, Israel is the only non-EU country which has been fully associated with the EU's FRAMEWORK Programme since 1996. The renewal of the Science & Technology Cooperation Agreement between the EU and Israel was approved by the Council and the European Parliament and concluded by the Israeli Government in March 2004, although the provisional application of this agreement allowed Israeli research entities to participate in the 6th RTD FRAMEWORK Programme

(FP6 2003–2006) activities from the beginning. The FP6 is a key part of the EU's strategy to create a true European Research Area, an Internal Market for science and knowledge in which Israel plays an active role.

From a bilateral perspective, Israel has reacted positively to the ENP, and has shown interest in the initiative. The ENP's bilateral and differentiated basis of conducting relations with the EU's neighbours corresponds to Israel's preferred relations with the EU. Israel never really appreciated being put into the group of 'Southern Mediterranean states' within the EMP framework, together with real, perceived or potential rivals or foes, and it considers the EMP as disregarding the country's special features (Israel being more economically developed, having democratic institutions, etc.) or type of relations with the EU. Israel has traditionally considered the EMP as a 'straightjacket' (Del Sarto and Tovias 2001). Thus, the ENP offers Israel (and other southern and eastern neighbours) an opportunity to air its voice on its particular concerns. The bilateral, one-by-one approach with Israel, the Palestinian Authority of the West Bank and Gaza Strip and other Arab neighbours also offers the EU spill-over effects from the culture and education domain (through an indirect pathway) through which to influence the Middle East process, through its emphasis on political, social and economic reforms in the Southern Mediterranean partner countries. Yet in view of the top priority that Israel enjoys in the ENP framework, the EU has to tread very carefully with its role in the MEPP (as argued above). It may be that the ENP could result in a step backward from the EMP in terms of the EU's leverage in the MEPP. Thus, rather than adding value over existing programmes, the ENP may harm what the EU has so painfully been working on in establishing closer relations with Israel and its neighbours. The EMP is the only environment where Israeli and Arab neighbours sit together around the same table, despite the tragic ongoing events in the Middle East conflict. It is also the only environment where the Israeli government accepts the EU's involvement in matters relating to security of the Middle East (Pace 2006: 84). Moreover, since the EU tends to fund pro-peace (cultural and educational) organisations and NGOs there is no potential conflict with the role of the US in this area. Hence the US cannot act as a potential spoiler in cultural and educational affairs. Neither does the EU's engagement in Israel and Palestine in these fields have any negative impact on the role of other outside actors such as the UN or NATO. However, this does not mean that culture and educational domains do not attract any criticisms. NGO Monitor, for example, regularly challenges the EU's continuous funding to what it calls 'highly politicized NGOs' in Israel.[27]

Israel has a diversified civil society active in social, cultural, educational, economic, environmental and human rights matters. At the end of the 1990s, NGOs supporting peace efforts were prominent but following the outbreak of the second *Intifada* these NGOs were practically paralysed. However, grass roots contacts between Israelis and Palestinians have continued throughout the *Intifada*, albeit with a low profile. Yet in terms of people-to-people link-ages, Palestinians from the West Bank and Gaza Strip who work in Israel are not able to join Israeli trade unions or organise their own unions in Israel. Israeli legislation contains laws and regulations that favour the Jewish major-ity, despite the Declaration of Independence which proclaims equality for citizens. The Arab minority also suffers from discrimination in many areas including budget allocations, education and health. Moreover, the Nationality and Entry into Israel Law of 2003 severely affects the Arab minor-ity, suspending for a renewable one-year period the possibility of family unification, subject to limited exceptions.[28] In the Council conclusions of March 2004, the EU made its position on these issues clear when it stated that: 'The European Council expressed its sympathy for those on all sides who endure the effects of violence or whose lives are disrupted by the conflict ... It ... welcomed the Palestinian Authority's announcement of plans for improving Palestinian security performance ... and called on the Israeli Government to take action to alleviate the suffering of Palestinians by lifting prohibitions on movement, reversing its settlement policy ...' However, despite a supposedly 'fresh' policy (ENP), the EU has, so far, not moved beyond rhetorical action in this regard.

The *Intifada* has had its toll on various sectors of the Israeli economy. While unemployment stood at 9.4% in 2001, it rose to 10.3% in 2002 and to 10.6% by mid-2003. In 2002, youth unemployment stood at a high of 21% (Pace 2006). How can the EU, through the ENP, promote people-to-people linkages which can then impact the transformation of conflict situations as in the case of Israel and Palestine?

In its proposed EU/Israel Action Plan,[29] the Commission outlined the objectives under the people-to-people contacts area. Broadly, these aims, under the general themes of a) education, training and youth, b) culture and audio-visual issues, and c) civil society co-operation,[30] include:

- The creation of a 'European Higher Education and Vocational Training Area', increased mobility of teachers and students included.
- Enhanced co-operation in the field of Youth and Sport.
- Enhanced cultural co-operation.
- Promotion of civil society co-operation.

What is particularly notable in this document is that with regards to youth exchanges, there is no mention of or reference to the Anna Lindh Foundation, developed under the third basket of the EMP, which also has as one of its main target groups youth in the Mediterranean area. Hence the linkage between the ENP's people-to-people programmes and the EMP's existing programmes under the third basket remains void. One cannot overemphasise the importance of increased educational and cultural support and coopera-tion measures vis-à-vis the new EU neighbours in the East, and for stronger intercultural initiatives addressing the cross-Mediterranean countries; for this reason, the role that civil society organisations have to play is critical and so is the newly created Euro-Mediterranean Foundation for Dialogue between Cultures and Civilisations. After the events of September 11, cultural cooperation with the Southern Mediterranean area remains rather fragmented, impeded and sporadic. The creation of the new Foundation aims at narrowing the divisions between Northern and Southern Mediterranean neighbours through the promotion of education and cultural exchange programmes aimed mainly at young people. The Foundation can help address discrimination and racial as well as cultural stereotypes and encourage respect for human rights. Through the engagement of civil society representatives on all levels of decision-making the Foundation can ensure its transparency and legitimacy. The only vague reference to such a linkage may be found under the ENP EU–Israel Action Plan's culture and audiovisual issues section which stipulates the EU and Israel's aim to 'enhance Israel's participation in the relevant cultural cooperation programmes of the Euro-Mediterranean partnership'. But no specific reference is made to the Anna Lindh foundation. Furthermore, as regards the 'promotion of regular dialogue on civil society issues' no mention is made in this ENP document of the Euro-Mediterranean Human Rights Network or the Euro-Mediterranean Civil Fora. Again the potential for value-added through the ENP is lost in this particular context.

Although EU intentions are noteworthy and its main leverage is indirect in the case of Israel, the EU could have more impact on its neighbouring states if it coordinates its existing people-to-people programmes (EMP) with newly, emerging initiatives (ENP). The need for intercultural dialogue and deeper understanding between Islam, Judaism and Christianity is widely acknowledged within EU documents. But implementation requires more than just written agreements and conclusions between governments on all sides concerned. Robust and resilient cultural relations require a process of activating more grass roots levels of cultural cooperation that will need time to grow gradually, and personal commitment from all those involved, especially in countries where the independent sector (as in Southern Mediterranean countries) is relatively weak. With the formal opening of negotiations for Turkey's EU accession process, and Israel's strong links with this country, the potential for cross-cultural understanding and cross-border exchanges are positive and promising. Since both Turkey and Israel are members of the EMP, it would be a real shame if the ENP strays away from the regional dimension of existing EMP structures and does not effectively build on the latter's regional cooperation programmes, especially those relating to culture and education.

Conclusion

Culture and education have for a long time been referred to by policy-makers and administrators alike as 'soft issues' when compared to the 'real, tough issues' of the economy, trade, security, migration, etc. (see the relevant other chapters, this volume). In the ENP documents analysed, these tough issues still seemingly dominate the agenda of the EU's relations with its new neighbours.[31] This need not be the case. Culture and education can be fruitful bridges across issues, fostering dialogue and exchange between the EU-25 and their neighbours. Cultural and educational diplomatic efforts can be pro-active activities and influential instruments which help further the development of open and inclusive partnerships within the 'wider' European context. This is particularly important with neighbours like the FSU and Israel.[32] However, post-9/11, the US-led war on terrorism, the second Iraq war and current talks on Iran emphasise the need to take culture and education seriously as the conceptual gap between cultures is by no means a 'soft' issue, as these current events clearly show.

For this to become a 'reality', all parties involved have to take their commitments seriously and share their contributions in activating this potential. From the EU's perspective of 'good governance', its institutions have to show strong leadership and vision in securing educational and cultural cooperation programmes with the necessary mechanisms and financial support. A stated goal of the Wider Europe/New Neighbourhood Policy of the Commission is the extension of existing community programmes to neighbouring countries not already benefiting from them. Yet, the budget for Neighbourhood programmes beyond 2006 is still (at time of writing) uncertain. Although 'people-to-people' actions, including cultural and educational exchanges and cooperation, are mentioned in the relevant documents, it is not yet clear whether culture and education will be acknowledged amongst the main sectors of cooperation. On a positive note, within the ENP framework, culture and education have assumed positions of relevant factors with respect to challenges arising in European as well as non-European societies (particularly with the fifth EU enlargement to the east and south, in light of 9/11, 7/7 and other events).

However, although ENP actors are now talking of sequencing priority areas with neighbours,[33] the 2005 Communication is not very encouraging for observers of culture and educational programmes (European Commission 2005a). Under the document's 'Priorities and expectations' section, strengthened people-to-people contacts are noted as 'high in the priorities of partners' but nothing is said about the ranking of these issues on the EU's list of priorities – and it is noticeable that the human and cultural dimension of the ENP is always mentioned last in ENP documents. In Annex 1 of the same communication, under Israel's country priorities, education and culture are not mentioned, although 'the detailed list of objectives and actions' adopted by the Commission in December 2004 is mentioned. This chapter has argued that in the case of Israeli relations with their Arab neighbours, the ENP is a step backward from the EMP. The Civil Fora complementing the EMP's Summits have initiated a new arena for dialogue and stronger linkages between the EMP's cultural, political and economic baskets (Pace 2005b and 2005c). The potential exists for the ENP to add value to this important dimension of the EMP yet it is too early to predict what this value-added could be.

On a positive note, the 2005 Communication mentions education as a priority for Moldova and Ukraine in order to help them 'work towards the implementation of educational reform in line with the Bologna Process'. Another encouraging feature of this Commission Communication is the urgency given to the creation of an ENP-specific scholarship scheme for participants. However it is not yet clear whether the funds devoted to culture and education will merely be of a symbolic nature. The decision about the ENP budget is of utmost significance for putting rhetoric into practice.

Moreover, for a truly European-Neighbourhood cultural and educational space to flourish, the Commission and national governments of the EU-25 and neighbouring countries have to facilitate transnational (that is, bilateral and multilateral) collaborative endeavours and create the appropriate legal, financial and operative frameworks. Local and regional authorities have to take advantage of these opportunities by developing 'bridging' schemes in the educational and cultural fields reflecting the needs of their regions. The role of independent sectors in strengthening and supporting civil society across borders can be put to practice through the promotion of cross-border networks. For an improved mutual understanding, the media have a great responsibility in contributing to this process through the mobility of journalists and cooperative endeavours across the regions.

ENP Action Plans should therefore be more specific about the EU budget lines for cultural and educational cooperation and the mechanisms for fruitful integration of the neighbours into existing EU cultural and educational programmes. Cultural exchange could also be stimulated through the provision of a comprehensive mobility scheme for cultural professionals, artists and journalists. This will entail the removal of mobility barriers and bureaucratic obstacles, especially with regard to visa regulations. Within the ENP structures and instruments, the extension of existing and the creation of complementary regional funds for cross-cultural cooperation and support for networks and platforms could provide useful schemes for cultural cooperation. As envisioned in ENP documents, monitoring processes of the independence of the media and freedom of expression should also be firmly in place.

The EU's investment into its own future and that of its neighbours promises rich dividends in terms of increased tolerance, trust, stability, security and cohesion. The ENP framework put forward by the Commission of the EU represents a timely approach to consider the opportunities and implications of the enlarged and enlarging EU from a wider European context. Involvement and mutual commitment by all parties on a people-to-people level in the areas of culture, education, arts and media are promising long-term strategies in this direction. It is a truly challenging task of the EU's educational and cultural foreign policies to lead the way for integrating the civil societies of the neighbouring countries into the EU, especially since the absence of a tangible accession perspective for most neighbouring countries remains. A bottom-up foreign policy of educational and cultural exchange and cooperation is of particular significance in this context. High politics often produce media headlines which in turn produce images of confrontation between the EU and its neighbours. Cultural and educational issues have, post-9/11, found their way into these headlines. The EU has an important role to play in advocating a strong awareness of a more differentiated view of diverse cultures, and cultural and educational policies are key to this endeavour. Finally, it is imperative for the EU and its neighbours to work towards full democratic participation especially of young people, across Europe and its neighbourhood, through institutions – particularly those of education and culture – that encourage public debate and empower the future generations to come. Moving beyond Europe's geographical borders, these young people will present a critical core group to the larger world.

Notes

1   I am grateful to Michael E. Smith, Katja Weber and Michael Baun for their stimulating inputs, constructive criticisms and support in the preparation of this chapter, as well as Kataryna Wolczuk and Anand Menon for their comments and suggestions. Thanks also to the ENP officials I interviewed for this chapter. An early version appeared in *Evropa* (in Russian), a journal of the Polish Institute of International Affairs, Warsaw, entitled 'Partners or Periphery? Russia and Israel in the EU's European Neighbourhood Policy'. I would also like to thank participants who attended the international conference on *European Neighbourhood Policy: Old Challenges, New Chances?* on 20–21 May 2005 in Prague which was organised by the Association for International Affairs and the Friedrich-Ebert Stiftung, Prague, Czech Republic, where I presented an earlier draft of this chapter.
2   Since Russia is not an 'official' ENP partner, this chapter will focus on the FSU as one of its case studies. In doing so it covers other FSU countries beyond Russia.
3   The Treaty on European Union, signed in Maastricht on 7 February 1992 entered into force on 1 November 1993.
4   Article 128 of the Maastricht Treaty.
5   Telephone interview held by the author, European Commission, ENP Task Force, 30 August 2005.
6   European Parliament, resolution of 5 September 2001 on cultural cooperation in Europe. See European Commission 2003g; see also: http://europa.eu.int/comm/culture/eac/sources_info/pdf-word/study_on_cult_coop.pdf for a comprehensive overview of cultural policies in the European context, especially the 'Study on Cultural Cooperation in Europe' published by Interarts and the European Forum for

the Arts and Heritage or EFAH, June 2003.

7   Telephone interview held by the author, European Commission, ENP Task Force, 30 August 2005.

8   Interviews held by the author, European Commission, DG Regional Policy, 23 January 2004 and 24 February 2005.

9   Culture 2000 was initially set to run from 2000 to 2004 with an annual budget of approximately €32 million. Since 2001 the programme has also been open to most of the candidate countries. It has been extended for two more years (2005/6) with approximately €34 million reserved for each.

10 Telephone interview, European Commission, ENP Task Force, 30 August 2005.

11 The 10th Euro-Mediterranean Economic Transition Conference held on 6 and 7 June 2006 in Brussels aimed to specifically clarify the 'stake in the EU Internal Market' and to enhance awareness of the potential economic benefits of that 'stake' as articulated in the ENP. See EuroMed Synopsis, Issue No. 351, 20 April 2006.

12 Personal communications, Prague, 2005 during the international conference *European Neighbourhood Policy: Old Challenges, New Chances?* organised by the Association for International Affairs and the Friedrich-Ebert Stiftung, Prague, 20–21 May 2005.

13 A protocol to the PCA was signed by the EU and Russia on 27 April 2004 to extend the agreement to the 10 new member states as of 1 May 2004. The PCA determines a dense network of bilateral institutional contacts between the EU and its Russian partner, in various formats including: two summits each year, cooperation committee (senior official level) and at the St Petersburg Summit in May 2003, it was decided to strengthen the existing Cooperation Council as a Permanent Partnership Council (PPC). Moreover, there are nine sub-committees (working level) as well as a Parliamentary Cooperation Committee.

14 Russian Federation: Strategic Partnership – 4 Common Spaces. Work on common spaces draws on elements of ENP that are of common interest to the EU and Russia.

15 It is important to note the work on Justice and Home Affairs (JHA) including implementation of the Europol–Russia agreement, the conclusion of negotiations on readmission, and signature and ratification of outstanding border agreements with Estonia and Latvia. See http://ec.europa.eu/comm/external_relations/russia /intro/index.htm (last accessed 17 August 2006) for more on this.

16 This was also made clear in the context of work to create a common space of research and education, including culture, where the Commission wants to promote intensified cooperation on science and technology, education and culture, including Russian participation in EU education exchange programmes.

17 The University of Birmingham, UK and the Russian State University – Higher School of Economics (SU-HSE) have, during 2005/6, submitted a BRIDGE application for the development of such a dual masters programme between the UK and Russian higher education institutions.

18 http://europa.eu.int/comm/europeaid/projects/TACIS/publications/annual _programmes/cbc_2004_en.pdf.

19 Ibid. p. 2.

20 Telephone interview held by the author, Commission ENP Task Force, 30 August 2005.

21 Notably, EuropeAid in close cooperation with DG Relex, DG Regio and DG Enlargement.

22 Differences arise in the mismatched levels of funding, the programming process, project selection, project implementation and project monitoring (different reporting, monitoring and evaluation procedures) which limit the impact of cooperation along the external borders.

23 Programme of Cross Border Cooperation of the Republic of Karelia, 1.4, Tarja Cronberg quoted in Prozorov (2005).

24 Including Romania and Bulgaria borders with Western NIS and Western Balkans. TACIS will provide support in Russia, Ukraine, Belarus and Moldova.

25 During the Bush–Putin meeting in Bratislava, Slovakia, 24 February 2005 and their question and answer session to the media, questions were posed regarding 'democracy' in Russia as well as in the US. See www.whitehouse.gov/news/releases /2005/02/20050224–9.html.

26 Following the outbreak of the second *Intifada*, it has been increasingly difficult for Israel to find partners in the Mediterranean area.

27 See www.ngo-monitor.org/funding/eu_ngo_funding_2005–290306.pdf.

28 ENP Country Report, Israel, 2004, p. 10.

29 Available at: http://europa.eu.int/comm/world/enp/pdf/action_plans/Proposed _Action_Plan_EU-Israel.pdf (accessed 30 January 2005).

30 Public health is another theme included under these broad aims.

31 See for example the ENP Country Reports for Israel and the Palestinian Authority.

32 Russia is the EU's fifth largest trading partner (after the US, Switzerland, China and Japan) while the enlarged EU is Russia's largest trading partner, accounting for more than 50% of its total trade; some 40% of Europe's gas supplies come from Russia. See www.europa.eu.int/comm/external_relations for more on this

33 Luigi Narbone, ENP Task Force, Berlin, November 2005.

PART III

Alternative perspectives on the ENP

Michael Baun

10

Wider Europe, transatlantic relations and global governance

The ENP has significant implications for the United States and transatlantic relations. EU policies could affect important US economic, political, and strategic interests in particular parts of the European neighbourhood, just as American regional policies will no doubt affect the implementation of the ENP and its chances for success. Through its impact on transatlantic relations and its consequences for the EU's emerging role as an external actor, the ENP also has significant implications for international politics and the broader global system.

On the surface, the US and EU appear to have broadly similar goals and interests in the European neighbourhood. Both favour the spread of stability and democracy in Europe's neighbouring regions. Both also seek to limit Russian influence in the former Soviet space and the growth of Islamic radicalism in the broader Middle East. Because of these shared general goals and interests, there would seem to be considerable potential for US–EU cooperation in the European neighbourhood. In addition to solving regional problems and advancing common interests, such cooperation could give new purpose and vitality to a troubled transatlantic partnership, thus making a major contribution to global peace and security. Whether this potential for transatlantic cooperation will be realised, however, or whether the increased strategic engagement of the EU in its 'near abroad' will create new tensions and problems for transatlantic relations, remains to be seen.

This chapter examines the transatlantic and global dimensions of the ENP. It begins by analysing the interaction of US and EU policies in particular parts of the European neighbourhood. The strategic situation of specific regions, their potential for integration with the EU, and their relative importance for the United States vary considerably. To assess the potential impact of the ENP on US interests and transatlantic relations, therefore, it makes sense to disaggregate the European neighbourhood into specific regions and analyse them separately. The chapter then examines the general prospects for cooperation between the US and EU in the European neighbourhood in view of their sometimes divergent regional interests, priorities, and policy approaches. The final substantive section considers the larger implications of the ENP for the US and international politics, arguing that the ENP represents a potentially significant normative challenge for US global hegemony and leadership.

Eastern Europe

Eastern Europe is the EU's true 'backyard', with each of the countries of this region sharing land borders with one or more current or future member states. The EU occupies a prominent position here due to its geographical proximity, economic weight, and the close social and cultural ties of some member states, especially the newest ones, with the countries of this region. The aspirations of Ukraine and Moldova, and perhaps someday Belarus as well, to eventually join the EU also give Brussels tremendous influence. However, Eastern Europe is also part of the EU's 'shared neighbourhood' with Russia, meaning that relations with Moscow are a major factor affecting EU policy and transatlantic cooperation in the region (Emerson 2004a; Lynch 2004).

The US also has important interests and plays a key role in this part of the European neighbourhood. Since the break-up of the Soviet Union in the early 1990s, Washington has supported the independence of the Eastern European states and their integration into Euro-Atlantic institutions. More recently, the Bush administration has strongly supported democratic developments in Ukraine and Moldova, and increased its efforts to promote democratic change in Belarus as part of its broader strategy of democracy promotion. Resolution of the frozen conflict in the Transnistria region of Moldova is another US priority, to prevent this breakaway enclave from becoming a source of regional instability and a haven for international terrorists and criminal activity.

US goals and interests in Eastern Europe largely coincide with those of the EU, so it is not surprising that there has been considerable cooperation between Washington and Brussels in this region in recent years. One example is the coordinated response to Ukraine's 'Orange Revolution'. Both Washington and Brussels immediately denounced the November 2004 presidential elections in Ukraine, claiming that they were unfair and did not adhere to accepted democratic standards. Joint US–EU diplomatic intervention then helped to ensure a new vote in December, which resulted in the election of Western-leaning Viktor Yuschenko (Kempe and Solonenko 2005; Tefft 2005). While European leaders such as CFSP chief Javier Solana and

Polish President Aleksander Kwasniewski took the public lead in efforts to mediate the election crisis, the US played a crucial behind-the-scenes role. Throughout the course of the election crisis, US and EU authorities worked closely together and coordinated their efforts to influence developments.

Since the Orange Revolution, both Washington and Brussels have supported the new democratic government in Ukraine with diplomatic, economic, and other forms of assistance. They have differed, however, on how rapidly Ukraine should be integrated into Euro-Atlantic institutions. While Brussels has reacted cautiously to political developments in Ukraine, merely updating the ENP Action Plan it had previously agreed to with the authoritarian Kuchma government and refusing to offer Ukraine a prospect of EU membership, the US has supported the position of the new member states – especially Poland and Lithuania – who argue that Ukraine should be given a firm prospect of membership as a means of encouraging further reform and cementing its pro-Western orientation (Gromadzki et al. 2005). The US also strongly supports the NATO ambitions of President Yuschenko and other pro-Western leaders, in contrast to some European governments, such as France and Germany, who feel that offering Ukraine membership in the Alliance would only antagonise Russia (Fried 2005).

Washington and Brussels have also cooperated to promote democratic change in Belarus. In an increasingly coordinated fashion, both have condemned the political repression and non-democratic practices of the Belarusian government and imposed diplomatic and other sanctions as a means of exerting pressure for change. Joint US–EU pressure on Belarus increased significantly following the Orange Revolution in Ukraine. In April 2005, while on a visit to neighbouring Lithuania, US Secretary of State Condoleezza Rice called the regime of President Alexander Lukashenko 'the last true dictatorship in central Europe' and declared that it was 'time for change to come' (*New York Times*, 21 April 2005). Responding to Russian criticism of 'outside' interference in Belarusian affairs, Rice insisted that both the US and EU have a legitimate role to play in Belarus, providing support, 'as both we and the European Union are doing, to the development of civil society groups and the training of independent media and independent political and civil society forces' (*RFE/RL* 2005c). Washington and Brussels stepped up their joint pressure on the Lukashenko regime in advance of the March 2006 presidential elections, and both reacted to the non-democratic vote and the repression of opposition protests which followed with additional measures, including the imposition of visa bans and freezing the assets of certain Belarusian officials. In official statements both before and after the elections, the US and EU have stressed the importance each places on continued close coordination of their policies towards Belarus (Council of the EU 2006).

There has also been increased transatlantic cooperation on Transnistria. US engagement in international efforts to resolve the Transnistria conflict dates back to the mid-1990s, but American concern about the enclave's role as a haven for terrorist-related criminal activity, including arms smuggling and the illegal trafficking of persons, has grown after 9/11 (Hyde Smith 2005). By contrast, the EU's role in the Transnistria conflict before 2003 was 'negligible', because of the region's geographical remoteness, and because member states did not want to harm relations with Russia by interfering in its 'near abroad' (Vahl and Emerson 2004).

The EU's increased attention to the Transnistria conflict since 2002 has enabled greater transatlantic cooperation on this issue, however. In early 2003, Washington and Brussels jointly imposed visa bans on Transnistrian leaders as a means of pressuring the separatist regime in Tiraspol. Later the same year, both advised the Moldovan government not to accept a Russian proposal for ending the conflict – the 'Kozak Memorandum' – because it called for the creation of a Moldovan federation that would preserve Transnistrian autonomy and allow the continued presence of Russian troops in the region. Both have also pressed Moscow to abide by its 1999 OSCE commitment to remove its troops and weapons stocks from the disputed region. In late 2005, both the US and EU officially joined the five-party talks on ending the dispute (also involving Russia, Moldova, Ukraine, Transnistrian authorities and the OSCE) (Beatty 2005a). The EU also deployed a border-monitoring mission along the Ukraine–Transnistria border, to prevent smuggling and increase economic pressure on the separatist regime (Ferrero-Waldner 2005). It has also raised the possibility that EU forces could be part of a peace stabilisation force inside Transnistria, replacing departing Russian troops, as part of an eventual settlement (Beatty 2005b). Indeed, the increased 'Europeanisation' of the Transnistria conflict will likely mean that the US plays more of a 'backseat role' on this issue in the future (Vahl 2005: 5), something which the US government would no doubt welcome given its preoccupation with security concerns elsewhere.

In summation, the US and EU appear to have broadly similar goals in Eastern Europe, as well as a good record of cooperation in this region in recent years. Nevertheless, some notable differences of approach and points of disagreement exist. These chiefly concern the pace of democratic change in the region and relations with Russia. Generally speaking, the US favours a more aggressive promotion of democratic change in the former Soviet space, in keeping with its strategic values and interests and its broader democratisation strategy. Many EU officials and member states, however, favour a more cautious approach to promoting democratic change, because they do not want to upset relations with Russia, and because they worry that democratising governments in Ukraine, Moldova, and potentially even Belarus, will demand EU membership. With the EU having difficulty digesting the 2004 enlargement, and with growing resistance to possible further enlargements to include the Western Balkans and Turkey, new demands for membership are something that the EU does not want to face.

The EU is divided on the question of 'Eastern policy', however, with most of the new member states favouring a more proactive approach to democratisation as well as a tougher stance towards Russia. The new members also argue that the EU should offer the prospect of membership to its Eastern neighbours, in order to encourage democratic reforms and promote their Western re-orientation. This is a view that is shared, for the most part, by Britain and the Nordic member states. These internal divisions could limit the coherence and effectiveness of EU policy towards Eastern Europe and inhibit transatlantic cooperation in the region. They could also become a source of tension in transatlantic relations if they lead to EU inaction, or if the US seeks to exploit or manipulate these divisions to promote its own goals in the region.

The South Caucasus

Strategically located between Russia, Iran, Turkey and Central Asia, and forming a land bridge linking the oil-rich Caspian Basin and the Black Sea, the South Caucasus is a vitally important region of the European neighbourhood. Although more geographically distant from the EU than Eastern Europe, the three countries of this region – the former Soviet republics of Georgia, Azerbaijan and Armenia – are each members of the Council of Europe, the OSCE, and NATO's 'Partnership for Peace' programme, providing an institutional basis for their claims to be part of the Wider Europe. Each has also expressed a desire to some day join the EU. The region is bedevilled by a number of frozen conflicts, however, between Armenia and Azerbaijan in Nagorno-Karabakh, and over the separatist regions of Abkhazia and South Ossetia in Georgia. Russia also continues to exercise considerable influence in this part of the former Soviet space, while Turkey and Iran are also key players.

Despite the region's inclusion in the ENP, EU attention to the South Caucasus is relatively recent. In fact, EU policy towards the South Caucasus before 2003 has been termed a 'non-strategy', reflecting the absence of clear EU interests and objectives in the region (Lynch 2003a; MacFarlane 2004). Some individual member states have been active in the region, however. France has served as co-chair (along with the US and Russia) of the OSCE Minsk Group mediating between Armenia and Azerbaijan on Nagorno-Karabakh, while Germany, France and the UK are members of the Group of Friends assisting the UN Secretary-General in intermediating the Abkhazia conflict in Georgia.

The US has been actively involved in the South Caucasus since the early 1990s, in an increasingly fierce contest for regional influence with Russia and Iran. Energy security is a major US interest in the region, as it is for the EU. American companies are active in the exploitation of Caspian Basin energy resources, and the US government has been a primary supporter of projects to construct new oil and gas pipelines across the region, running from Baku (Azerbaijan) through Georgia to Turkish ports on the Mediterranean. The first of two major pipelines, the Baku-Tbilisi-Ceyhan (BTC) oil pipeline, began operation in 2005, and the second, the Baku-Tbilisi-Erzerum (BTE) natural gas pipeline, is due to begin operations in 2007.

The post-9/11 struggle against terrorism has further increased US interest in the region, given its proximity to both Central Asia and Iran and the security dangers posed by the region's various frozen conflicts (Shaffer 2003). Cooperation with the governments of the region to control borders and prevent the movement of terrorists, WMD proliferation, and international criminal activity, is a key aspect of US policy in the South Caucasus, which Washington has termed a 'frontline region' in the global 'war on terrorism' (Jones 2004).

Among the South Caucasus states, the US has particularly close ties to Georgia. Washington has been a major supporter of the new democratic government in Tbilisi following the 2003 'Rose Revolution', with the Bush administration proclaiming Georgia a 'beacon of liberty' and a model of peaceful democratic change for other authoritarian regimes in the former Soviet Union to follow (Grant 2005). In addition to considerable economic and financial assistance, the US has provided Georgia with vital diplomatic and security support. It has backed Georgia's territorial integrity and political independence by pressing Russia to close its remaining military bases in the country and end its support for the separatist regions of Abkhazia and South Ossetia (*Wall Street Journal*, 3 August 2005). US military assistance to Georgia includes the Georgia Train and Equip Program (GTEP) that was launched in 2002 to train local counter-insurgency forces, and a follow-up programme, the Sustainment and Stability Operations Program (SSOP), that was launched in 2004 (US Department of State 2005c). The United States also supports Georgia's NATO ambitions, including the signing of an Individual Partnership Action Programme (IPAP) in 2004 that is viewed as the precursor to Georgia's eventual application for NATO membership (CES 2005: 60–2).

Azerbaijan is another crucially important country for the US, because of its energy wealth and strategic geographic location. Concern about pipeline security, as well as increased anti-terrorism and counter-proliferation efforts in the Caspian Sea and along Azerbaijan's borders with Iran and Russia, have led to an expanding military relationship between Washington and Baku since early 2002 (Shaffer 2003). The US has increased its direct military assistance to Azerbaijan and supported Baku's efforts to improve its ties with NATO, including the signing of an IPAP agreement in 2005. Given its proximity to Central Asia, Azerbaijan is a possible future location for US military bases, especially in the wake of Uzbekistan's decision in 2005 to close down its US air base. As a predominantly Muslim society with a secular government,

Azerbaijan is also a valuable ally of the United States in the struggle against Islamist terrorism, as evidenced by the symbolically useful deployment of Azeri troops to support US-led efforts in Kosovo, Afghanistan and Iraq. Precisely because of its strategic importance, the US has joined with the EU to encourage democratic reforms in Azerbaijan, fearing that continued authoritarianism could provoke political unrest and destabilise the country. Joint US–EU pressure did not lead to democratic parliamentary elections in November 2005, however, and the US response to these elections was relatively tepid in comparison to its reaction to non-democratic elections in Ukraine and Belarus.

The US has also sought closer ties to Armenia. With the support of a strong Congressional lobby, the US has provided nearly $1.5 billion in assistance to Armenia since the early 1990s, the highest on a per capita basis for countries of the former Soviet Union. Much of this has been in the form of humanitarian aid, but recent US assistance has focused on democracy building and economic reform (US Department of State 2005b). Washington has provided nearly $7.5 million to Armenia since 2001 to promote the development of Armenian law enforcement capabilities, especially in the area of counter-narcotics and border control (*RFE/RL* 2005d). In late 2005, it awarded Armenia a $235 million Millennium Challenge Account (MCA) grant to promote rural economic development (*New York Times*, 20 December 2005), the second largest amount provided to any country under the MCA programme, exceeded only by the $295 million awarded to Georgia earlier the same year. Washington has also supported Armenia's growing cooperation with NATO, including the signing of an IPAP agreement in 2005.

US policies in the South Caucasus are basically complemented by the EU's increased involvement in the region since 2003. The ENP Action Plans that have been proposed for each of the three South Caucasus states emphasise progress towards democracy, good governance, rule of law, and respect for human rights as a condition for improved economic and political ties with the EU. They also focus on the resolution of outstanding regional conflicts and improved interstate relations as a condition for further integration (European Commission 2005a). Although the EU has no direct involvement in international efforts to mediate the region's frozen conflicts, limiting its involvement to economic rehabilitation projects in Georgia and support for existing UN and OSCE mediation efforts, Brussels has indicted its willingness to play a larger role. The EU's consideration of a Georgian government request to help monitor that country's border with Russia, following Moscow's decision in December 2004 to block the extension of an OSCE border-monitoring mission (Beatty 2005c) – although it ultimately decided against this request – as well as suggestions that European troops could be deployed as peace-keepers in Nagorno-Karabakh, also hint at the possibility of an expanded EU security role in the South Caucasus in the future.

In the final analysis, US and EU interests in the South Caucasus appear broadly convergent and their policies in the region mutually reinforcing. The EU's increased engagement in the South Caucasus has been enthusiastically welcomed by the US, which would like the EU to do much more, especially when it comes to resolving the region's frozen conflicts. In addition to promoting stability and democracy, the US and EU also have common energy security interests in the South Caucasus, with both seeking the establishment of secure alternative routes for the trans-shipment of Caspian oil and gas to existing pipelines through Russia.

These generally convergent interests create the basis for a joint approach to the region that could yield huge benefits for each. However, as in Eastern Europe and other parts of the former Soviet space, EU involvement in the South Caucasus is inhibited by the reluctance of Brussels and some member states to upset relations with Russia by interfering in Moscow's 'near abroad'. Such reluctance was the basis for the EU's decision not to dispatch an ESDP mission to the Georgia–Russia border in 2005, and it is a major reason for the EU's refusal to become more directly involved in international efforts to resolve the region's frozen conflicts (ICG 2006). As in other parts of the former Soviet Union, therefore, EU inaction in the South Caucasus could become an increasing source of tension in US–EU relations. Another point of contention is Iran's role in the region. Generally speaking, while the US favours a strategy of containment towards the Islamic republic, the EU prefers a strategy of engagement, and would be more willing than Washington to accept an Iranian role in the region (for instance, as the price for securing access to Iranian energy). Despite the potential benefits, therefore, the prospects for greater transatlantic cooperation in the South Caucasus remain problematic.

The Middle East and Northern Africa

The southern portion of Europe's neighbourhood is a region of tremendous economic and strategic importance for the US and EU alike. EU efforts to build a systematic relationship with this region began in 1995, with the launching of the Barcelona Process and the European-Mediterranean Partnership (EMP). This multilateral framework will now be supplemented, and to some extent superseded, by the ENP, which adds a potentially valuable bilateral component to EU relations with the region (Balfour 2004; Emerson and Noutcheva 2005). Despite its significant ties to the region, however, EU influence is limited by the fact that none of the Southern Mediterranean countries has a realistic prospect of EU membership. Thus, EU efforts to promote reform in the region will have to proceed without the 'golden carrot' of membership, a source of leverage that is at least potentially available in other parts of the European neighbourhood.

US involvement in the Middle East is longstanding, but American engagement in the region has greatly intensified since 9/11 and the Iraq war. US Middle East strategy has also undergone a major change, shifting from a predominant focus on the security of Israel and regional stability to a more ambitious attempt at political and economic transformation. In late 2003, the Bush administration announced sweeping plans for advancing freedom and democracy in the 'Greater Middle East', a zone of predominantly Islamic countries stretching from Mauritania to Pakistan (White House 2003). After intense criticism from Arab and European governments that the initiative was merely an attempt to impose US designs on the region, and that it could divert attention from efforts to resolve the Israeli–Palestinian conflict, the US proposal was substantially modified before the 'Broader Middle East and North Africa' (BMENA) initiative was adopted by world leaders at the June 2004 G8 summit.[1] In another change of strategy, since the November 2004 elections the Bush administration has departed from its unilateralist approach in the Middle East and has instead sought to coordinate its policies in the region more closely with Europe (Daalder et al. 2006).

As their initial criticism of the 'Greater Middle East' proposal indicates, however, many Europeans view increased US involvement in the Middle East with considerable wariness. They doubt the wisdom of launching high-profile initiatives – especially given US unpopularity in the region – 'rather than working quietly to achieve change' (Ottaway and Carothers 2004: 2), and they fear that increased US intervention could produce even greater instability and anti-Western sentiment in the region, generating negative spill-over effects for Europe such as increased immigration and terrorism. A particular concern is the spread of Islamic radicalism within the growing Muslim minority populations of many European countries. Some Europeans also fear that US policies could undermine the effectiveness of the EU's own initiatives in the region. According to one study, the EU could have difficulty becoming a driving force for reform in the Middle East if it has 'to face an uphill struggle against negative tendencies, for example in the widening and deepening of radical Islam', engendered by US policies (Emerson and Noutcheva 2005: 22). Having invested so much effort and money in the region over the past decade, many Europeans no doubt resent US efforts to reset and dominate the agenda in this important part of their direct neighbourhood.

Thus, despite formally endorsing the BMENA initiative, the EU remains wary of identifying too closely with US policies in the Middle East, instead jealously guarding the independence of its own programmes and preferring to follow a course of 'complementary but separate' (or 'distinct but complementary', Chapter 12) initiatives in the region (Beatty 2005d). This approach is justified, according to one former EU official, because 'Given the dismal image of the US in the [Middle East] region, it is questionable whether the EU would gain anything from too open an association with the US.' The EU should informally cooperate with the US as much as possible, he argues, 'but [Washington and Brussels] should operate separately rather than appear together in the Middle East' (Cameron 2005: 10).

Nevertheless, there has been a convergence of US and European approaches in the Middle East since 2003 that could lead to increased cooperation in the future. Perhaps influenced by its difficult experiences in Iraq, the US appears to have moved from an emphasis on military solutions and coercive regime change to a greater focus on the underlying social, economic and political sources of terrorism and instability, an approach long favoured by the EU. As one European official puts it, 'the BMENA marks the adoption by the US of policy objectives long pursued by the EU itself in [the Middle East] region' (Chapter 12). The US also appears to be giving a higher priority to resolving the Israeli–Palestinian conflict, something which the EU has also long urged.

EU policy towards the region has also undergone change. While EU assistance to the Southern Mediterranean countries has traditionally focused on economic development and infrastructure projects – a 'developmentalist' approach to democratisation, according to Youngs (2004: 11) – the EU has now begun placing greater emphasis on the rule of law, human rights, and democracy, bringing its policy more in line with the US approach. The EU has also begun supplementing its traditional civilian or soft-power approach with a new emphasis on hard security issues, particularly the struggle against terrorism and WMD proliferation. The ENP Action Plans that were signed with Jordan, Morocco and Tunisia in 2005, and that are being negotiated with Lebanon and Egypt, make progress on democratic reforms and human rights a key condition of closer ties with the EU, as well as the commitment to preventing terrorism, WMD proliferation, and illegal immigration. The limited success of EU Mediterranean policies to date, as well as the disappointing results of the December 2005 conference to celebrate the ten-year anniversary of the Barcelona Process, also suggest the limits of EU influence in the region acting alone and argue for greater cooperation with the US (*Financial Times*, 29 November 2005).

Both the US and EU have also begun questioning their traditional preference for regional stability over democratic change and human rights, and both seem to increasingly acknowledge a link between past Western support for authoritarian regimes and the growth of Islamic radicalism and political extremism in the Middle East (Balfour 2004). Evidence for this new thinking is provided by joint US–EU pressure on the authoritarian governments of Egypt and Saudi Arabia, both key Western allies in the Middle East, to allow greater democratic freedoms in their countries, although it remains to be seen how hard they will push for such reforms.

There has also been greater transatlantic cooperation on specific regional issues. Especially in its second term, the Bush administration has emphasised the need for US–EU partnership to resolve the Israeli–Palestinian conflict (US Department of State 2005a). The US and Europe have also cooperated in pressing Syria to withdraw its military and security forces from Lebanon, including joint US–French sponsorship of a UN Security Council Resolution in September 2004. US–European pressure on Syria intensified following the assassination of Lebanese Prime Minister Rafiq al-Hariri in February 2005. Perhaps most notable, however, is the close transatlantic cooperation on Iran. Since 2003, the US has quietly supported the efforts of the 'EU-3' (the governments of Germany, France and the UK, acting on behalf of the EU) to negotiate an end to Iran's uranium enrichment programme. After the apparent failure of these negotiations in late 2005, the European governments have forged a common front with the US in pushing for action against Iran by the UN Security Council, against the opposition of Russia and China. Nevertheless, there remains considerable potential for transatlantic divergence on all of these issues in the future, due to unwavering US support for Israel (exemplified once again in the summer 2006 Lebanon conflict), as well as diverging policy inclinations; in the final analysis, when it comes to dealing with the Hamas-led Palestinian government, Hezbollah in Lebanon, and the anti-Western governments of Syria and Iran, Washington continues to favour a strategy of isolation, punishment, and regime change, while the EU generally prefers a strategy of negotiation and engagement (Daalder et al. 2006).

In summation, of all the regions of the European neighbourhood the Middle East represents perhaps the greatest contrast of threat and opportunity for the transatlantic relationship. While there is real potential for conflict in this region between the EU's neighbourhood goals and US strategic security objectives in the 'war on terrorism', there is also huge potential for cooperation to achieve the mutual goals of enhanced stability, security and democracy. As one American analyst has put it, although perhaps over-dramatically, 'If the United States and Europe do not have a joint policy (with whatever differences of emphasis there may be) in the Middle East, then they have little use for each other in international politics' (Mead 2004: 125). Thus far, however, the US and EU have been notably 'unsuccessful in forging a common approach to the region' (Daalder et al. 2006: 1). Whether this continues to be the case remains to be seen, with major implications for the overall US–EU relationship.

Transatlantic relations in the European neighbourhood

The preceding discussion has shown that, while the US and EU have broadly similar goals in the European neighbourhood – stability, security, democracy – they often define these in different ways and favour different approaches to achieving them. They also have different regional interests and priorities, stemming from geography and their different economic, social and historical ties to the concerned regions and countries, which could inhibit cooperation and even become sources of transatlantic friction in the future.

In the former Soviet space, differing views on relations with Russia pose a major problem for transatlantic cooperation. While the US regards Russia from a distance, as a geo-strategic partner (in the 'war on terrorism', for instance, or in international efforts to deal with Iran's nuclear ambitions) or rival, for the EU Russia is a large and powerful neighbour, with whom it shares a common border and neighbourhood. Many EU countries are heavily dependent on Russia for energy, especially natural gas, with this dependence projected to grow in the future. Russia is also an important trade and investment partner for many European countries, while some, such as Germany and Italy, are major Russian creditors. From a security perspective, the EU needs Russian cooperation to resolve the troublesome frozen conflicts and other security problems in their shared neighbourhood, providing yet another reason to maintain cordial relations. Some member states, most notably France, also view Russia as a potential geo-strategic partner in efforts to counterbalance US global dominance and promote a more multipolar world system (Burwell 2005; Cameron and Ac 2005).

Washington and Brussels are not always going to be on the same page when it comes to dealing with Russia, therefore. US policy is more likely to be inconsistent, veering from confrontation and a willingness to challenge Russia in its 'near abroad', to passivity in the face of disagreeable Russian actions whenever Moscow's cooperation is needed on other pressing global issues. The EU, on the other hand, seeks a more balanced and stable long-term relationship with its powerful neighbour, leading it in some cases to defer to Russian interests in the former Soviet Union in the interest of preserving good overall relations with Moscow. Different strategic considerations in relations with Russia, therefore, are a key factor inhibiting closer US–EU cooperation in the former Soviet space and a potential source of transatlantic discord.

American and European interests are also not identical when it comes to the Middle East. Because of its geographical proximity to the Middle East and the existence of sizeable Muslim minorities in many European countries, the EU is much more vulnerable to the negative consequences of instability in the region than is the US. Europe also has extensive trade and economic ties with the Southern Mediterranean countries that could be disrupted by regional instability. Thus, as in the case of the former Soviet Union, the EU's relations with the Middle East are 'strongly influenced by its position as a neighbour' (Leigh 2005: 123), which gives it fundamentally different interests in this region from those of the more geographically distant US. As discussed previously, the EU has sought to protect its interests in the broader Middle East by preserving the autonomy of its own policies and not associating too closely with the policy initiatives of the US.

The US and EU also favour different approaches to promoting security and democracy in the European neighbourhood. Especially under the Bush administration, the US has tended to emphasise the hard power dimension of security, including the actual deployment of American military force (or in the case of the 2006 Lebanon conflict, support for the Israeli use of force). It also favours rapid political change ('regime change') as the best way to promote democracy, focusing on the overthrow of authoritarian (anti-Western) governments and the adoption of formal democratic institutions. Popular elections are viewed as the main legitimising device of the US approach to democratic regime change, and little thought is given to the social and institutional bases of democracy. As one prominent commentator has put it, the 'Bush doctrine' policy of 'democracy promotion via coercive regime change' seems to assume 'that democracy is some kind of default condition to which societies reverted once tyrants were removed, rather than a collection of complex institutions that need to be painstakingly built over the years' (*Financial Times*, 11 October 2005).

The EU, by contrast, has preferred a more gradual or 'developmentalist' approach to promoting democratic change, which focuses on creating the economic and social conditions for democracy. It has also emphasised the use of civilian power resources, including economic and technical assistance, political dialogue, and 'people-to-people' educational and cultural exchanges. With the ENP, the EU will supposedly make such assistance and access to the single market more conditional on progress in adopting democratic reforms. In the struggle against terrorism, the EU prefers to focus on attacking the 'root causes' of political extremism by providing assistance for long-term economic, social and political development, although it has also begun to develop deployable hard security capabilities within the context of ESDP.

These different approaches reflect a number of factors, including differences of political culture and geographical proximity to regions of concern, as well as differing institutional capacities and capabilities. These are factors that are either permanent or unlikely to change very quickly. As a result, the preference for different approaches to promoting security and democracy is something that is likely to remain a problem for US–EU cooperation in the European neighbourhood, especially in the Middle East. This does not mean that cooperation is impossible, however. In many instances, the careful coordination of different but complementary foreign policy strengths and approaches can be highly productive and beneficial. Such cooperation also creates the possibility for mutual learning and adaptation, leading to greater policy convergence. Equally possible, however, is that the continued preference for different approaches could lead to greater transatlantic discord and friction.

The ENP as a 'normative challenge' for the United States

The ENP represents a fairly unique model of engagement with neighbouring countries and regions. As former Commission President Romano Prodi has proclaimed, it represents in some ways 'our own new philosophy of international relations, combining the extending of bilateral relations and the promotion of integration and cooperation between nearby areas' (Agence Europe 2002). The EU model of external governance seeks to spread stability and security by embracing neighbouring countries and regions in networks of economic, political, and institutional ties of varying density. The prospect of greater integration with the EU encourages neighbouring countries to change their behaviour and introduce economic and political reforms ('conditionality'). Change is also induced through socialisation and learning processes that result from intensified contact and interaction with the EU. The overall result is a transformative dynamic: as one observer has commented, 'upon entering the EU's sphere of influence countries are changed forever' (Leonard 2003).

Moreover, the EU external governance model contrasts favourably – in the eyes of many people around the world – with the current US model of international relations, which also seeks to influence and transform. However, while the EU model relies on attraction and integration, or 'soft power', the US model uses imposition and coercive military force. While the EU model emphasises gradual, evolutionary, and deep social change, the US model demands rapid and often merely superficial political transformation ('regime change'). While the EU model offers neighbouring or partner countries 'joint ownership', or the prospect of a voice in newly created transnational structures, the US model is based on unilateral domination and offers, 'at best ... economic opportunities' (*Financial Times*, 2 February 2005), and maybe military assistance and cooperation as well. In short, while the EU model aims at community-building, the US model creates the impression of 'empire-building'.

The EU's 'gravity model' of democratisation, relying on Europe's power of attraction and best exemplified by the ongoing process of enlargement, has also arguably been more effective than other democratisation strategies, including the US advocacy of universal democracy (Emerson and Noutcheva 2004a). Compared to the EU, other democratic powers, including the US, have been less successful at transforming their neighbouring regions into spheres of democracy and good governance. In the US neighbourhood of Latin America, for instance, apparent democratisation in the 1980s and the embrace of neo-liberal capitalism in the 1990s now seems to be giving way to populism, 'creeping authoritarianism', and rejection of the neo-liberal 'Washington consensus' economic model (*New York Times*, 1 March 2005).

The effectiveness of the EU model is no doubt due to the lure of prospective membership in a prosperous, stable, and secure club of countries. Whether it will be effective beyond the sphere of planned or likely future enlargements, without the lucrative 'golden carrot' of membership to induce difficult political and economic reforms, is an open question. On the answer to this question hinges the ultimate success of the ENP. However, the EU's chances of success are also bolstered by the basic attractiveness of its integrative and community-building approach to neighbourhood relations. To the extent that the ENP and the EU model of external governance is effective and successful, the EU's attractiveness and status as a 'normative power' (Manners 2002) will also be enhanced.

It is reasonable, therefore, to view the ENP, and the model of international relations on which it is based, as representing a significant 'normative challenge' for the US. By presenting an alternative, inherently more attractive and possibly more effective approach to international relations and world order, the EU model of external governance not only potentially enhances the EU's relative global power and influence, but also challenges the underlying normative structure of the international system (nation-state based realism) upon which US hegemony and leadership are based. Another way of thinking about this challenge is in terms of Cooper's (2003) conceptualisation of the international order as being composed of 'pre-modern', 'modern', and 'post-modern' spheres. If successful, the ENP could lead to an expansion of the EU-cantered 'post-modern' world at the expense of the state-centric 'modern' world in which the US remains anchored. Whether the ENP will be successful, of course, is another matter.

Conclusion

The ENP is a development with significant implications for the US and transatlantic relations. Viewed positively, the EU's increased engagement in its own neighbourhood provides the US with a potentially valuable and much-needed partner for its efforts to promote stability and democracy in Eurasia and the broader Middle East. US–EU cooperation in the European neighbourhood could also be a means of rebuilding the transatlantic partnership, giving it new purpose and direction following the divisions over Iraq.

As this chapter has argued, however, such cooperation is not automatic or assured. Despite broad agreement on the general goals of promoting stability and democracy, the regional interests and priorities of the US and EU are not always identical, and the US and Europe also often favour different approaches for achieving these common goals. The active US promotion of democratic change in the former Soviet Union and broader Middle East, for instance, has created problems for the EU, complicating relations with Russia and generating instability on the EU's borders to which it now must respond. The increased mutual engagement of the US and EU in the European neighbourhood, therefore, may not necessarily lead to greater cooperation and improved transatlantic relations; instead, the inability of Washington and Brussels to cooperate, or even increased policy competition between them in specific regions, could be something which seriously undermines the transatlantic relationship. In this sense, the ENP represents as much a challenge or danger for transatlantic relations as it does an opportunity.

The ENP also presents a normative challenge for the US. If successful, the

EU model of external governance, based on integration, partnership, and the exercise of soft power, could pose an alternative, inherently more attractive and possibly more effective approach to international relations than the more traditional hard power model currently favoured by Washington. A successful ENP would not only enhance the EU's relative global power and influence, but it could also challenge the underlying normative structure of the international system on which US leadership and hegemony is based. In this manner, the ENP has implications for international politics and the global system that go beyond its potential impact on transatlantic relations.

Notes

1   Key elements of the BMENA include the Forum for the Future, a conference of ministerial-level representatives from G8 states and regional governments meeting on a regular basis to discuss democratic and economic reform, and two proposed new funds: one to promote democratisation in Arab and Islamic countries, and one to provide venture capital for businesses. For additional details on the BMENA, see the US State Department website: http://bmena.state.gov/.

Ulrich Sedelmeier

11

The European Neighbourhood Policy: a comment on theory and policy

This volume is extremely topical and timely in attempting a first systematic and conceptual stock-taking of the EU's efforts to create a broad system of governance for cooperation with its neighbours. The volume sets out to answer two main questions. First, how can we explain the specific form and substance of the European Neighbourhood Policy and the characteristics of the system of governance that it creates? Second, how effective is the ENP in achieving the goals that the EU pursues through it?

With regard to the second question, most contributions point out that it is still too early to provide more than a tentative answer in view of the recent nature of the ENP. The contributors therefore examine primarily the set-up of cooperation in the various sectors to assess the likelihood of effective cooperation. Most contributors draw on precedents in the EU's external relations – primarily Eastern enlargement – to assess whether the transfer and adaptations of instruments used in such precedents into the various domains of the ENP is likely to allow the EU to achieve its goals. As assessments of the likely effectiveness therefore have to rely largely on the emerging patterns of governance in the ENP, the first question becomes even more pertinent.

To explain the characteristics of the ENP's system of governance, the editors propose to draw on theories of governance and regional integration. Governance theories serve primarily to categorise the 'dependent variable', i.e. the forms, content and instruments of cooperation. Accordingly, the editors distinguish between different forms of governance with regard to the degree of integration that they provide for, the extent to which they are hierarchical or based on mutual coordination, and the extent to which they involve private actors. Integration theories provide (alternative) 'independent variable(s)' that explain (variation in) the emerging patterns of governance and cooperation. The editors emphasise in particular transaction costs and threat perceptions, as well as bargaining power asymmetries. At the same time, they also remain open to consider social or 'ideational' factors.

The editors' framework of analysis thus resembles more a flexible set of markers for pertinent explanatory factors than a rigid template with clearly specified competing hypotheses for the case studies to test. The contributions do not tightly follow a common format in analysing their individual policy domains, which makes it somewhat difficult to assess the explanatory power of the framework of analysis. However, the various contributions clearly corroborate a central conceptual assumption of the volume. The nature of the explanatory variables that the editors emphasise and the organisational set-up of the volume suggest that the system of governance that the ENP creates is to be differentiated at the sectoral level. And indeed, the various contributions confirm that the governance patterns and forms of cooperation vary significantly according to the policy domain in question.

To locate the analysis at the sectoral level thus appears highly appropriate in order to capture the central dynamics underpinning the ENP. Yet the focus on individual policy domains has a drawback. It makes it difficult to capture the tensions between the overall objectives of the ENP and policy patterns in particular sectors. Such a tension results if the main intra-EU conflicts over policy are not simply, or not even primarily, according to national lines, but rather reflect transgovernmental cleavages between sectoral policy-makers and the group of policy-makers in charge of the overall policy. Most chapters in this volume emphasise the striking similarities between the ENP and the EU's enlargement policy with regard to the instruments used (Del Sarto and Tulmets 2006; Kelley 2006; Lavenex and Schimmelfennig 2006). The salience of this tension between sectoral dynamics and overall policy is another similarity between Eastern enlargement and the ENP.

In this commentary I concentrate primarily on the tensions between the overall ENP and its various policy dimensions to examine the obstacles that those policy-makers in EU institutions and member states face collectively if they want to use the full potential of sectoral cooperation to achieve the broader goals of the ENP. This focus serves both as a critical comment on the theoretical framework of this volume, and on the policy itself.

The concept of a 'composite policy'

The ENP and the EU's Eastern enlargement (association) policy share key characteristics of a 'composite policy' (Sedelmeier and Wallace 2000; Sedelmeier 2005). The composite nature of both the ENP and the Eastern enlargement policy stem from the EU's attempts to create ever more 'special' and 'privileged' partnerships in its external relations. Policy-makers in charge of external relations therefore aim to draw on the entire range of EU policies in order to maximise the potential benefits and incentives that they can hold out to non-member states.

The main feature of a composite policy is that different groups of policy-makers are in charge of different components of policy. One group of policy-makers is in charge of agreeing the overall goals and instruments of the policy – the 'macro-policy'. In the area of external relations, these 'macro-policy-makers' usually comprise officials from member state foreign ministries (and the Commission's DG for External Relations) and possibly the heads of state and government in the European Council. The other groups of policy-makers include the various officials in charge of specific policy domains which are included in the macro-policy. The key point is that while the macro-policy-makers are in charge of setting the overall goals and choosing the instruments to be used to this end, they cannot decide on the specific settings of these instruments in the various policy domains included, or in other words, the specific policies in the sub-systems of the overall policy from which it draws its substance.

A fundamental requirement of policy-making in a 'composite policy' is thus horizontal coordination between the macro-policy-makers and the respective groups of sectoral policy-makers. The main challenge for such coordination is that the preferences of macro- and sectoral policy-makers might diverge due to their different organisational positions that imply different goal hierarchies. As the preferences of the sectoral policy-makers reflect the constellation of interest group preferences or dominant policy paradigms in their specific policy domain, incompatibility between the goals of the macro-policy and sectoral interests and paradigms is a key obstacle to the strategic coherence and efficiency of the macro-policy.

In the early stages of Eastern enlargement, the main question that arose from the association policy's characteristics as a composite policy was to what extent the EU would be able to use its policy instruments, such as trade liberalisation in specific sectors, in order to support the economic and political transformation in the associated countries. In the case of the ENP a central challenge arising from its composite character is whether the incentives that specific policy domains could generate can be used effectively in order to foster its broader goals. To understand how salient the challenges of a composite policy are in the case of the ENP, I first examine the macro-policy of the ENP, namely the extent to which there is a consensus among macro-policy-makers about the goals to be pursued and the types of instruments used. I then turn to three key policy domains: market access, free movement of persons, and political dialogue. In each of these domains, I examine the potential incentives that it can generate, and whether they are domain-specific or sizeable enough to provide the ENP participants with incentives for compliance with the broader goals of the ENP. I then consider the prospects for an effective use of these potential incentives by the EU macro-policy-makers in view of the domain-specific constellation of societal preferences in the EU and the dominant sectoral policy paradigm.

The 'macro-policy' of the ENP

Consensus on policy goals

A key condition for coherence and effectiveness in a composite policy like the ENP is a consensus among the macro-policy-makers on the goals of the policy and the instruments to be used. Such a consensus is necessary if they are to be able to promote collective preferences successfully vis-à-vis the various groups of sectoral policy-makers whose respective preferences for policy in their issues areas might differ.

In the case of the ENP, the consensus on the key goals among the chiefs of government and foreign ministries of the member states is fairly strong. The overall goals of the ENP are clearly stated and shared among the member states. The ENP's main rationale is to increase the EU's security; stability in the neighbourhood is to be achieved through promoting welfare and democracy in the ENP participants (see also Chapters 3 and 12). In this regard, the consensus among the macro-policy-makers is stronger than in the case of Eastern enlargement, where national positions differed on the balance between the goals of security and stability on the one hand, and of integration as a goal in its own right, on the other.

This consensus on the overall goals notwithstanding, there are potential dividing lines. One cleavage concerns the geographic focus of the ENP. The relative importance of the EU's eastern and southern neighbours for individual member states differs according their geographical location. This geographical cleavage was reflected in the late inclusion of the Mediterranean countries on the insistence of the southern member states. It significantly increased the diversity among the ENP participants, which poses a challenge for the coherence of the ENP. The formula of 'differentiation' on the basis of how far individual ENP participants are prepared to go in meeting the EU's expectations solved this challenge creatively, at least for the time being.

A second issue that could undermine the overall consensus is the potential goal conflict that might emerge between the ENP's security rationale and democracy promotion, as Maier and Schimmelfennig (Chapter 3) point out. A strict enforcement of democratic conditionality can conflict with commercial or security concerns. Member states might be reluctant to jeopardise relations with undemocratic governments that appear to guarantee stability and with countries with which they have important commercial ties.

More fundamentally, EU macro-policy-makers do not seem to have confronted the question of whether democracy promotion is a subordinate goal, as an instrument in the pursuit of promoting stability, or a goal in its own right. Moreover, it remains an open question whether democracy promotion in the context of the ENP can rely on the same conditionality-based mechanisms as Eastern enlargement. The less conducive starting conditions in most ENP participants and the weaker incentive structure that the EU can offer might favour a policy of continued engagement of ENP participants rather than a strict enforcement of conditionality even if their governments' record on democracy and human rights deteriorates.

In sum, while the consensus on the ENP's goals among macro-policy-makers across member states and EU institutions appears stronger than in the case of Eastern enlargement, divergences might emerge with regard to the hierarchy among the goals, notably the status of, and strategies for, democracy promotion.

Coherence of policy instruments

The last point already relates to the question of a consensus on the instruments to be used in the ENP, and their coherence. In broad terms, the EU can draw on two main strategies and instruments to promote its goals in its neighbourhood (Kubicek 2003; Kelley 2004b; Schimmelfennig and Sedelmeier 2005a). 'Conditionality' is a strategy in which the EU offers (material) rewards for the target governments to comply with its demands. 'Socialisation' relies on processes of persuasion by the EU and identification of target governments with the EU, which lead them to accept the rules that the EU promotes as normatively legitimate. The two strategies can be complementary and mutually reinforce their effectiveness, but under certain conditions, they might also undermine each other.

As virtually all contributions to this volume point out, the fundamental difference between Eastern enlargement and the ENP is that the incentive of accession is explicitly off the agenda, and hence the main leverage for EU conditionality absent. While the framework and many instruments of the ENP are emulated from Eastern enlargement, the ENP reflects the need to adapt these instruments to the different context. Conditionality still figures very prominently in the ENP, but the EU puts a much stronger emphasis on 'soft' and participatory mechanisms involving the ENP partners (see also Chapter 12, this volume; Del Sarto and Tulmets 2006; Kelley 2006).

The key expression of the continued prominence of conditionality in the ENP is the principle of 'differentiation' among the ENP participants, in which the EU rewards those countries that go furthest in conforming to its priorities. These rewards include market access, facilitation of visa requirements, financial assistance, or participation in EU programmes. In addition, even in the absence of the membership perspective, the EU's 'constructive ambiguity' about the ultimate membership prospects of the (European) ENP participants functions as an additional incentive to meet the EU's expectations (see Chapter 12). The hope that membership will eventually become an option might explain why the Eastern ENP participants agreed in their Action Plans to put a greater emphasis on improving democracy and human rights than the Mediterranean participants. However, the experience of Eastern enlargement also shows that costly adjustments are undertaken only once the membership perspective becomes much more tangible, specifically after the start of accession negotiations.

On the other hand, the EU acknowledges that these incentives and its bargaining power vis-à-vis the ENP participants are not sufficiently strong to illicit compliance with its goals. Consequently, there is a much stronger emphasis on 'soft' mechanisms conducive to socialisation through joint goal-setting and assessment with the ENP participants, as opposed to conditions set unilaterally by the EU. Greater participation and input, and hence 'joint ownership' of the ENP participants, relates, for example, to negotiations of Action Plan priorities and their monitoring by joint bodies (see for example, Chapter 12).

Despite this creative adjustment of enlargement practices to the ENP, doubts remain about the effectiveness of this particular combination of conditionality and socialisation mechanisms in practice. First, the EU faces an obvious trade-off: while joint ownership is indeed a precondition for sociali-sation processes to work, it reduces the likelihood that bilateral Action Plans reflect the EU's objective precisely in relations with those countries which are furthest from conforming to the conditions preferred by the EU. For example, Noutcheva and Emerson (Chapter 5) point out with regard to economic governance that the jointly identified priorities in the Action Plans only provide broad guidelines about desirable improvements and do not prescribe clear targets for measuring achievement. Second, the shift towards softer governance instruments might undermine the effectiveness of the ENP's conditionality-based strategies. As Vachudova (Chapter 6) argues, the use of more consensual arrangements deprives the ENP of a key mechanism to influence domestic change in the ENP partners. 'Joint ownership' is at odds with the tough monitoring and reporting by EU institutions that was a precondition for reform-oriented forces to mobilise pressure against reform-adverse governments in East Central European accession countries.

At the same time, the conditions in the ENP partners are generally less conducive to successful socialisation than in the context of Eastern enlargement. Factors such as identification of governments with the EU or the resonance of EU requirements with domestic rules that the literature hypothesises as pre-conditions for the effectiveness for social learning (Schimmelfennig and Sedelmeier 2005b) are much less salient in the ENP participants. Nonetheless, as Leigh (Chapter 12) points out, governments in the EU's neighbours have generally considered participation in the ENP desirable, even if their domestic practices clashed with the EU's emphasis on human rights, the rule of law, and good governance. Leigh attributes this desire to 'competitive pressures' that the fear of exclusion from the ENP induced among the EU's neighbours. Such competitive pressures suggest that the ENP participants are indeed susceptible to the EU's 'social influence'

(Johnston 2001). In this sense, governments appear to attribute a legitimising effect on participation in the ENP, which in turn gives the EU a certain extent of non-material leverage. Still, it may be doubtful whether this leverage will extend to inducing costly domestic changes and it can be expected to vary significantly across countries, depending on the extent of positive identification with the EU.

In sum, the ENP macro-policy-makers appear to share a consensus on the instruments to be used, but it seems that they have not confronted certain ambiguities. The stronger emphasis on soft mechanisms in the ENP is consistent with the much less favourable conditions for exercising influence on domestic change in the ENP participants through conditionality than in the case of Eastern enlargement. At the same time, this instrument implies that the outcomes desired by the EU are much less certain, more contingent on domestic politics in the ENP participants, and subject to a much more long-term process. Moreover, the peculiar mix of incentive-based and socialisation-based strategies in the ENP has the potential to undermine their respective potential. Finally, while the incentives that the EU can offer in the absence of membership are much weaker than in Eastern enlargement, a key question related to the ENP's composite nature is whether the EU macro-policy-makers are able to use the available incentives in the sectoral policy domains for the purposes of their broader goals.

Sectoral policies of the ENP

Market access
As Noutcheva & Emerson and Vachudova (Chapters 5 and 6) point out, access to the EU's internal market is the key incentive for non-member states to forge closer relations with the EU. In its more limited form market access consists of trade liberalisation. The most far-reaching form is full participation in the internal market, including the removal of non-tariff barriers (NTBs) and the absence of trade defence measures, such as safeguards or anti-dumping action, as well as the extension of the free movement of goods to services, capital and labour. As the internal market is still the core of EU membership, the incentive of 'a stake in the internal market' is an incentive that is potentially sufficiently large for ENP participants to comply with EU conditions in a range of policy areas. Vachudova suggests that 'the promise of greater participation in the internal market will be the catalyst for any reform momentum that develops within the ENP process'. However, obstacles to the effective use of this particular material incentive to enable a package deal on compliance with the EU's broader conditions exist both on the side of the ENP participants and the EU itself.

On the one side of the ENP participants, the reward of participation in the internal market might still not be sufficiently high for governments to undertake costly domestic change. As Maier and Schimmelfennig (Chapter 3) point out with regard to democratic reforms, even the prospect of full membership is not sufficient if the changes demanded by the EU threaten governments' power bases. To what extent market access might provide the EU with effective leverage to demand compliance with less costly policy reforms depends on the specific benefits that the ENP partners might reap from trade liberalisation and a 'stake in the internal market'. However, first, these benefits appear somewhat vaguely defined in the ENP. Second, the tensions between macro-policy-makers and sectoral policy-makers in the EU might prevent the effective use of these benefits as rewards for compliance.

With regard to *sectoral trade liberalisation*, the key question is whether the ENP can offer the participants additional improvements over their current trade regimes with the EU, which are either based on the Partnership and Cooperation Agreements (PCAs) or the Association Agreements with the Mediterranean countries. Vachudova suggests that further trade liberalisation of industrial products is in particular an incentive for the Eastern ENP partic-ipants, since they – in contrast to the Mediterranean participants – still face significant EU protectionism in this area. Furthermore, market access for agricultural products is an obvious incentive for all ENP participants. However, the prospects for the EU to offer these potential rewards are low: the EU's Eastern enlargement offers plenty of evidence that EU interest groups in the 'sensitive sectors' successfully influenced sectoral policy-makers across member states and in the Commission to block concessions in these areas. A similar split between macro- and sectoral policy-makers in the ENP will then undermine the use of sectoral trade liberalisation for the purposes of external governance. As Vachudova puts it: 'If EU politicians … do not [trump domestic interests and open markets] they will severely undermine … the ENP as an effective foreign policy instrument.'

Full *participation in the internal market* presents additional benefits to trade liberalisation for ENP participants. It eliminates NTBs and eliminates the use of trade defence instruments by the EU. Crucially, it also includes, for example, the services market, where the ENP partners have potential compet-itive advantages in certain sectors (see also Chapter 5). For the EU, the advantages of a regulatory alignment of the ENP participants are obvious: the EU's exporters and investors could work in a familiar regulatory environ-ment. At the same time, alignment with EU competition policy and regulations of production processes, such as in environmental policy or health and safety in the workplace, would reduce some competitive advan-tages of producers in the ENP participants. Moreover, alignment would promote some of the EU's broader goals, such as higher levels of environ-mental protection. For the ENP participants, however, it is less obvious whether the necessary adjustment is worth the potential benefits.

The most obvious drawback for the ENP participants is that regulatory alignment involves high costs. If the ultimate goal cannot be EU membership, then it is not clear why they would implement the costly and complex regulatory regimes, especially those that do not affect the nature of goods to be traded, such as in environmental or social policy. There might be an intrinsic value in adopting elements of, say, EU competition policy, but it is limited by their lower levels of economic development. As Noutcheva and Emerson point out, the ENP acknowledges this problem. Rather than full harmonisation, the EU only expects selective alignment 'in areas where it makes economic sense, suits the development levels and serves the development goals of the neighbours'. Yet such flexibility has a flipside. The key problem of regulatory alignment concerns EU reciprocity. The ENP's reference to 'a stake' in the internal market does not entail a clear commitment by the EU of how it will reciprocate alignment efforts. Reciprocity involves an obvious trade-off: the more flexible the ENP partners' alignment, the less likely are binding concessions from the EU.

In the context of Eastern enlargement, the Commission's policy-makers in charge of relations with the candidates proposed one option for such reciprocity: in return for alignment with EU competition policy, particularly state aids, the EU should renounce the use of trade defence instruments. Once the candidates applied EU competition policy, then there were no grounds to use, for example, anti-dumping measures or countervailing duties. However, this initiative was blocked by sectoral policy-makers in the Commission and the member states. The most binding form of EU reciprocity for regulatory alignment by non-members is the European Economic Area (EEA) agreement between the EU and most EFTA members. This option was also discussed in the context of the 'pre-accession' strategy for Eastern enlargement and it is sometimes floated in the context of the ENP. Without the membership perspective, ENP participants might be more inclined to consider this option as a 'halfway house' than the Eastern enlargement candidates who feared that it might simply serve as a waiting room to delay their full membership. Yet all the other drawbacks of an EEA-type regime still hold.

The main political flaw of the EEA, as Noutcheva and Emerson point out, is its asymmetrical nature. The non-member states have to apply rules that they had no say in. For the EFTA members who joined the EEA, this obvious disadvantage was acceptable, since it was only considered a transitional regime on the way to full membership (Smith 1999). Moreover, the parallel nature of accession negotiations meant that their representatives participated in the various Council bodies after the signing of accession treaties and hence the asymmetrical nature was never felt as strongly. Second, the exclusion of agriculture from the EEA – which many EFTA members even found desirable in view of their higher levels of subsidy – is a much more serious drawback for the ENP participants. Finally, even if the ENP participants found unconditional market access worth the costs of complete regulatory alignment, sectoral policy-makers in the EU are unlikely to grant it unless the ENP partners create similar enforcement institutions to the EFTA surveillance authority and the EFTA court (see also Chapter 5), which is rather unrealistic; both for the ENP participants to create such joint institutions and for EU authorities to trust their regulatory capacities.

In sum, in the absence of a membership perspective, it is doubtful whether a rather vaguely specified 'stake in the internal market' provides sufficient incentive for the ENP participants to engage in comprehensive regulatory alignment, let alone comply with the EU's broader political conditions. It appears unlikely that sectoral policy-makers in the EU will be prepared to grant the ENP participants access to all areas of the internal market and in those areas where access is granted, it is unlikely to be unconditional. The sectoral policy-makers in charge of the 'sensitive' sectors are likely to resist concessions to the ENP participants in their issue areas and the policy-makers in charge of the internal market are likely to insist on strict regulatory pre-conditions for unconditional market access. Such strict domain-specific conditions for rewards in this domain significantly restrict the ability of the macro-policy to use access to the internal market as effective leverage for the broader goals of the ENP.

Free movement of people and JHA

The free movement of people relates to two very different issues. On the one hand, it concerns the free movement of workers as part of the internal market. On the other hand, it relates to issues in the context of Justice and Home Affairs (JHA), such as questions of external border controls and free travel inside the EU. The latter type of free movement of people particularly relates very directly to the key objectives that the EU pursues with the ENP. The threats of illegal migration and transnational crime are among the key security risks that the ENP seeks to combat.

The domain of cooperation in JHA is therefore not simply an issue area on which the macro-policy-makers of the ENP might want to draw in order to generate incentives for the ENP participants to comply with the EU's broader objectives, but where the sectoral policy-makers themselves have a keen interest in cooperation that furthers the ENP's broader goals. Moreover, in the terminology of the editors, the EU's threat perception in this domain is high; it is less characterised by asymmetrical interdependence between the EU and the ENP participants than other domains.

At the same time, as Occhipinti (Chapter 7) points out, a key element of EU policy was to persuade the ENP participants that effective border management and the fight against organised crime were not simply in the EU's interest, but mutual interests. Such interest convergence in strengthened state capacities in the ENP participants facilitated cooperation, especially when the EU provided financial assistance for related initiatives.

For issues where the balance of costs and benefits is more unevenly distributed, such as re-admission agreements, the EU also has potential rewards within this domain that it can use as leverage for inserting its internal security priorities into the Action Plans. The most important incentive relates to the EU's visa regime; ranging from a facilitation to the complete lifting of the visa requirement for specific countries. While the experience of Bulgaria and Romania in the context of Eastern enlargement shows that the lifting of visa requirements can be a highly valued incentive, it requires an extremely strict alignment with EU JHA conditions. Occhipinti points out that the ENP used visa facilitation as a direct incentive for the re-admission agreements with Morocco and Ukraine.

At the same time, this evidence also suggests that it will be very difficult for macro-policy-makers to argue for the use of concessions in the JHA domain to encourage broader political reforms. While the facilitation of the visa regime might be seen as a reward for democratisation in Ukraine, it was not granted until a re-admission agreement was signed. Conversely, it might prove difficult to provide incentives from outside the policy domain for achieving domain-specific objectives. Occhipinti reports plans in the Commission to link, in the longer term, cooperation on border management and the fight against organised crime with EU concessions with regard to legal economic migration. However, to deliver this reward in practice might prove difficult, if we consider the strong opposition in the old member states to granting workers from the new member states the freedom of movement.

Political dialogue

There is a certain ambiguity with regard to the role of the Political Dialogue in the ENP, which is also reflected in the contribution by Smith and Webber (Chapter 4). On the one hand, the ENP partners are a subject of the EU's Common Foreign and Security Policy (CFSP). In this sense, CFSP might use the bilateral Political Dialogue as one instrument that provides a forum to directly raise with ENP participants issues of concern. The two case studies on the Middle East and the former Soviet Union largely fall into this category of the ENP participants as a subject of concern for the CFSP.

On the other hand, the Political Dialogue is traditionally an instrument to provide non-member states with information about CFSP activities. Thus, 'closer cooperation' through the Political Dialogue usually involves more intense exchanges about foreign policy, aimed at sharing assessment of international events and if possible, generating mutual support for common foreign policy positions. In this case, the aim of the Political Dialogue is not primarily to address specific issues of international concern that involve the ENP participant, but rather to promote greater convergence between the foreign policies of the two parties. This function of the Political Dialogue was its central role in the EU's Eastern enlargement policy and it also appears particularly prominent in the ENP.

Interdependence in this policy domain is generally less asymmetrical than in other domains and potential gains from cooperation are mutual (see also Chapter 4). On the one hand, CFSP can benefit if consultations lead to the support of the ENP participants for its positions. On the other hand, the ENP participants might find it desirable to be consulted at an early stage of CFSP decision-making which might give them an opportunity to shape CFSP positions. To assess the prospects for such mutually beneficial cooperation on foreign policy through the Political Dialogue in the ENP, its precedent in the Eastern enlargement policy is instructive.

The most tangible outcome of the Political Dialogue with the East Central European candidate countries was their 'association' with CFSP outputs, i.e. declarations of support for CFSP positions. Smith and Webber explain the impressive record of alignment as the result of the candidates' 'socialisation' through the Political Dialogue. Yet, they also point out that in the context of accession, this was not the full story. Association with CFSP outputs was not simply the result of socialisation, but also an instrumental strategy of the associated countries to present themselves as attractive candidates for membership by demonstrating the convergence of their foreign policies with CFSP. Even in the absence of a formal requirement by the EU, the implicit adjustment pressure also explains why their association with CFSP positions was generally a process of unilateral adjustment, rather than a joint elaboration of such positions.

In the ENP, the possibility of an association with CFSP outputs – on a case by case basis – has also been raised, for example with Ukraine (Chapter 4). In general, the implicit pressures for the ENP participants to align themselves unilaterally are much more limited in the absence of the membership perspective. If the EU wants to induce a convergence of ENP participants' foreign policy position with CFSP, it has to rely primarily on 'socialisation'. Successful socialisation requires a much greater involvement of the ENP participants through consultation at early stages of CFSP decision-making, and hence a certain scope for them to influence CFSP.

The extent to which non-members have an opportunity to shape CFSP through the Political Dialogue was also the central question in this domain in the EU's enlargement policy (Sedelmeier 2005). The formula of 'dialogue and cooperation', which the ENP maintains, resulted from a compromise between the EU's preferred language of 'dialogue' – which in EU terminology refers to 'third countries' and the associated countries' preference for 'cooperation' – which the EU usually reserves for consultations among member states. In the context of Eastern enlargement, the EU incrementally developed the Political Dialogue into a highly developed multilateral framework for consultations. Consultation included regular exchanges at all levels of the CFSP decision-making structure, as well as a complex mechanism through which the associated countries could feed their positions through the Council Secretariat into the intra-EU decision-making process.

However, despite this significant institutional investment and innovation, the Political Dialogue never developed into a meaningful forum of two-way consultation. A fundamental obstacle to consultations and decision-shaping was the policy paradigm on which the Political Dialogue is based. This paradigm draws a sharp distinction between insiders and outsiders and considers the involvement of the latter a threat to the integrity of CFSP and its viability. This paradigm shapes the understanding of CFSP policy-makers of the possible functions that the Political Dialogue can serve and they therefore cannot conceive of an involvement of non-member states – even if they are candidates for membership – that allows them to influence the policy process.

The precedent of the Political Dialogue in the Eastern enlargement policy suggests that the domain-specific policy paradigm presents an obstacle to substantive consultations of the ENP participants. The Political Dialogue appears therefore unable to create the necessary precondition for their social-isation through CFSP. In the absence of the membership perspective which might have induced pressures for non-members to align themselves with CFSP positions, the scope for the Political Dialogue in the ENP to induce convergence through socialisation also appears seriously circumscribed. Thus, as Smith and Webber (Chapter 4) conclude, the Political Dialogue might be a further domain of the ENP in which the potential is not fully realised.

Conclusion

The editors suggest that the system of governance will be significantly influ-enced by patterns of interdependence, as reflected in transaction costs and threat perceptions. These patterns of interdependence differ across the domains of the ENP and the contributions to this volume demonstrate that the patterns of governance vary considerably across domains. I have suggested that the highly appropriate focus on the sectoral level of the ENP should be complemented by a perspective that focuses explicitly on the tensions between the 'macro-policy' of the ENP – its broader objectives for the EU's external governance – and the sectoral dynamics in specific domains included in the ENP.

In the absence of the accession perspective, which in the context of Eastern enlargement provided an overarching rationale for compliance with the EU's conditions across policy domains, the ENP has to rely to a much greater extent on the ability of macro-policy-makers to use the benefits that can be generated in specific policy domains to induce the ENP participants to comply with its broader objectives. However, an overview of key policy domains that could generate such benefits – market access, free movement and political dialogue – suggests that there are significant domain-specific obstacles, either in the form of interest group pressures or dominant policy paradigms, to use such benefits for the purpose of the broader objectives of the ENP. Despite the apparent consensus among foreign policy-makers across the member states and the Commission DG for External Relations on the broader goals to be pursued through the ENP, the governance patterns created through the ENP may be therefore more likely to follow intra-domain dynamics.

MICHAEL LEIGH

12

Making a success of the ENP: challenge and response

The European Union entered a 'period of reflection' on its own future following the referenda on the draft Constitutional Treaty in France, in May 2005, and the Netherlands, in June 2005. This reflection focuses on the EU's internal structures and policies as well as its role in international relations. The defeat of the Constitutional Treaty was attributed to a wide range of doubts and hesitations on the part of public opinion. Among these were perceptions, or misperceptions, of the effects of the 2004 enlargement. Under these conditions, the EU indicated that it would honour existing enlargement commitments, provided that conditions were met by the remaining candidates, step up its efforts to dispel misunderstandings but undertake no new enlargement commitments for the time being.

Nonetheless the need to foster political and economic development in the countries surrounding the EU had never been greater. In Ukraine, the 'Orange Revolution' required EU support for it to become truly entrenched. In Moldova, the government's choice of a reform agenda, based on EU standards and principles, needed to be translated into concrete measures. Both countries appealed to the EU for support in trying to resolve the Transnistria conflict. Georgia looked to the EU to support its reforms and to help unfreeze conflicts in south Ossetia and Abkhazia. Azerbaijan and Armenia were edging in a similar direction, though far more tentatively, looking also for a greater EU role in efforts to resolve the conflict over Nagorno-Karabakh. Jordan and Morocco sought EU backing for home grown reform programmes. Lebanon's fragile democracy required a new vision to overcome the effects of Syrian occupation and the risks of sectarian splits. Egypt and Tunisia needed encouragement to ease restrictions on political life, to improve governance and to build a broader base for the secular state. Israel and the Palestinians favoured greater European engagement in efforts to bring stability to the region. The

EU and all its neighbours faced threats from terrorism and from trafficking in arms, drugs and people, and recognised the inability of individual states to tackle these problems alone.

These problems would not wait for the EU to conclude its period of reflection. The EU was in no position to offer its neighbours the prospect of membership, as it had to countries in Central and Eastern Europe, Malta, Cyprus and Turkey in the 1990s. In any event, the neighbours of the enlarged union were either ineligible for membership, as non-European countries, or unlikely to be given such a 'perspective' within the foreseeable future. A policy was needed which took these constraints into account but which nonetheless enabled the EU to respond effectively.

Fortunately such a policy had been enunciated two years earlier in different circumstances (European Commission 2004a). Known initially as 'Wider Europe', the European Neighbourhood Policy had never seemed more timely than in mid-2005. The objectives, geographic scope, ways and means and achievements of this policy have been set out elsewhere (Leigh 2005). Rather than recap these, this chapter looks at some of the particular challenges the policy faces in the years ahead.

Objectives

The ENP's short- to medium-term objectives are clear: to project the EU's own security, stability and relative prosperity into its neighbouring region by drawing the countries concerned into a network of political cooperation and economic integration with the EU. EU policy documents have indicated from the outset that this goal is entirely separate from the possibility for European countries, which share the EU's political principles and values, to apply for membership (Leigh 2005).

The ENP does not put forward a vision of the final state of the participants' mutual relations. For a certain period, such ambiguity is constructive, combined with the promise that the further a country is ready to go in taking concrete measures, based on common principles and priorities, the further the EU will be willing to go in bringing that country into its own policies and activities. However, as implementation of the Action Plans advances and the EU contemplates new bilateral agreements with participants, further thought will have to be given to the destination and not just to the journey.

Some observers take for granted that the end state will be participation in the European Economic Area or a similar arrangement. Indeed, this model may suit more developed partners but may be ill-adapted to the needs and capacities of others. Some partners assume that the natural final outcome will be EU membership, despite the EU's unwillingness to endorse this objective. While making full use of constructive ambiguity to leverage reform, the EU might well wish to address the ENP's final destination during its period of reflection.

Geographic scope

In 2005 ENP Actions Plans were in force with Ukraine, Moldova, Morocco, Tunisia, Jordan, Israel and the Palestinian Authority. They were being developed with Armenia, Azerbaijan and Georgia, as well as Egypt and Lebanon. Potentially the ENP covers all countries participating in the Barcelona Process. Their active participation depends on an Association Agreement being in place. Russia prefers a separate bilateral track with the EU in the form of a 'strategic partnership', whose content largely parallels the ENP (European Commission 2003d), while Belarus does not qualify, at the moment, given the nature of the Lukashenka regime.

There are three main challenges stemming from the ENP's geographic coverage: first, to help create the conditions for active participation by potentially eligible countries which are not today in a position meaningfully to endorse the ENP's underlying principles or common values (this concerns mainly Libya and Belarus); second, to avoid creating new divisions with countries in adjacent areas, which are beyond the ENP's scope (this concerns mainly Central Asia to the east, Mauritania to the south, and the Gulf countries to the south-east); and third, to convince Russia that it, too, can benefit from the increased security and economic growth prospects arising from ENP participation by countries which were part of the Soviet Union.

Libya is moving towards acceptance of the *acquis* of the Barcelona Process, a move that would bring it within the scope of the ENP. The EU is strengthening its support for civil society in Belarus and stepping up its condemnation of human rights violations by the Lukashenka regime. It is also signalling to the population that it too can benefit from closer links with the EU once free and fair elections have been held.

The EU is promoting regional cooperation with Central Asia, in strategic areas including energy, transport, border management and counter-terrorism. This takes on additional importance given the involvement in the ENP of the three Southern Caucasus countries, which are linked both to Central Asia and to Europe. The EU named a Special Representative to Central Asia in June 2005 and set up a political dialogue with the region as a whole. In 2005 Mauritania signalled its interest in joining the Barcelona Process which would reinforce links with other North African countries and with the EU. Clearly such a step would require a credible commitment to the principles underlying the Barcelona Process.

Russia agreed in 2005 to develop four major areas of cooperation with the EU, including political dialogue on 'adjacent areas' (of the former Soviet Union) (European Commission 2005e). This was a step towards viewing the common neighbourhood as an area where both parties could benefit from increased stability, rather than as a zero-sum game or the theatre for a new version of the great game.

Thus ways and means have been found to address the challenges arising from the ENP's geographic scope and limits. They will, however, require considerable political will, creativity, and resources to yield their full potential benefits in the years ahead.

Brand

A related question concerns the initiative's label. 'Wider Europe' seemed inappropriate, as most partners are located beyond Europe itself. ENP is a more accurate label: it applies to countries which are indeed neighbours of the enlarged European Union, whether located to the east or to the south. It does not, however, wholly convince governments that consider their countries, rightly, to be profoundly European and that did not wish to be confined to the status of 'neighbour'.

Some initial descriptions of the initiative implied that the EU would involve partners in 'everything but institutions'. However this telescoped a long and complex process and, thus, was open to misinterpretation. Others, such as the idea of creating a 'ring of friends' around the EU, seemed too diffuse, and too self-centred, to project a clear and attractive image of the project's goals.

The EU would do well to stick to 'ENP' as a widely recognised brand, while avoiding slogans which raise expectations that will be hard to satisfy in the short run. Rather than a second effort at rebranding, the EU should retain the label but avoid its use as a qualifier to every initiative taken with countries which do not wish to be confined to the status of neighbours.

Visibility

One of the reasons for doubts and hesitations about enlargement, as reflected in the referenda, was a weak feeling of ownership of the process beyond a relatively narrow circle of politicians, diplomats and policy elites. Opinion leaders made few efforts to explain that enlargement had been undertaken, not as a form of charity or as a reward for overthrowing communism, but because it was in the interests of the existing EU and its citizens. This easy-to-grasp message could have turned opinion around if bolstered by examples demonstrating the positive impact of enlargement on investment, economic growth, jobs and security.

Despite this weak feeling of ownership, enlargement was a palpable development which none could ignore. The ENP, by contrast, is an incremental policy, whose impact will take time to be felt. It has the political support of the European Commission, the European Council, the European Parliament and participating governments but so far there has been little trickle down to those whose commitment and involvement are essential for the policy's success.

This means raising the ENP's profile, the greater involvement of civil society actors on both sides of the border of the enlarged EU, and active efforts to promote discussion and debate. Clearly no 'communications strategy' will provide a quick fix. Actions speak louder than words. Understanding and support will grow as concrete benefits are felt. All the same, a lesson is to be learned from the enlargement experience. The ENP's proponents in the EU and in partner countries need to mobilise public support through a constant, measured and realistic presentation of the ENP's aims and achievements.

Incentives

Some observers, including a number of authors in the present volume, have questioned whether the ENP contains sufficient incentives to induce partner countries to adopt significant reforms in the absence of an offer of EU membership. Indeed, the prospect of membership provides a powerful inducement to candidate countries to adopt political and economic reforms based on EU principles, rules and laws. Indeed, there is general recognition that such reforms are in the interests of the population whether followed by EU accession or not.

The EU does not expect the ENP to exert the same kind of inducement. It does not expect to become as intimately involved in reforms as it has in candidate countries. The ENP follows the principle of 'joint ownership', meaning that action plan priorities cannot be stipulated by the EU but rather must be agreed jointly.

Nonetheless, the ENP has proved sufficiently attractive to convince partners to sign up to domestic reforms and foreign policy goals which are surprisingly far-reaching. Participation in the ENP is itself an incentive, as was clear from the reaction of some neighbouring countries which were initially excluded. Some other countries were at first disinclined to become involved because of the ENP's strong accent on human rights, the rule of law and good governance. They did, however, decide to engage partly because of competitive pressures and the wish to avoid exclusion.

Other incentives include participation in EU policies and programmes, new forms of technical advice and support, a new financial instrument, the European Neighbourhood and Partnership Instrument (ENPI), to provide grant assistance (European Commission 2004j), and the EU's commitment to negotiate new and more comprehensive bilateral agreements once a critical mass of Action Plan priorities has been fulfilled. The World Bank has adapted its own country strategies to ENP priorities, a trend likely to develop further in the future. Thus loans from IFIs, including the World Bank, the European Investment Bank and the European Bank for Reconstruction and Development (in Eastern Europe), can be mobilised, in addition to EU grant assistance, to help participating countries fulfil ENP commitments.[1]

Making the ENPI operational provided a twofold challenge for the EU. On the one hand, sufficient resources needed to be allocated to the instrument to convince partners that it represents genuine added value by comparison with its predecessors MEDA and TACIS. In the 2007–2013 budgetary period, approximately €12 billion in funding will be available for the ENPI to support these partners' reforms, an increase of 32 per cent in real terms over the funding provided by MEDA and TACIS in 2000–2006. On the other hand, the ENPI required new financial engineering to permit a single set of rules and procedures to apply to projects implemented on both sides of the border of the enlarged EU. This will bring gains in efficiency and visibility but will require considerable flexibility and openness to change on the part of the institutional actors involved.

Besides these general incentives, each partner has negotiated the inclusion in its Action Plan of EU commitments on specific issues of major national concern. In the case of Ukraine, for example, these include the establishment of a free trade area, once the country has acceded to the WTO, the granting of market economy status, and an agreement on visa facilitation. The EU offered to speed up and extend other commitments to Ukraine, in recognition of the contribution of the Orange Revolution to meeting Action Plan political priorities.

The credibility of these different incentives depends on their effective *delivery* without undue delay. This poses challenges to both sides. The partner must deliver on its reform and foreign policy commitments while the EU must deliver on a balanced set of incentives, keyed to the partner's own progress. On the EU side, this takes us back to the need for the policy to have sufficient visibility and political support for the necessary resources and openness towards partner countries to be forthcoming.

Action Plan priorities now constitute the agenda for bilateral cooperation with each country. There will be systematic monitoring and reporting, creating further incentives for governments to demonstrate good performance both to the EU and to their own electorates. Time will tell whether the incentives and the procedures provided by the ENP will prove attractive enough to supply an additional stimulus for governance and market-oriented reforms.

Conditionality

The ENP has eschewed the concept of negative conditionality, that is, the withdrawal of benefits in the event of a breach of basic principles, in favour of the concept of positive reinforcement. The further a partner country is willing to go in implementing specific, measurable, priorities, the further the EU is willing to go in integrating that country into EU policies and programmes. This will also be reflected in the allocation of financial assistance. While all countries will receive support based on objective criteria and needs, additional support could be made available from special reserves for countries which do particularly well in addressing Action Plan political priorities.

This approach puts a premium on performance, both in using EU funds effectively and in advancing with political and economic reforms. It poses a number of challenges though. The first is to ensure adequate monitoring, making use of the bodies set up by the cooperation or association agreements with each country. The second is mustering the political will to act on the basis of *differentiation*, one of the main principles of the ENP's tailor-made, country by country approach. In an EU of 25, with some member states oriented towards the south and others towards the east, this challenge should not be underestimated.

Multi-level cooperation

Following the introduction of the ENP, some perplexity has been expressed as to the existence of multiple forms of cooperation with the same partners. Mediterranean countries, for example, have bilateral association agreements with the EU, they are part of the Barcelona Process, they engage in 'sub-regional' cooperation with their immediate neighbours, and, now, they are covered by the Broader Middle East and North Africa initiative sponsored by the G8 (White House 2004). Partners in Eastern Europe are involved in some forms of cooperation among CIS countries (such as the 'Common Economic Space', which comprises Russia, Ukraine, Belarus and Kazakhstan[2]), while being linked to the EU by Partnership and Association Agreements and, now, the ENP. Aspirations to eventual NATO membership further complicate the picture in Eastern Europe.

Such perplexity is understandable but to a considerable extent a reflection of the complexity of the international system in the post-Cold War world. The crucial point is that the objectives and operating methods of these different initiatives should be complementary and, preferably, mutually reinforcing.

In the south, the ENP strongly reinforces the bilateral aspect of the Barcelona Process, mainly represented hitherto by the Association Agreements. The ENP will enable each country to draw closer to the EU at its own speed, according to its own needs and capacities. Thus, Israel, for example, will be able to push ahead with cooperation in areas linked to its own level of economic and technological development. Jordan and Morocco will become more involved in EU activities, as they implement their ambitious domestic reform agenda. This will strengthen the multilateral Barcelona process, too, by removing any impression that countries are held back in developing closer links with the EU by slower moving members of the group.

Both the ENP and the Barcelona Process are compatible with sub-regional cooperation, such as the 'Agadir Process.'[3] The ENP should also favour new forms of sub-regional cooperation as countries develop their links with the EU in similar areas. Provided the Middle East Peace Process gathers momentum, Israel, Jordan and the Palestinian Authority could develop such cooperation, with support from the ENPI and the EIB, in areas such as energy, water, information technology and trade.

The Broader Middle East and North Africa (BMENA) initiative is a looser framework involving a much wider group of states. It shares with the ENP the goal of strengthening the respect for the rule of law, human rights, and democratisation, in keeping with the findings of successive UNDP Arab Human Development reports (United Nations Development Programme 2004). From an EU perspective, BMENA marks the adoption by the United States of policy objectives long pursued by the EU itself in this region. It should lead to the allocation of additional resources by the US to the attainment of these objectives and encourage the pursuit of distinct but complementary projects.

Questions have been raised about the coexistence of the ENP with the 'Single Economic Space' and other forms of cooperation among members of the CIS. The EU has shown understanding for regional cooperation in the CIS framework provided it is voluntary and compatible with the goals of the countries concerned vis à vis the EU and the wider international system. Thus a free trade area, for example, between Russia, Ukraine, Belarus and Kazakhstan would be compatible with WTO accession and a free trade area with the EU, whereas a customs union, or a monetary union, would not.

A certain degree of overlap is inevitable in a fast-developing international system which is not neatly divided into distinct blocs. It is for the proponents of each policy to enunciate clearly its objectives and methods, and how to ensure compatibility with other initiatives. This will undoubtedly remain one of the challenges in explaining the ENP and its specific additional value in the years ahead.

Conclusion

The successful implementation of the ENP is one of the main external challenges facing the EU in the first decade of the twenty-first century. The area immediately surrounding the EU is the area where it can expect to have most influence in the international arena. The period of reflection, induced by the rejection of the Constitutional Treaty in 2005, makes the ENP all the more timely. It provides a framework and a methodology, largely inspired by the enlargement experience, to structure relations between the EU and its neighbours. This chapter has highlighted a number of detailed issues which must be tackled to enable the policy to succeed. Lucidity about the ENP's objectives, its scope and its limits, are preconditions for establishing a sense of common ownership and a common will to make it succeed on the part of all concerned.

Notes

1 Moldova must establish full creditworthiness before being eligible for EIB loans.
2 Founded by Russia, Belarus, Kazakhstan and Ukraine, initial decision taken in February 2003, agreement signed in September 2003, in force since May 2004.
3 Free Trade Agreement between Jordan, Egypt, Tunisia and Morocco signed on 25 February 2004 in Agadir.

KATJA WEBER, MICHAEL E. SMITH AND MICHAEL BAUN

13

Conclusion: the ENP and external governance in theory and practice

Enlargement is arguably the European Union's most effective foreign policy tool, and the 2004 enlargement has dominated the EU's external relations energies for well over a decade now. As this process winds down, the EU is now looking to the ENP as the primary framework for handling a range of problems and relationships along its new borders. This initiative could be one of the EU's most important foreign policy instruments once the limit of new EU member states is reached. The ENP programme enables the EU to offer its partners a range of incentives and cooperative mechanisms to solve various problems, all bound by an institutional framework that can be tailored to the needs of individual ENP countries. In this way the EU intends to significantly improve upon its earlier approaches to foreign policy with non-member states, such as Common Strategies or Partnership and Cooperation Agreements. And by using a single framework for relations with all neighbouring countries, the EU also hopes to both reduce concerns among its neighbours about their relative status to each other and mitigate internal EU divisions about prioritising relations (including prospects for accession) among the partners to the east and south.

In this volume we have attempted to explain the emergence of the ENP, and offer a preliminary evaluation of its performance, through the conceptual lens of 'external governance'. Overall, our answers to the questions posed at the end of Chapter 1 vary greatly depending on the policy domain and ENP partner being evaluated. Given this range of findings, our primary tasks in the Conclusion are to revisit the utility of governance theory for explaining the ENP, evaluate the possible success of the ENP in terms of performance and effectiveness, and offer some thoughts about the implications of the ENP for the EU's neighbourhood and beyond. Before proceeding, it bears repeating here that the arguments and evaluations presented throughout this entire volume must always be qualified in light of the unfinished, even open-ended, nature of the ENP programme. And, to mention but one further caveat, it is quite likely that, aside from the EU, other structural variables such as globalisation or the rise of new powers like China and India may play an indirect role in shaping the ENP.

External governance revisited

Earlier in this volume we defined 'external governance' as a certain type of structured international cooperation that differs from other types of international relationships, such as those based on hegemonic leadership, strategic games, international regimes, global norms, asymmetric interdependence, collective goods provisioning, or *quid pro quo* bargaining. This is not to say, however, that external governance is the only or even best way to understand the ENP. Nor does it mean that external governance cannot be combined with other concepts to give a more complete understanding of the ENP programme. Still, we believe that certain key aspects of the overall ENP programme, particularly its character as a formal 'meta-regime' used to manage virtually all aspects of a valued international relationship, are best described as emerging forms of external governance.

For the purposes of advancing theoretical analysis, external governance can be treated as both a dependent variable and an independent variable. In the rest of this section we attempt to revisit external governance as a dependent variable: what explains the overall range of policy domains and rule types found within the ENP programme, as reflected in the agreements between the EU and its ENP partners? In the sections that follow, we treat external governance – through the ENP – as an independent variable: how might the ENP actually impact the policy problems and other issues covered in the ENP Action Plans (i.e. the questions of implementation and performance)?

Viewing the ENP as a dependent variable, we argued in Chapter 1 that a functionalist-based transaction costs approach provides a useful starting point for explaining some aspects of the ENP programme. This is reflected in several of the case studies. Specifically, there is little doubt that security concerns on the part of both the EU and certain bordering countries helped to instigate the entire project, primarily in anticipation of the 2004 enlargement. The rise of conservative sentiment within certain EU states, fears of immigration and crime, and the agenda-setting effects of high-profile events (particularly the terrorist attacks on Spain, the UK and the US since 2001) helped keep the ENP on the EU's policy agenda. Some of these problems were originally framed as 'eastern' sourced problems, suggesting an initial ENP focus on Belarus, Moldova and Ukraine, and the question of justice and home affairs cooperation was a key centrepiece of the original ENP plan. This was followed closely by the questions of energy security and political stability/dialogue (see Chapters 4, 7 and 8). And since membership was not an option, the primary EU incentive on offer was some degree of market access, the terms of which were to be negotiated along with other central aspects of the ENP programme (i.e. those associated with security and political stability).

However, internal EU politics and pressures from non-member states led the EU – chiefly in the form of the Commission – to expand both the geographical coverage and policy scope of the ENP. To avoid privileging one region – South or East – over another, and to restrain a membership perspective for certain states, the final ENP plan included all actual and potential bordering countries (including the Southern Caucasus), and allowed all of them a potential stake in the EU's internal market, but not full membership in the EU. From the perspective of the ENP partners, virtually all would like greater access to the internal market, a lowering of barriers with the EU, and better management of certain bilateral problems. In this sense a transactions costs approach focused on economic incentives helps explain the general receptiveness of most ENP partners to the new programme, even those that would otherwise prefer full EU membership (particularly Ukraine).

Within these overall parameters, however, the ENP programme does vary widely, in terms of the partners involved, the specific problems covered by the ENP Action Plans, and the specific policy tools and rules used to manage those problems. Here we must move beyond a functional transactions cost approach to shed light on these factors. For example, one of the more obvious findings of this volume is the importance of the EU's past approaches to the states/problems covered by the ENP. Institutional history is extremely important in explaining two facets of the ENP: the general political conditionality clause (democracy and human rights) and the wide range of issue coverage in the ENP beyond the central issues of stability/security and the effective management of economic relations. The political conditionality norm has been institutionalised as a basic EU goal with non-members, and many subsidiary policy issues (such as economic development or cultural exchanges) had been included in previous EU policy frameworks and the accession process. It was therefore fairly easy and even normatively appropriate for the Commission to incorporate these goals into the ENP programme. However, it is also worth asking whether the central functional problems covered by the ENP programme – particularly those involving security and market access – will ever be served if political conditionality is actually imposed on the ENP partners, nearly all of which have problems in this area. In other words, the EU will almost certainly have to subordinate political conditionality to its threat-based problems when dealing with most if not all of the ENP partners (see Chapter 3). Similarly, the EU will also face pressures to subordinate friendly relations with ENP partners to certain aspects of the EU–Russian relationship, particularly in the area of energy security (see Chapter 8). The EU's reluctance to play a more direct role in Russia's gas pricing dispute with Ukraine shows how difficult it will be to find the right balance between ENP partners and outside parties. Similarly, its willingness to deal with ENP outsiders (such as Kazakhstan) that also violate norms of democracy and human rights while holding ENP partners (such as Belarus) to a higher standard also calls into question the EU's actual priorities in foreign policy.

Looking at the policy tools/rules found within the ENP plan (i.e. the questions of incentives and bindingness), the EU similarly drew upon the 'report card' approach of past accession negotiations to outline the types of behaviour expected of ENP partners and to assess where they now stand on certain policy issues of interest to the EU. However, again there is a major disparity between institutional/normative legacy and potential functional/ instrumental application. First, the EU could virtually dictate the terms of past accessions, yet ENP partners are not offered this major incentive for their good behaviour (although there is a possible difference here between south- ern and eastern ENP partners, particularly Ukraine). Second, conditional market access may not be enough of an incentive (as compared to accession) to encourage cooperative behaviour, except for states (such as Ukraine) that may eventually be able to join the EU (see Chapter 6). Here the lack of a firm 'final reward' (like accession) means the ENP must function as an on-going process of negotiations, with no clear end point if full access to the single market is not allowed (although incremental and/or sectoral incentives may be useful). As a general rule, open-ended talks are inherently more difficult than those where a clear point of closure is possible. Third, the issue of differ- entiation will be far more important and prominent in the ENP as compared to the accession process. ENP partners differ widely across a range of dimen- sions, economic and political, and the EU will have little choice but to treat them accordingly. Thus the EU could be very mistaken (that is, unduly opti- mistic) about its prospects for the ENP, which might therefore limit the utility of an external governance approach to its external relations.

The practical result of these factors greatly *increases* the importance of simple policy bargaining or logrolling, plus the strategic use of side-payments by the EU, within the overall ENP plan, and also greatly *reduces* the EU's own bargaining power relative to previous accession processes. Without a credible membership perspective, and without offering the incentive of market access, the EU will have to work out ongoing package deals on a case-by-case basis with its ENP partners to facilitate external governance. These deals are likely to be so unique – or differentiated – that it may make little sense to even consider the ENP as a single policy tool or normative framework. However, we must return to our consideration of the ENP as a meta-regime rather than as a mere basket of individual policy problems and goals. With the right combination of tailor-made incentives (limited market access, financial aid, security support, logrolling, etc.), with a pragmatic relaxation of political conditionality (at least in the short term), and with some attention to long-term socialisation efforts (i.e. civil society building through people-to-people contacts or economic training/development), the external governance approach to the ENP might actually be feasible in principle. ENP partners also may come to feel a certain degree of ownership or 'buy-in' to the project, which may increase its legitimacy and therefore its effectiveness. This possibility of course is largely theoretical; whether it is happening in actual practice will be examined in the rest of this chapter.

Before turning to the ENP in practice, it may be helpful to summarise the range of general incentives for building the ENP programme. These have been described as both 'push' factors and 'pull' factors. Push factors involve the motivations among prospective ENP partners to join the programme; pull factors represent the attractive features of regular cooperation with the EU. These factors and their theoretical relationship to the prospects for external governance are summarised in Table 13.1.

As suggested in Chapter 1, the notion of 'high' transaction costs generally refers to a greater difficulty in arranging stable, mutually beneficial cooperation among a set of actors. This difficulty can be manifested in several ways: concerns over the high stakes involved, difficulties in measuring or distributing costs/benefits, technical complexity, etc. 'Low' transaction costs refer to the general lack of such problems in managing a relationship. These problems can be arranged along a continuum, with 'medium' transaction costs falling somewhere in the middle. Obviously the actual measurement and prioritisation of these factors will vary considerably across and even within different ENP partners as the programme is implemented, which is why it is necessary to consider issue and country-specific variables in the analysis. This task is taken up in the rest of this chapter.

Evaluating the policy performance of the ENP: a preliminary view

In its Strategy Paper of 12 May 2004, the Commission clearly expected the ENP to bring 'added value' to the EU and its partner countries and outlined eleven specific benefits. Among other things, the ENP is expected to advance the EU's foreign policy objectives; move relations with certain countries beyond cooperation to integration; upgrade the scope and intensity of political cooperation; encourage reform and reduce trade barriers; resolve outstanding issues; define priorities; introduce a new financial instrument; increase existing funds, and provide technical assistance. As noted above, where we stand now is difficult to determine since we are dealing to some extent with a 'moving target'. In many instances it is much too early to ascertain how specific Action Plans will be implemented and whether EU member states will assign sufficient financial means for the proposed ENP policies to succeed as a new instrument of EU foreign policy.

Still, it is possible at this point to make an educated guess to suggest what

Table 13.1 General incentives for governance mechanisms across ENP policy sectors

ENP policy areas	Push factors (that motivate ENP partners)	Pull factors (that increase attractiveness of the EU and its ENP programme)	Nature of functional transaction costs (high vs. low)	General likelihood of ENP partners agreeing to robust external governance mechanisms (i.e. binding rules)
1. Shared values	Desire for domestic political reforms	EU as monitor of progress and source of reform ideas	High	Fairly high for democracies; low for non-democracies
2. Political dialogue	Fear of external threats and internal stability	Cost of exclusion	High	Low to moderate if no EU security guarantee or no external threat
3. Economic/ social development	Desire for internal reforms	EU as model for economic development	Low	Low/moderate for non-market economies; high for market economies
4. Trade and internal market	Desire for market access; Fear of economic Competition	Fear of exclusion	High	High if market access is offered
5. Justice and home affairs	Desire to manage border controls on crime/ immigration/ trade/tourism	Role of EU as target of illicit activity and as source of best practices	High	High
6. Connecting the neighbourhood	Desire to manage common resources and develop networks; fear of being cut off from resource supplies	Role of EU as market player and as source of best practices	High	High
7. People-to-people contacts	Desire to promote/protect own cultural/ educational heritage	Desire to enjoy EU's cultural/ educational heritage	Low	Low

may determine whether the ENP is likely to be effective or at least a step in right direction. For a policy initiative this broad in terms of both functional and geographic scope, it makes sense to apply several measures of effectiveness at different levels of analysis. For example, at the macro level one can compare the ENP to past history/policies and ask whether the ENP overall is likely to do a better job of dealing with specific problems than previous arrangements. At a more micro level we can assess the degree of support by ENP partners – their sense of 'ownership' or legitimacy regarding the ENP plan. This assessment of course is likely to vary widely, so that the ENP might be a 'success' with one country and/or policy sector(s) and a 'failure' with others. And with both levels we can further examine the nature of rules to govern certain policy problems, in terms of both explicit bindingness and in terms of actual rule implementation in solving joint problems (including voluntary vs. involuntary defection).

Thus, the case studies not only make clear that we need to use multiple yardsticks to measure ENP performance/success, but also sensitise us to the question of a time horizon. What may be deemed a short-term success may be judged quite differently in the long run. While several EU neighbours, for example, are struggling to replace authoritarian governments with democratic structures and moving away from command to free market economies, EU member states are likely to give their partners credit for even small steps in the right direction. Once this initial transition has been completed, however, EU countries can be expected to be much less lenient. And with respect to several sectors scrutinised in this volume we can shed light on general trends, although it is too early to make a definitive judgment on specific outcomes (success or lack thereof). Given that Action Plans are the product of joint negotiations between the Commission and individual partner states, and that the partners may negotiate different reforms depending on their national priorities, it is not surprising that the EU and its partners use a variety of institutional arrangements in search of success.

Certain external governance patterns do stand out. For instance, the EU's gravitational pull is weaker in the more distant periphery and where EU instruments shift from hierarchical governance to softer modes of cooperation. It is also somewhat weaker towards the south than the east. Sectorally, economic relations between the EU and its ENP partners tend to be less hierarchical and largely based on mutual agreement and cooperation. Or, whereas fiscal policy tends to be subject to hard coordination, employment policy is characterised by soft coordination. In the environmental sector, there is a need for 'detailed rules and procedures for cooperation, and binding obligations and detailed review mechanisms'– greater structural sophistication – than in the energy sector (Chapter 8). And, when it comes to ENP security relations, these are not highly institutionalised, thus increasing the likelihood of defection. However, there is some degree of 'soft' security cooperation through the Political Dialogue and JHA aspects of the ENP, as well as a potential for ENP partners to participate in security operations outside of their own territory. Whether these arrangements will hold up in the event of an actual security crisis remains to be seen.

Similarly, we are able to suggest preliminary answers to a host of (empirical) questions raised in this volume. Of obvious interest is whether the EU is willing to treat ENP partners as equals and is capable of doing so. Not surprisingly, given the joint nature of the Action Plans, some partners appear to be 'more equal' than others. As Smith and Webber make clear (Chapter 4), there is an asymmetry between ENP partners and the EU in the security realm and 'broad terms of partnership are set by the Commission'. In the energy sector, on the other hand, there appears to be rough parity between the EU and its neighbours, due to mutual vulnerabilities and complementary interests (Chapter 8). Likewise, in the social and economic realm, partners are treated as equals and asked to emulate EU member states to create prosperity, although not to the same degree as acceding countries (Chapter 5).

When it comes to the relative priority of ENP goals, as viewed from the EU's perspective, in principle, human rights should stand above all. In practice, however, we observe significant variance, depending upon the specific ENP partners involved. Examining the EU's relations with the Western Balkans, for example, 'Post-war reconstruction, state- and institution-building come first' (Chapter 5). In the south, the EU seems hesitant to pursue democratisation policies forcefully and instead emphasises economic reform. As Lavenex and Stulberg have shown (Chapter 8), environmental cooperation is not a main priority of the ENP; in fact, it seems to be much more important to promote political transformation in general. In the case of Georgia, the ENP premises regional stabilisation on economic and social levers; political dialogue is clearly secondary (see Chapter 4). According to Pace (Chapter 9), security ranks higher than cross-border mobility, and cultural and educational cooperation is subsumed well below other EU foreign policy concerns. And, as Maier and Schimmelfennig observed in their chapter on shared values (Chapter 3), stringent political conditionality might prevent useful functional cooperation in other issue areas.

It is equally important to understand how ENP partners prioritise across ENP goals. In the East, political elites seek to lean on the European project to legitimise their domestic agenda and thus, their Action Plans are strong on democracy and human rights (see Chapter 5). In the South, greater emphasis appears to be placed on the economic benefits of regulatory convergence. Or, as Lavenex and Stulberg found, 'strong economic disincentives may run counter to ... "hard" enforcement mechanisms in the environmental realm'. Moreover, afraid of antagonising Russia, nearly all NIS are reluctant to forge closer relations with the EU in the energy sector.

With respect to internal EU politics, do the 25 EU member states agree on ENP goals? Issues related to environmental security, for instance, are less politically divisive among member states than issues dealing with energy.

Also, throughout the 1990s, a split in priorities could be observed that continues to this day. More specifically, while some EU members favour a Mediterranean orientation, others have a clear preference for an Eastern agenda (see Chapter 4). Similar disagreement exists with respect to EU policies toward Ukraine. As a rule of thumb it can be suggested that, for the most part, each member state seeks to stabilise its own backyard, leading to inherent intra-EU tensions between the southern and eastern dimensions of the ENP.

Should the ENP activities be viewed as a new form of regional cooperation? As the Barcelona Process with the Mediterranean Countries and the Partnership and Cooperation Agreements with the NIS demonstrate, the EU has maintained relations with its southern and eastern neighbours for a decade now. Although there is some evidence of a regional focus with respect to ENP environmental governance as illustrated by DABLAS and ICPDR (see Chapter 8), and the possibility of greater multilateral/regional cooperation in the security realm with the Euro-Arab Dialogue, by and large the Europe Agreements, Partnership and Cooperation Agreements, and Stabilisation and Association Agreements are *bilateral* and do not represent real multilateral cooperation. However, the ENP combines bilateral and regional approaches to EU relations with neighbouring countries. An example is the South Caucasus, where the EU has sought to negotiate separate Action Plans with each of the three South Caucasus states in parallel. While this approach may hold back the development of EU relations with the most democratically advanced of these countries – Georgia – it also increases the EU's leverage in dealing with interconnected regional problems (e.g. conflict resolution, energy, transportation).

Regarding the short-term versus long-term impact of the ENP, our initial evaluation is that, due to intra-regional heterogeneity an uneven pattern of progress is likely. But it is by no means certain whether the ENP can lead to better governance and improved economic performance without the powerful lure of membership. Incentives for change, it appears, will largely have to come from the economic field. As Vachudova has argued (Chapter 6), good standing in the ENP could become a valuable economic asset for ENP states if it becomes a 'credible commitment device' for assuring investors regarding the country's progress with economic reforms. In the energy sector, the EU's long-term interaction with its new neighbours, moreover, will be heavily dependent on extra-regional suppliers, in particular Russia and OPEC. And, given the absence of mention of several trouble spots in the ENP Country Reports, the EU's influence in the security area appears to be limited. Maier and Schimmelfennig, similarly, predict that the ENP will not have a significant direct impact on democracy and human rights in ENP countries, largely because EU policy has been inconsistent, fragmented, and often undermined by strategic and economic goals. But it is premature to paint too bleak a picture, particularly for the long run. It is certainly possible for cooperation in areas that have seen some success (like JHA) to spill over to sectors that are struggling at the moment.

One further issue our volume sheds light on is the role played by the United States, Russia and international organisations in implementing the ENP. As Noutcheva and Emerson put it (Chapter 5), there is an 'implicit competition' between the EU and Russia regarding their 'overlapping neighbourhoods'. From Russia's perspective the EU is interfering in its sphere of influence, whereas EU member states see Russia holding their energy policy in the neighbourhood hostage. The United States and the EU, to a large extent, seem to be seeing eye-to-eye on the ENP. The Americans, much like the EU, view the ENP as a way to stabilise the territory of the former Soviet Union and to spread democracy and promote human rights (see Chapter 10). For the most part, US and EU interests converge with respect to Eastern Europe and the Southern Caucasus, although there are differences over how to deal with Russian interests in the former Soviet space and the integration of democratising Eastern countries into Euro-Atlantic structures. In the Middle East, as Baun has shown (Chapter 10), the EU prefers 'complementary but separate' initiatives from the United States, but, ultimately, has to settle for a secondary role. In fact, according to Smith and Webber (Chapter 4), in the security realm, actors like Russia, the United States, the UN, the OSCE and NATO often appear to be doing more than the EU, and therefore may undermine the latter's effectiveness in the neighbourhood in the long term.

Next steps: toward a theory of external governance

If, theoretically speaking, our governance model is underdetermined (i.e. it may be able to account for regional and/or sectoral variations but not specific institutional outcomes), do we revisit other theoretical frameworks/alternative modes of organising cooperation to investigate whether they can shed greater light on the ENP? More specifically, does the study of hegemons, strategic games, regimes, global norms, asymmetric interdependence, collective goods theory, or bargaining yield greater insights than the governance framework outlined in this book?

Clearly, each of these frameworks can account for certain aspects of the ENP. But in our view, ultimately none of these fully specify the conditions that underlie the demand for and supply of particular institutional structures, and thus do not provide greater explanatory power than the conceptual framework outlined by the contributors of this volume.

Hegemonic stability theory, for instance, maintains that a dominant state organises cooperation among self-interested states in a situation of actual or potential discord. International cooperation is seen as a public good and, since free-riding and buck-passing make the provision of public goods in the international realm problematic, a benevolent or coercive hegemon often-times solves this dilemma in an anarchic environment (see Kindleberger 1973; Krasner 1976; Keohane 1980). Yet, as game theorists – focusing on strategies of reciprocity, iteration, and *quid pro quo* bargaining (Axelrod 1984; Oye 1986) – make abundantly clear, cooperation is possible in the absence of a hegemon, even when conflicts of interest exist. 'Structure and sectors,' as Stein (1990: 53) explains, 'play a role in determining the constellation of actors' preferences, but structural and sectoral approaches are both incom-plete and must be supplemented by an emphasis on strategic interaction between states.'

Game theoretic models are not without problems either, though. First, they tend to be information intensive, requiring information about payoff structures, time horizons, number of players, relative gains, etc. Moreover, they are subject to perceptional issues and, when dealing with multi-level games, the outcome may be mutually contingent. In presuming simultaneous choice, game theory also fails to capture the dynamic nature of international relations that occurs in an ongoing context of action and reaction. And when we look at the literature on regimes, global norms creation and diffusion, bargaining, or asymmetric interdependence, we, similarly, run into problems making sense of particular facets of international cooperation.

In sum, we suggest that our volume provides a plausible conceptual framework to shed light on the ENP; we do not claim to have rigorously tested a fully-formed theory of external governance at this point. The next step clearly will have to be the specification of hypotheses and the operationalisa-tion of our main variables. The threat/transaction cost model sketched in Chapter 1 may be a step in this direction. Put differently, given the multi-faceted nature of the ENP and the fact that the EU employs a mixed strategy and a variety of tools to promote cooperation, our claim is that a focus on external governance allows us to make meaningful observations concerning the ENP. Like Hemmer and Katzenstein (2002: 583), rather than establish the superiority of one conceptual framework over another, 'we develop eclectic explanations that offer compelling insights into a specific empirical puzzle'. Thus our claim is modest. As these scholars (2002: 599) expressly state, '... analytical eclecticism leaves room for disagreement about the shape of partic-ular causal arguments and the sequence in which variables interact'.

The EU and external governance: prospects and implications

What are the future prospects for the ENP and EU external governance? To a great extent, the ENP will succeed or fail on the basis of its own merits and effectiveness as a policy. However, it will also be affected by other issues and developments, including some that are beyond the control of the EU and its partners. An important factor affecting the ENP will be the EU's own internal development, with a major question being whether the EU can successfully absorb ten new member states and achieve a post-enlargement consensus regarding its institutional future. An EU preoccupied with its own internal crises, or unable to resolve them, would be less capable of focusing on external policies and priorities, including the development of the ENP. Also affecting the ENP will be the ongoing debate on enlargement. If opposition to further enlargement hardens, this could seriously weaken the EU's ability to exercise influence in neighbouring countries and regions by eliminating the prospect of membership (even if only distant) as a source of leverage. At the same time, the end of enlargement would only increase the importance of the ENP as a framework for relations with neighbouring countries, since an EU with permanently defined borders would find it even more necessary to develop ways of projecting influence and promoting reform beyond offering the prospect of membership.

For the present, however, the EU's borders are not fixed and further enlargement is still planned or possible, and these prospective enlargements have significant implications for the future development of the ENP. The accession of Bulgaria and Romania in 2007 will increase the importance of both Moldova and Ukraine for the EU, necessitating closer ties with these countries. It will also extend the EU to the Black Sea, and thus give further impetus to the development of a coherent strategy for this important part of the EU neighbourhood, which also includes the Southern Caucasus. Whether or not Turkey eventually joins the EU, the accession negotiations with Ankara alone create increased pressure on the EU to deal seriously with the South Caucasus states, all of which share a land border with Turkey; they also give the EU additional leverage and influence in this region. Turkish accession, moreover, would increase EU interest and influence in Central Asia, providing an additional argument for including this key region in an expanded ENP.

The ENP will also be affected by the policies of other powerful regional actors. As discussed by Lavenex and Stulberg (Chapter 8), and as demonstrated by the January 2006 gas disputes between Russia and several ENP partners (Ukraine, Moldova and Georgia), Moscow has the potential to play a 'spoiler' role in the EU's eastern neighbourhood. ENP success in the former Soviet Union, therefore, hinges on the development of EU–Russia relations, just as these will be affected by the ENP and its consequences for Russian interests in the former Soviet space. Another key actor is Iran, which projects considerable influence in the South Caucasus region as well as throughout the broader Middle East. As Baun reminds us in Chapter 10, the United States is also an important actor in the EU neighbourhood, with interests and priorities that do not always coincide with those of the EU. And finally, disputes between ENP participants themselves, such as the Israeli–Hizbollah–Lebanon military conflict of mid-2006, can seriously challenge the EU's capacity to use (mostly) soft power incentives to encourage good behaviour among its neighbouring states.

A key question for the future is whether the ENP should be expanded beyond the current partner countries. In addition to Central Asia, consideration for inclusion could be given to the states of the Persian Gulf region, including possibly Iran. Aside from the prospect of Turkish accession, which would give the EU increased presence and influence in both regions, several other factors argue for such a geographical expansion of the ENP. Both the Persian Gulf and Central Asia are important or potentially important sources of energy for Europe, as well as sources of insecurity stemming from terrorism and WMD proliferation. Instability in these regions could also spill over and undermine EU efforts in current partner countries. The United States would no doubt welcome greater EU involvement in these strategically vital regions. Indeed, an ENP zone that included Central Asia and the Persian Gulf would more closely conform to the post-9/11 US strategic map of the world, with its focus on the 'crescent of crisis' stretching from Northern Africa to Central Asia (Daalder et al. 2006), thus creating new possibilities for US–EU strategic cooperation. As Leigh points out in his contribution to this volume (Chapter 12), the Northern African country of Mauritania is another potential ENP participant.

In the end, the success or failure of the ENP is a question with significant implications not only for the EU and its immediate neighbourhood, but for the entire international system. A successful ENP would be a major contribution to global peace and security, and it could provide a useful example for other democratic powers. For the United States especially, the ENP could provide a model for dealing with the countries and regions of its own southern neighbourhood, an area where US policies appear to be failing. After a wave of democratisation and economic liberalisation in the 1980s and 1990s, Latin American governments now appear to be turning away from the neoliberal model and embracing once again populist-authoritarian and statist policies. This backlash could be a response to the traditional US approach to dealing with its immediate neighbourhood, which has emphasised free trade, rapid political and economic change, and coercive diplomacy (and occasionally military intervention). A US neighbourhood strategy that adopts the ENP approach of integration, gradual change, and joint ownership might prove more attractive and successful. While both the United States and the EU have an asymmetrical relationship with their respective neighbourhoods, a successful ENP could demonstrate that asymmetrical power does not have to be exercised in a coercive and imposing way, and that external governance can be more effectively achieved through integration and cooperation.

A successful ENP would also impact the international system by expanding the EU's external influence and role. British analyst Mark Leonard has written of the 'Euro-sphere', the 84 countries and 1.5 billion people surrounding Europe that are 'umbilically linked' to the EU through trade and economic ties, and that constitute an EU 'zone of influence which is gradually being transformed by the European project and adopting European ways of doing things' (2003: 22). While not all of the countries comprising Leonard's 'Euro-sphere' are addressed by the ENP, it is not difficult to see how a successful, and possibly expanded, ENP could contribute to the building of such a zone of influence. The growth of EU influence, in turn, would have important consequences for the United States and transatlantic relations, leading possibly to a more vigorous partnership to advance common goals and shared values, or to geopolitical competition and rivalry. As Baun argues in his chapter (Chapter 10), the ultimate impact of the ENP on transatlantic relations remains an open question.

Of course, we must also consider the consequences if the EU's efforts at external governance do not succeed – if for whatever reasons the ENP does not prove effective, be it lack of adequate funding, incoherent design and implementation, or insufficient incentives for partner countries to alter their behaviour and adopt EU norms. In this case, not only would the EU's external influence be considerably diminished, but the EU itself would be much less secure. Such an outcome would be a major blow to global peace and security, and would certainly not be in the interests of the United States and other democratic actors. In addition to the potential costs of the ENP and the difficult challenges it poses for both the EU and others, therefore, we must also consider the potential dangers resulting from the failure or inability of the EU to extend its stabilising influence into neighbouring areas. And these could be very substantial indeed.

ℛEFERENCES

Abbott, K. and D. Snidal (2000), 'Hard and Soft Law in International Governance', *International Organization* 54: 421–56.

Adams, J. (2002), 'Russia's Gas Diplomacy', *Problems of Post-Communism* 49: 14–22.

Agence Europe (2002), 'Prodi Says EU has to "Shoulder its Responsibilities and Create a New Political Project for the Mediterranean"', *Europe Daily Bulletin*, No. 8229, 10–11 June, p. 17.

Albi, R. (2005), 'The Geopolitical Implications of European Neighbourhood Policy', *European Foreign Affairs Review* 10.

Allen, D. and M. Smith (1990), 'Western Europe's Presence in the Contemporary International Arena', *Review of International Studies* 16.

Alston, P. et al. (eds) (1999), *The EU and Human Rights*, Oxford: Oxford University Press.

Andonova, L.B. (2003), *Transnational Politics of the Environment: The EU and Environmental Policy in Central and Eastern Europe*, Cambridge: MIT Press.

Åslund, A. (2002), *Building Capitalism: The Transformation of the Former Soviet Bloc*, Cambridge: Cambridge University Press.

Åslund, A. (2003), 'Looking Eastwards to Bridge the Trade Divide', *Financial Times*, 17 January.

Åslund, A. and A. Warner (2004), 'The EU Enlargement: Consequences for the CIS Countries', in Marek Dabrowski, Ben Slay and Jaroslaw Neneman (eds), *Beyond Transition: Development Perspectives and Dilemmas*, Burlington VT: Ashgate.

Axelrod, R. (1984), *The Evolution of Cooperation*, New York: Basic Books.

Axelrod, R. (1986), 'An Evolutionary Approach to Norms', *American Political Science Review* 80: 1095–111.

Aydin, M. (2004), *Europe's Next Shore: The Black Sea Region After EU Enlargement*, Paris: EU Institute for Security Studies, Occasional Paper No. 53.

Balmaceda, M.M. (2003), 'EU Energy Policy and Future European Energy Markets: Consequences for the Central and East European States', *Oil, Gas, and Energy Law and Intelligence* 1.

Balmaceda, M.M. (2004), *Explaining the Management of Energy Dependency in Ukraine: Possibilities and Limits of a Domestic-Cantered Perspective*, Mannheimer Zentrum fur Europaische Sozialforschung, Mannheim, Working Paper No. 79.

Bales, K. (2000), *Disposable People: New Slavery in the New Economy*, Berkeley: University of California Press.

Balfour, R. (2004), *Rethinking the Euro-Mediterranean Security Dialogue*, Paris: EU Institute for Security Studies, Occasional Paper No. 52.

Barbé, E. (1998), 'Balancing Europe's Eastern and Southern Dimensions', in J. Zielonka (ed.), *Paradoxes of European Foreign Policy*, La Haya: Kluwer Law International.

Barbé, E. and F. Izquierdo (1997), 'Present and Future of Joint Actions for the Mediterranean Region', in Martin Holland (ed.), *Common Foreign and Security Policy: The Record and Reforms*, London: Pinter Publishers.

Barkin, J.S. and G.E. Shambaugh (1999), 'Hypotheses on the International Politics of Common Pool Resources', in J.S. Barkin and G.E. Shambaugh (eds), *Anarchy and the Environment: International Relations of Common Pool Resources*, Albany: SUNY Press.

Beatty, A. (2005a), 'EU to Join Negotiations on the Future of Transdniestria', *European Voice* Vol. 11, No. 34, 29 September.

Beatty, A. (2005b), 'EU "Set to Give OK" to Monitors in Transdniester', *European Voice* Vol. 11, No. 24, 23 June.

Beatty, A. (2005c), 'Observers on Stand-By for Caucasus Flashpoint', *European Voice* Vol. 11, No. 5, 10 February.

Beatty, A. (2005d), 'US Official Calls For a United Voice in Middle East Policy', *European Voice* Vol. 11, No. 37, 20 October.

Biscop, S. (2004), 'The European Security Strategy and the Neighbourhood Policy: A New Starting Point for Euro-Mediterranean Security Partnership', in A. Fulvio and R. Rossi (eds), *European Neighbourhood Policy: Political, Economic and Social Issues*, Faculty of Political Sciences: University of Catania.

Börzel, T.A. and T. Risse (2003), 'Conceptualising the Domestic Impact of Europe', in K. Featherstone and C. Radaelli (eds), *The Politics of Europeanisation*, Oxford: Oxford University Press.

Botcheva, L. and L. Martin (2001), 'Institutional Effects on State Behaviour: Convergence and Divergence', *International Studies Quarterly* 45: 1–26.

Bulmer, S.J. (1994), 'The Governance of the European Union: A New Institutionalist Approach', *Journal of Public Policy* 13: 351–80.

Bulmer, S.J. (1997), *New Institutionalism, the Single Market and EU Governance*, Arena Working Paper Series WP 97/25.

Burwell, F. (2005), *Re-Engaging Russia: The Case for a Joint US-EU Effort*, Policy Paper, February, Washington, DC: The Atlantic Council.

Cameron, D. (2001), 'The Return to Europe: The Impact of the EU on Post-Communist Reform', paper presented at the Annual Meeting of the American Political Science Association, San Francisco, California.

Cameron, D. (2003), 'The Challenges of Accession', *East European Politics and Societies* 17: 24–41.

Cameron, F. (1999), *The Foreign and Security Policy of the European Union: Past, Present and Future*, Sheffield: Sheffield Academic Press.

Cameron, F. (2005), *Promoting Political and Economic Reform in the Mediterranean and the Middle East*, Brussels: European Policy Centre.

Cameron, F. and J.M. Dománski (2005), *Russian Foreign Policy with Special Reference to its Western Neighbours*, Brussels: European Policy Centre, EPC Issue Paper No. 37, 13 July.

Caporaso, J. and J. Jupille (1998), 'States, Agency and Rules: The EU in Global Environmental Politics', in C. Rhodes (ed.), *The European Union in the World*, Boulder: Lynne Reinner.

Carius, A., I. Homeyer and S. von Bär (2000), 'Eastern Enlargement of the European Union and Environmental Policy: Challenges, Expectations, Multiple Speeds and Flexibility', in K. Holzinger and P. Knöpfel (eds), *Environmental Policy in a European Union of Variable Geometry? The Challenge of the Next Enlargement*, Basel: Helbig & Lichtenhahn.

Carmin, J. and S.D. Vandeveer (2004), 'Enlarging EU Environments: Central and Eastern Europe from Transition to Accession', *Environmental Politics* 13: 3–24.

Cederman, L.-E. (ed.) (2000), *Constructing Europe's Identity: The External Dimension*, Boulder: Lynne Rienner.

CES (2005), *NATO's New Role in the NIS Area: Final Project Report*, CES Project, May, Warsaw: Centre for Eastern Studies.

Checkel, J.T. (2005), 'International Institutions and Socialization in Europe: Introduction and Framework', *International Organization* 59: 801–26.

Christensen, T.J. and J. Snyder (1990), 'Chain Gangs and Passed Bucks: Predicting Alliance Patterns in Multipolarity', *International Organization* 44: 137–68.

Claes, D.H. (2001), *The Politics of Oil-Producer Cooperation*, Boulder: Westview Press.

Clapham, A. (1999), 'Where is the EU's Human Rights Common Foreign Policy, and How is it Manifested in Multilateral Fora?', in Philip Alston et al. (eds), *The EU and Human Rights*, Oxford: Oxford University Press.

Cleutinx, C. (2005), 'The Energy Dialogue EU–Russia', Presentation, October 2005, http://ec.europa.eu/energy/russia/presentations/doc/2005_luxembourg_en.pdf.

Clingendael Institute for International Relations (2004), *Study on Energy Supply Security and Geopolitics*, Final Report, The Hague.

Collignon, S. (2003), 'Is Europe Going Far Enough? Reflections on the Stability and Growth Pact, the Lisbon Strategy and the EU's Economic Governance', *European Political Economy Review* 1: 222–47.

Cooper, R. (2002), 'Why we still need empires', *Guardian*, 7 April.

Cooper, Robert (2003), *The Breaking of Nations: Order and Chaos in the Twenty-first Century*, New York: Atlantic Monthly Press.

Coppieters, B., M. Emerson, M. Huysseune, T. Kovziridze, G. Noutcheva, N. Tocci and M. Vahl (2004), *Europeanization and Conflict Resolution: Case Studies from the European Periphery*, Ghent: Academia Press.

Cornes, R. and T. Sandler (1996), *The Theory of Externalities, Public Goods, and Club Goods*, Cambridge: Cambridge University Press.

Cortell, A.P. and J.W. Davis Jr (1996), 'How Do International Institutions Matter? The Domestic Impact of Rules and Norms', *International Studies Quarterly* 40: 451–78.

Cosgrove-Sacks, C. (ed.) (1999), *The European Union and Developing Countries: The Challenges of Globalisation*, London/New York: Macmillan/St. Martin's.

Cottrell, R. (2005), 'Meet the Neighbours: A Survey of the EU's Eastern Borders', *The Economist*, 25 June.

Council of the European Union (2002a), 2421st Council meeting, Press release 7705/02, Luxembourg, 15 April.

Council of the European Union (2002b), 2450th GAERC, 30 September.

Council of the European Union (2002c), 2463rd Council meeting, Doc. 14183/02, 18 November.

Council of the European Union (2003a), 2518th GAERC, 16 June.

Council of the European Union (2003b), 2541st GAERC, 17 November.

Council of the European Union (2004), 2590th Council Meeting, Luxembourg, 14 June.

Council of the European Union (2005), 'Financial Perspective 2007–2013', 15915/05, 19 December.

Council of the European Union (2006), 'Declaration by the Presidency on Behalf of the European Union on the Presidential Elections in Belarus', EU Press Release, ESC/06/51, 22 March.

Crawford, B. and P.W. Schulze (eds) (1990), *The New Europe Asserts Itself: A Changing Role in International Relations*, Berkeley: University of California Press.

Cronberg, T. (2000), 'Euregios in the Making: The Case of Euregio Karelia', in Pirkkoliisa Ahponen and Pirjo Jukarainen (eds), *Tearing Down the Curtain, Opening the Gates: Northern Boundaries in Change*, Jyväskylä: SoPhi.

Crowe, B. (2003), 'A Common European Foreign Policy after Iraq?', *International Affairs* 79: 533–46.

Crowe, B. (2005), *Foreign Minister of Europe*, London: Foreign Policy Centre.

Daalder, I., N. Gnesotto and P. Gordon (eds) (2006), *Crescent of Crisis: U.S–European Strategy for the Greater Middle East*, Washington, DC: Brookings Institution Press.

Dannreuther, R. (ed.) (2004), *European Union Foreign and Security Policy: Towards a Neighbourhood Strategy*, New York: Routledge.

Del Sarto, R. and A. Tovias (2001), 'Caught between Europe and the Orient: Israel and the EMP', *The International Spectator* 4: 61–75.

Del Sarto, R. and T. Schumacher (2005), 'From EMP to ENP: What's at Stake with the European Neighbourhood Policy towards the Southern Mediterranean', *European Foreign Affairs Review* 10.

Del Sarto, R. and E. Tulmets (2006), 'The European Neighbourhood Policy: Policy Transfer from the Enlargement Policy and the Mediterranean Policy', paper presented at Robert Schuman Centre Luncheon Seminar, Florence.

Devdariani, J. and Hancilova, B. (2002), *Georgia's Pankisi Gorge: Russian, US and European Connections*, Brussels: Centre for European Policy Studies, Policy Brief No. 23.

Dienes, L. (2005), 'The Present Oil Boom', *Johnson's Russia List* 8399, 6 October.

Dietz, T. (2000), *The Imposition of Governance: Transforming Foreign Policy Through EU Enlargement*, Copenhagen Peace Research Institute, paper.

Dimitrova A.L. (ed.) (2004), *Driven to Change: The European Union's Enlargement Viewed from the East*, Manchester: Manchester University Press.

Dunsire, A. (1993), 'Modes of Governance', in Jan Kooiman (ed.), *Modern Governance: New Government-Society Interactions*, London: Sage.

Eberlein, B. and D. Kerwer (2004), 'New Governance in the European Union: A Theoretical Perspective', *Journal of Common Market Studies 2004* 42: 121–42.

Ecotec et al. (2000), *Administrative Capacity for Implementation and Enforcement of EU Environmental Policy in the 13 Candidate Countries*, Birmingham: Ecotec.

Ecotec et al. (2001), *The Benefits of Compliance with the Environmental Acquis for the Candidate Countries*, Birmingham: Ecotec.

Edwards, G. and E. Regelsberger (eds) (1990), *Europe's Global Links: The European Community and Inter-Regional Cooperation*, London: Pinter Publishers.

Eising, R. and B. Kohler-Koch (1999), 'Introduction: Network Governance in the European Union', in Beate Kohler-Koch and Rainer Eising (eds), *The Transformation of Governance in the European Union*, New York: Routledge.

Emerson, M. (1988), *The Economics of 1992: The E.C. Commission's Assessment of the Economic Effects of Completing the Internal Market*, Oxford: Oxford University Press.

Emerson, M., D. Gros, A. Italianer, J. Pisani-Ferry and H. Reichenbach (1992), *One Market, One Money*, Oxford: Oxford University Press.

Emerson, M. et al. (2002), *Navigating by the Stars: Norway, the European Economic Area and the European Union*, Brussels: Centre for European Policy Studies.

Emerson, M. (2003), *Institutionalising the Wider Europe*, Brussels: Centre for European Policy Studies, Policy Brief No. 42.

Emerson, M. (2004a), *The EU–Russia–US Triangle*, Brussels: Centre for European Policy Studies, Policy Brief No. 52.

Emerson, M. (2004b), *European Neighbourhood Policy: Strategy or Placebo?*, Brussels: Centre for European Policy Studies, Working Document No. 215.

Emerson, M. (2004c), *The Wider Europe Matrix*, Brussels: Centre for European Policy Studies.

Emerson, M. (2005a), *EU–Russia – Four Common Spaces and the Proliferation of the Fuzzy*, Brussels: Centre for European Policy Studies, Policy Brief No. 71.

Emerson, M. (2005b), *The Black Sea as Epicentre of the After-Shocks of the EU's Earthquake*, Brussels: Centre for European Policy Studies, Policy Brief No. 79.

Emerson, M. and G. Noutcheva (2004a), *Europeanisation as a Gravity Model of Democratisation*, Brussels: Centre for European Policy Studies, Working Document No. 214.

Emerson, M. and G. Noutcheva (2004b), *From Barcelona Process to Neighbourhood Policy: Assessments and Open Issues*, Brussels: Centre for European Policy Studies monograph, 10 December.

Emerson, M. and G. Noutcheva (2005), *From Barcelona Process to Neighbourhood Policy:*

Assessments and Open Issues, Brussels: Centre for European Policy Studies, Working Document No. 220.

Emerson, M., S. Aydin, G. Noutcheva, N. Tocci, M. Vahl and R. Youngs (2005), *The Reluctant Debutante: The European Union as Promoter of Democracy in its Neighbourhood*, Brussels: Centre for European Policy Studies, Working Document No. 223.

ENP Action Plan, Israel (n.d.), http://europa.eu.int/comm/world/enp/pdf/action_plans /Proposed_Action_Plan_EU-Israel.pdf (accessed 30 January 2005).

Epstein, R. (2006), 'Cultivating Consensus and Creating Conflict: International Institutions and the (De)Politicization of Economic Policy in Post-communist Europe', *Comparative Political Studies*.

ERM (2003), *Convergence with EU Environmental Legislation in Eastern Europe, Caucasus and Central Asia: A Guide*, London: ERM.

EU–Georgia Partnership and Cooperation Agreement (1999), http://europa.eu.int/comm /external_relations/ceeca/pca/index.htm (accessed 4 November 2005).

EU Action Plan on Justice and Home Affairs in Ukraine (2001), Agreed upon at the fourth session of the EU and Ukraine Co-ordination Committee, 12 December, www.eclc.gov.ua/new/html/eng/7/action_plan_eng.eng.html.

EU–Ukraine scoreboard on Justice and Home Affairs (2002), Official site of the Mission of Ukraine to the European Communities, 19 June, www.ukraine-eu.mfa.gov.ua/cgi-bin /valmenu_miss.sh?1p040606.html.

EU–Ukraine Action Plan (n.d), www.kmu.gov.ua/control/en/publish/article?art_id= 12854890&cat_id=12853974 (accessed 4 November 2005).

EuroMed Synopsis (2006), Issue No. 351, 20 April.

European Bank for Reconstruction and Development (2004), *Transition Report*, London: EBRD.

European Commission (1999), *Women Refugees: STOP Women's Sexual Exploitation and Trafficking*, (01/12/1998–30/11/1999) DAPHNE – JHA/98/DAF/070.

European Commission (2001a), *European Governance: A White Paper*, COM(2001) 428 final, 25 July.

European Commission (2001b), *Trafficking in Women. The Misery Behind the Fantasy: From Poverty to Slavery. A Comprehensive European Strategy*, http://europa.eu.int /comm/justice_home/news/8mars_en.htm.

European Commission (2001c), *Workshop 1: Application of the Concept of Prevention to Trafficking in Human Beings*, Brussels: European Commission.

European Commission (2001d), *Communication from the Commission to the Council and the European Parliament: Combating Trafficking in Human Beings and Combating the Sexual Exploitation of Children and Child Pornography*, COM(2000) 854 final/2.

European Commission (2001e), *Green Paper 'Towards a European Strategy for the Security of Energy Supply'*, Brussels: European Commission.

European Commission (2001f), *Communication from the Commission-Environmental Co-operation in the Danube–Black Sea Region*, COM(2001) 615 final, 30 October.

European Commission (2002a), *Commission Staff Working Paper: Energy Dialogue with Russia Update on Progress*, SEC(2002)1272.

European Commission (2002b), *Commission Staff Working Paper: Energy Dialogue with Russia Progress Since the October 2001 EU–Russia Summit*, SEC(2002) 333.

European Commission (2002c), *Commission Staff Working Paper: EU–Russia Energy Dialogue Second Progress Report*.

European Commission (2003a), *Wider Europe-Neighbourhood: A New Framework for Relations with our Eastern and Southern Neighbours*, COM(2003) 104 final, 11 March.

European Commission (2003b), Commission Communication, *Paving the Way for a New Neighbourhood Instrument*, COM(2003) 393 final, 1 July.

European Commission (2003c), Communication from the Commission to the Council and the European Parliament, *Reinvigorating EU Actions on Human Rights and Democratisation with Mediterranean Partners: Strategic Guidelines*, COM(2003) 294 final, 21 May.

European Commission (2003d), *Eleventh EU–Russia Summit, St. Petersburg*, 31.05, IP/03/768, 28 May, http://europa.eu.int/comm/external_relations/russia/sum05_03/ip03_768.htm.

European Commission (2003e), *Communication on Pan-European Environmental Cooperation after the 2003 Kiev Conference*, COM(2003) 62 final, 6 February.

European Commission (2003f), *Commission Staff Working Paper: Energy Dialogue with Russia Update on Progress Since the November 2002 EU–Russia Summit*, SEC(2003) 473.

European Commission (2003g), *Designing the Future Programme of Cultural Cooperation for the European Union after 2006, Directorate-General for Education and Culture, Public Consultation Document*, April.

European Commission (2004a), *European Neighbourhood Policy: Strategy Paper*, COM(2004) 373 final, 12 May.

European Commission (2004b), *Action Plan EU–Moldova*, Brussels: European Commission.

European Commission (2004c), *Action Plan EU–Ukraine*, Brussels: European Commission.

European Commission (2004d), *Action Plan EU–Jordan*, Brussels: European Commission.

European Commission (2004e), *Action Plan EU–Israel*, Brussels: European Commission.

European Commission (2004f), *Proposal for a Regulation of the European Parliament and of the Council Laying Down General Provisions Establishing a European Neighbourhood and Partnership Instrument*, COM(2004) 628 final.

European Commission (2004g), *European Neighbourhood Policy: the First Action Plans*, Press Release IP/04/1453, 9 December.

European Commission (2004h), *Commission Staff Working Paper: Energy Dialogue with Russia Update on Progress*, SEC(2004) 114.

European Commission (2004i), Communication from the Commission to the Council, *On the Commission Proposals for Action Plans under the European Neighbourhood Policy (ENP)*, COM (2004) 795 final, 9 December.

European Commission (2004j), *Proposal for a Regulation of the European Parliament and of the Council Laying Down General Provisions Establishing a European Neighbourhood and Partnership Instrument*, COM(2004) 0626 final – COD 2004/0219, 29 September.

European Commission (2005a), Communication to the Commission, *Implementing and Promoting the European Neighbourhood Policy*, SEC (2005) 1521, 22 November.

European Commission (2005b), *10 Years of Barcelona Process: Taking Stock of Economic Progress in EU Mediterranean Partners*, Brussels: DG for Economic and Financial Affairs, Occasional Papers No. 17.

European Commission (2005c), *European Neighbourhood Policy: Economic Review of ENP Countries*, Brussels: Directorate General of Economic and Financial Affairs.

European Commission (2005d), *European Neighbourhood Policy: Recommendations for Armenia, Azerbaijan, Georgia and for Egypt and Lebanon*, COM(2005) 72 final, 2 March.

European Commission (2005e), 'Conclusions: EU-Russia Summit, Moscow, 10 May 2005', Press release.

European Commission (2005f), *Commission Staff Working Paper: European Neighbourhood Policy Country Report, Georgia*, COM(2005) 72 final.

European Commission (2006), *Attitudes Towards Energy*, Special Eurobarometer 47/WAVE 64.2–TNS Opinion & Social.

European Communities (2003), *From Aarhus to Kiev and Beyond: The EU's Contribution to*

Environment for Europe, Brussels.

European Council (1999), 'Presidency Conclusions', Cologne, 3–4 June.

European Council (2002a), *Council Framework Decision on Combating Trafficking in Human Beings*, COM(2000) 854 final/2, 2002/629/JHA, July 19.

European Council (2002b), *Declaration on the Middle East, Annex III attached to the Danish Presidency Conclusions, Copenhagen European Council*, 12–13 December 2002.

European Council (2003), *Presidency Conclusions*, Thessalonica, 19–21 June.

European Council (2004), *ESDP Presidency Report* (Endorsed by the European Council), http://ue.eu.int/uedocs/cmsUpload/ESDP%20Presidency%20Report%2017.12.04.pdf (accessed 4 November 2005).

European Environmental Agency (2003), *Europe's Environment: The Third Assessment. Summary*, Copenhagen: EEA.

European Parliament (1996), *Resolution on Trafficking in Human Beings*, A4–0326/95, C 32/88–93, 5 February.

European Parliament (2003), *Draft Report on Wider Europe – Neighbourhood: a New Framework for Relations with our Eastern and Southern Neighbours*, 2003/2018(INI), 25 September.

European Parliament (2004), EU–Georgia Parliamentary Cooperation Committee, fifth meeting (Brussels), draft minutes, 16–17 June 2003 (PV/CAUS/543490EN.doc, 4 October).

European Parliament (2006), 'Parliament Wants New Targets on Energy Security and Supply', *EU Parliament Press Service*, 22 March, www.europarl.eu.int/news/expert /infopress_page/051–6627–08.

European Union Draft Constitutional Treaty (n.d.), CONV 724/02.

Europol (2004a), 'Drugs', The Hague: January.

Europol (2004b), 'Trafficking of Human Beings: A Europol Perspective', The Hague: January.

Europol (2004c), 'Trafficking of Human Beings for Sexual Purposes in the EU: A Europol Perspective', The Hague.

Europol (2005), 'Organised illegal immigration into the European Union', The Hague: February.

Europol–Russia agreement (n.d.), http://europa.eu.int/comm/external_relations/russia /intro/.

Everts, S. (2002), *Shaping a Credible EU Foreign Policy*, London: Centre for European Reform.

Fantini, M. and M. Dodini (2005), 'The economic effects of the European Neighbourhood Policy', in Alan Mayhew and Nathaniel Copsey (eds), *European Neighbourhood Policy and Ukraine*, Sussex: Sussex University Press.

Featherstone, K. and C.M. Radaelli (eds) (2003), *The Politics of Europeanization*, Oxford: Oxford University Press.

Ferrero-Waldner, B. (2004), Press Conference to Launch First Seven Action Plans under the European Neighbourhood Policy, Brussels, 9 December, press release.

Ferrero-Waldner, B. (2005), 'Communication to the Commission: Implementing and Promoting the European Neighbourhood Policy', SEC(2005) 1521, Brussels, 22 November.

Fierro, E. (2002), *The EU's Approach to Human Rights Conditionality in Practice*, The Hague/London/New York: Martinus Nijhoff Publishers.

Florini, A. (1996), 'The Evolution of International Norms', *International Studies Quarterly* 40: 363–89.

Forbrig, A. and P. Demeš (eds) (2007), *Reclaiming Democracy: Civil Society and Electoral Change in Central and Eastern Europe*, Washington, DC: German Marshall Fund.

Fried, D. (2005), 'Ukraine: Developments in the Aftermath of the Orange Emerging

Threats', Testimony of the Assistant Secretary for European and Eurasian Affairs before the House International Relations Subcommittee on Europe and Emerging Threats, Washington, DC, 27 July, www.state.gov/p/eur/rls/rm/50304.htm.

Fried, D. (2006), 'U.S. and Europe: Advancing the Freedom Agenda Together', Address to the Baltimore Council on Foreign Relations, 18 January.

Fried, J. (2004), *Cultural Cooperation within the Wider Europe and Across the Mediterranean: Issues at Stake and Proposals for Action*, paper commissioned by the European Cultural Foundation (ECF) to the author, Amsterdam, 1 March, www.eurocult.org (accessed 4 March 2005).

Friis, L. (1997), *When Europe Negotiates: From Europe Agreements to Eastern Enlargement?*, Copenhagen: University of Copenhagen.

Friis, L. and A. Murphy (1999), 'The European Union and Central and Eastern Europe: Governance and Boundaries', *Journal of Common Market Studies* 37: 211–32.

Frost, M. (1996), *Ethics in International Affairs: A Constitutive Theory*, Cambridge: Cambridge University Press.

Gatev, I. (2004), 'The EU's New Neighbourhood Policy Towards Ukraine', European Foreign Policy Conference, London School of Economics, 2–3 July.

General Affairs and External Relations Council (2003), *Council Conclusions*, Luxembourg, 16 June, 10370/03 Press 167.

Ghebali, V.-Y. (2004), 'The OSCE Mission to Georgia (1992–2004): The Failing Art of Half-Hearted Measures', *Helsinki Monitor* 15: 280–92.

Ginsberg, R.H. (1989), *Foreign Policy Actions of the European Community: The Politics of Scale*, Boulder: Lynne Rienner.

Ginsberg, R.H. (2001), *The European Union in International Politics: Baptism by Fire*, Lanham: Rowman and Littlefield.

Gordon, P.H. (1997/98), 'Europe's Uncommon Foreign Policy', *International Security* 22: 74–100.

Gorvett, J. (2005), 'Turkish Drive Towards EU Increases Possibilities for Change in the Caucasus', *Eurasia Insight*, 6 January, www.eurasianet.org/departments/insight /articles/eav010605a.shtml (accessed 14 March 2005).

Gotz, R. (2005), 'Pipedreams: Russia and Europe's Energy Supply', *Osteuropa* 10: 279–311.

Grabbe, H. (1999), *A Partnership for Accession? The Implications of EU Conditionality for the Central and Eastern European Applicants*, EUI Working Paper, RCS N 12/99, Florence: European University Institute.

Grabbe, H. (2001), 'How Does Europeanisation Affect CEE Governance? Conditionality, Diffusion and Diversity', *Journal of European Public Policy* 8:4, 1013–31.

Grabbe, H. (2002), 'Europeanisation Goes East: Power and Uncertainty in the EU Accession Process', in K. Featherstone and C. Radaelli (eds), *The Politics of Europeanisation*, Oxford: Oxford University Press.

Grabbe, H. (2004), 'How the EU should help its neighbours', Policy Brief, Centre for European Reform, London.

Grabbe, H. (2006), *The EU's Transformative Power: Europeanization through Conditionality in Central and Eastern Europe*, London: Palgrave Macmillan.

Grant, C. (2005), 'A Beacon of Liberty Flickers: Observations on Georgia', *New Statesman*, 18 July.

Grigorian, A. (2003), 'The EU and the Karabakh Conflict', in D. Lynch (ed.), *The South Caucasus: A Challenge for the EU*, Paris: EU Institute for Security Studies, Chaillot Paper, No. 65.

Gromadzki, G. et al. (2005), 'Will the Orange Revolution Bear Fruit? EU–Ukraine Relations in 2005 and the Beginning of 2006', May, Warsaw: Stefan Batory Foundation.

Gros, D., K. Durrer, J. Jimeno, C. Morticelli and R. Perotti (2002a), *Fiscal and Monetary Policy for a Low-Speed Europe*, Brussels: Centre for European Policy Studies.

Gros, D., M. Castelli, J. Jimeno, T. Mayer and N. Thygern (2002b), *The Euro at 25: a Special Report on Enlargement*, Brussels: Centre for European Policy Studies.

Gros, D., T. Mayer and A. Ubide (2004), *The Nine Lives of the Stability Pact*, Brussels: Centre for European Policy Studies.

Gros, D., T. Mayer and A. Ubide (2005), *EMU at Risk*, Brussels: Centre for European Policy Studies.

Gstoehl, S. (1995), *Patchwork Europe? Towards a Continent of Variable Cooperation*, Charleston, SC: European Community Studies Association.

Guillet, J. (2006), 'More on the Russian-Ukrainian Gas Dispute', *European Tribune*, 2 January: www.eurotrib.com.

Harding, G. (2005), *Analysis: EU at Loss over Migrant Crisis*, United Press International, 13 October.

Harris, G. (2004), 'The Wider Europe', in F. Cameron (ed.), *The Future of Europe: Integration and Enlargement*, London and New York: Routledge.

Haukkala, H. and A. Moshes (2004), 'Beyond "Big Bang": The Challenges of the EU's Neighbourhood Policy in the East', *Finnish Institute of International Affairs Report* 9.

Haukkala, H. and S. Medvedev (eds) (2001), *The EU Common Strategy on Russia: Learning the Grammar of the CFSP*, Helsinki/Berlin: Ulkopoliittinen instituutti/Institut für Europäische Politik.

Hemmer, C. and P. Katzenstein (2002), 'Why is There No NATO in Asia? Collective Identity, and the Origins of Multilateralism', *International Organization* 56: 575–607.

Heritier, A. (2002), 'New Modes of Governance in Europe: Policy-Making Without Legislating?', in A. Heritier (ed.), *Common Goods: Reinventing European and International Governance*, Boulder: Rowman and Littlefield.

Hill, C. (ed.) (1996), *The Actors in Europe's Foreign Policy*, London: Routledge.

Hill, F. (2004), *Energy Empire: Oil, Gas, and Russia's Revival*, London: The Foreign Policy Centre.

Hochschild, A. and B. Ehrenreich (eds) (2004), *Global Woman: Nannies, Maids and Sex Workers in the New Economy* (2nd edn), New York: Owl Books.

Hoffman, S. (1995), 'Europe's Identity Crisis: Between the Past and America', in Stanley Hoffman (ed.), *The European Sisyphus: Essays on Europe, 1964–1994*, Boulder: Westview Press.

Holland, M. (1995), *European Union Foreign Policy: From EPC to CFSP Joint Action and South Africa*, Basingstoke: Macmillan.

Hooghe, L. and G. Marks (2003), 'Unraveling the Central State, But How? Types of Multi-level Governance', *American Political Science Review* 97: 233–43.

Horsley, W. (2004), 'Italy feels strain of migrant exodus', BBC News, 4 October, http://newsvote.bbc.co.uk/.

Howorth, J. (2000), 'European Integration and Defence: The Ultimate Challenge?', Paris: Institute for Security Studies of WEU, Chaillot Paper, No. 43.

Hughes, D.M. (2001), 'The "Natasha" Trade: Transnational Sex Trafficking', *National Institute of Justice Journal* 246: 8–15.

Hyde Smith, P. (2005), 'Moldova Matters: Why Progress is Still Possible on Ukraine's Southwestern Flank', Washington, DC: Occasional Paper, March, The Atlantic Council of the United States.

ICG (2006), *Conflict Resolution in the South Caucasus: The EU's Role*, 20 March, Brussels: International Crisis Group, Europe Report No. 173.

Interarts and the European Forum for the Arts and Heritage (EFAH) (2003), 'Study on Cultural Cooperation in Europe', June, http://europa.eu.int/comm/culture/eac /sources_info/pdf-word/study_on_cult_coop.pdf (accessed 15 December 2004).

International Energy Agency (2002), *Russia Energy Survey*, Paris: OECD.

Jachtenfuchs, M. and B. Kohler-Koch (1995), *The Transformation of Governance in the*

European Union, paper prepared for the European Community Studies Association, Charleston, SC, May.

Jacoby, W. (2004), *The Enlargement of the European Union and NATO: Ordering from the Menu in Central Europe*, Cambridge: Cambridge University Press.

Jileva, E. (2004), 'The Europeanization of the EU's Visa Policy', *The Helsinki Monitor*, 2004: 1, 23–31.

Johansson, E. (2002), 'The distant neighbours – EU, Middle East, North Africa and the Euro-Mediterranean Partnership', *Observatory of European Foreign Policy Working Paper* 37/2002, Institut Universitari d'Estudis Europeus.

Johansson-Nogués, E. (2003), *Network Governance and EU's Near Neighbourhood*, Mannheimer Zentrum fuer Europaeische Sozialforschung.

Johansson-Nogués, E. (2004), 'A "Ring of Friends"? The Implications of the European Neighbourhood Policy for the Mediterranean', *Mediterranean Politics* 9:2, 240–7.

Johnson, D. (2003), *EU–Russian Energy Links: A Partnership Made in Heaven or Hell?*, Conference on Resource Politics and Security in a Global Age, Sheffield University, 28–29 June.

Johnston, A.I. (2001), 'Treating International Institutions as Social Environments', *International Studies Quarterly* 45: 487–515.

Jones, Elizabeth A. (2004), 'The Administration's Priorities in Europe', Testimony of the Assistant Secretary for European and Eurasian Affairs before the House International Relations Committee, Subcommittee on Europe, Washington, DC, 3 March.

Joseph, I. (1998), *Caspian Gas Exports: Stranded Reserves in a Unique Predicament*, Houston: Centre for International Political Economy and the James A. Baker III Institute for Public Policy, Rice University.

Karaganov, S. et al. (2005), *Russia–EU Relations: The Present Situation and Prospects*, Brussels: Centre for European Policy Studies, Working Document No. 225.

Kaufmann, D., A. Kraay and M. Mastruzzi (2004), *Governance Matters III: Governance Indicators for 1996–2002*, Washington DC: World Bank.

Kelley, J. (2004a), 'International Actors on the Domestic Scene: Membership Conditionality and Socialization by International Institutions', *International Organization* 58: 425–57.

Kelley, J. (2004b), *Ethnic Politics in Europe. The Power of Norms and Incentives*, Princeton: Princeton University Press.

Kelley, J. (2006), 'New Wine in Old Wineskins: Promoting Political Reforms through the New European Neighbourhood Policy', *Journal of Common Market Studies* 44: 29–55.

Kempe, Iris and W. van Meurs (2002), 'Toward a Multi-layered Europe: Prospects and Risks Beyond EU Enlargement', CAP Working Paper, Munich, November.

Kempe, I. and I. Solonenko (2005), 'International Orientation and Foreign Support of the Presidential Elections', Munich: Centre for Applied Policy Research.

Keohane, R. (1980), 'The Theory of Hegemonic Stability and Changes in International Economic Regimes', in Ole Holsti (ed.), *Change in the International System*, Boulder: Westview Press.

Keohane, R.O. (1984), *After Hegemony: Cooperation and Discord in the World Political Economy*, Princeton: Princeton University Press.

Keohane, R. (1989), *International Institutions and State Power*, Boulder: Westview Press.

Keohane, R.O., and J.S. Nye (1977), *Power and Interdependence*, Boston: Little, Brown.

Kindleberger, C. (1973), *The World in Depression, 1929–1939*, Berkeley: University of California Press.

King, Gilbert (2004), *Woman, Child for Sale: The New Slave Trade in the 21st Century*, New York: Chamberlain Brothers.

Knodt, M. (2004), 'International Embeddedness of European Multi-Level Governance', *Journal of European Public Policy* 11: 701–19.

Kohler-Koch, B. (2005). *European governance and system integration*, European Governance Papers, EUROGOV No. C-05–01.

Kooiman, J. (ed.) (1993), *Modern Governance: New Government-Society Interactions*, London: Sage.

Kotov, V. (2004), 'Greening of Policies': Perspectives in Russia, Berlin Conference on the Human Dimensions of Global Environmental Change, Berlin.

Kovtun, T. (2006), 'Hardening Orange: Economic Lessons from the Gas War, Tinged with Politics', *Ukrayina Moloda*, 12 January 2006, as translated in *Foreign Broadcast Information Service (FBIS)*, CEP20060114027054, 12 January.

Krasner, S. (1976), 'State Power and the Structure of International Trade', *World Politics* 28: 317–43.

Krasner, S.D. (ed.) (1983), *International Regimes*, Ithaca, NY: Cornell University Press.

Krenzler, H.-G. and H.C. Schneider (1997), 'The Question of Consistency', in Elfriede Regelsberger, Philippe de Schoutheete de Tervarent and Wolfgang Wessels (eds), *Foreign Policy of the European Union: From EPC to CFSP and Beyond*, Boulder: Lynne Rienner.

Kubicek, P.J. (ed.) (2003), *The European Union and Democratization*, London: Routledge.

Kuzio, T. (2003), 'EU and Ukraine: A turning point in 2004?', Paris: EU Institute for Security Studies, Occasional Paper No. 47.

Lake, D. (1999), *Entangling Relations: American Foreign Policy in Its Century*, Princeton: Princeton University Press.

Lamy, P. (2004), 'Europe and the Future of Economic Governance', *Journal of Common Market Studies* 42: 5–21.

Lavenex, S. (2004a), 'EU External Governance in "Wider Europe"', *Journal of European Public Policy* 11: 680–700.

Lavenex, S. (2004b), 'Justice and Home Affairs and the EU's New Neighbours: Governance Beyond Membership?', in K. Henderson (ed.), *The Area of Freedom, Security and* Justice in the Enlarged Europe, New York: Palgrave Macmillan.

Lavenex, S. (2005), 'Politics of Exclusion and Inclusion in "Wider Europe"', in J. DeBardeleben (ed.), *Soft or Hard Borders? Managing the Divide in an Enlarged Europe*, Aldershot: Ashgate.

Lavenex, S. and F. Schimmelfennig (2006), 'Relations with the Wider Europe', in U. Sedelmeier and A. Young (eds) *The JCMS Annual Review of the European Union in 2005*, Oxford: Blackwell.

Leigh, M. (2005), 'The EU's Neighbourhood Policy', in Esther Brimmer and Stefan Fröhlich (eds), *The Strategic Implications of European Union Enlargement*, Johns Hopkins University: Centre for Transatlantic Relations.

Leonard, M. (2003), 'The Road to a Cool Europa', *New Statesman*, June 16.

Leonard, M. and C. Grant (2005), *Georgia and the EU: Can Europe's Neighbourhood Policy Deliver?*, Policy Brief, Centre for European Reform.

Lenschow, A. (2005), 'Environmental Policy: Contending Dynamics of Policy Change', in H. Wallace, W. Wallace and M. Pollack (eds), *Policy-Making in the European Union* (5th edn), Oxford: Oxford University Press.

Levitsky, S. and L. A. Way (2006), 'Linkage versus Leverage: Rethinking the International Dimension of Regime Change', *Comparative Politics* 38: 4.

Lindh, A. and L. Pagrotsky (2002), 'EU's relationship with its future neighbours following enlargement' (dated 8 March 2002), Council of the European Union, 7713/02, 8 April.

Linsenmann I. and W. Wessels (2002), *Modes of Economic Governance in the EU: Towards a 'gouvernance économique?'*, paper presented at the Conference on Economic Coordination in EMU, College of Europe, Brugge, Belgium, 28–29 June.

Lipson, C. (1991), 'Why Are Some International Agreements Informal?', *International Organization* 45: 495–538.

Lobjakas, A. (2005), 'Georgia: Foreign Minister Pushes for Greater EU Involvement in South Caucasus', RFE/RL feature article, 2 March, www.rferl.org (accessed 10 March 2005).

Luciani, G. (2002), *Energy Policies in the European Union: Risk and Uncertainty in the Changing Global Energy Market*, Florence: Robert Schumann Centre for Advanced Studies.

Lynch, D. (2003a), 'The EU: Towards a Strategy', in Dov Lynch (ed.), *The South Caucasus: A Challenge for the EU*, Paris: EU Institute for Security Studies, Chaillot Paper No. 65.

Lynch, D. (2003b), 'Russia Faces Europe', Paris: EU Institute for Security Studies, Chaillot Paper, No. 60.

Lynch, D. (2004), 'The Russia-EU Partnership and the Shared Neighbourhood', Report presented to the 'Eastern Europe and Central Asia' Working Group (COEST), The Hague, July, EU Institute for Security Studies, www.iss-eu.org/.

Lynch, D. (2005), 'Catalysing Change', in Dov Lynch (ed.), *Changing Belarus*, Paris: EU Institute for Security Studies, Chaillot Paper No. 85.

Lynch, D. (2006), 'Why Georgia Matters', Paris: EU Institute for Security Studies, Chaillot Paper No. 86.

MacDougall, D. et al. (1977), *The Role of Public Finance in European Economic Integration*, Brussels: European Commission.

MacFarlane, S.N. (2004), 'The Caucasus and Central Asia: Towards a Non-Strategy', in Roland Dannreuther (ed.), *European Union Foreign and Security Policy: Towards a Neighbourhood Strategy*, New York: Routledge.

Malesky, E. (2005), 'Straight Ahead on Red: The Mutually Reinforcing Impact of Foreign Direct Investment and Local Autonomy in Vietnam', unpublished manuscript.

Manners, I. (2002), 'Normative Power Europe: A Contradiction in Terms?' *Journal of Common Market Studies* 40: 234–58.

Manners, I. and R.G. Whitman (eds) (2000), *The Foreign Policies of European Union Member States*, Manchester: Manchester University Press.

Marks, G., L. Hooghe and K. Blank (1996), 'European Integration from the 1980s: State-Centric Versus Multi-level Governance', *Journal of Common Market Studies* 34: 342–78.

Marks, Gary, L. Hooghe and K. Blank (1998), 'European Integration From the 1980s: State-Centric v. Multi-Level Governance', in Brent Nelsen and Alexander Stubb (eds), *The European Union: Readings on the Theory and Practice of European Integration*, Boulder: Lynne Rienner.

Mattli, W. (1999), *The Logic of Regional Integration, Europe and Beyond*, New York: Cambridge University Press.

Mayhew, A. (1998), *Recreating Europe: The European Union's Policy Towards Central and Eastern Europe*, Cambridge: Cambridge University Press.

Mayhew, A. and N. Copsey (2005), 'Introduction', in Mayhew and Copsey (eds), *The European Neighbourhood Policy and Ukraine*, Sussex: University of Sussex Press.

Mead, W.R. (2004), *Power, Terror, Peace and War: America's Grand Strategy in a World at Risk*, New York: Knopf.

Meunier, S. and K. Nicolaidis (2005), 'Trading Power', paper presented at the Ninth Biennial International Conference of the European Union Studies Association (EUSA), Austin, Texas.

Milov, V. and I. Selivakhin (2005), *Problemy energeticheskoi politiki*, Moscow: Centre of the Carnegie Endowment for International Peace, Working Paper 4.

Milcher, S. and B. Slay (2005), 'The Economics of the European Neighbourhood Policy: An Initial Assessment', paper presented at the conference 'Europe After Enlargement', Centre for Social and Economic Research, Warsaw, Poland.

Ministry of Economic Development and Trade, Russian Federation (2004), *Development Strategies for Leading Russian Economic Sectors Summarized*, 14 December 2004, as translated in *Foreign Broadcast Information Service (FBIS)*, *CEP20050114000257*, 14 December.

Missiroli, A. (2003), 'The EU and Its Changing Neighbourhoods: Stabilisation, Integration and Partnership', in J. Batt et al., 'Partners and Neighbours: A CFSP for a Wider Europe', Paris: EU Institute for Security Studies, Chaillot Paper No. 64.

Mitchell, R.B. (1999), 'International Environmental Common Pool Resources: More Common than Domestic but More Difficult to Manage', in J.S. Barkin and G.E. Shambaugh (eds), *Anarchy and the Environment: International Relations of Common Pool Resources*, Albany: SUNY Press.

Monaghan, A. (2005), *Russian Perspectives of Russia–EU Security Relations*, Surrey: Conflict Studies Research Centre.

Moravcsik, A. (1991), 'Negotiating the Single European Act: National Interests and Conventional Statecraft in the European Community', *International Organization* 45: 19–56.

Moravcsik, A. (1993), 'Introduction: Integrating International and Domestic Theories of International Bargaining', in P.B. Evans, H.K. Jacobson and R.D. Putnam (eds), *Double-Edged Diplomacy: International Bargaining and Domestic Politics*, Berkeley: University of California Press.

Moravcsik, A. (1998), *The Choice for Europe: Social Purpose and State Power from Messina to Maastricht*, Ithaca: Cornell University Press.

Moravcsik, A. and M.A. Vachudova (2003), 'National Interests, State Power and EU Enlargement', *East European Politics and Societies* 17: 42–57.

Mueller-Jentsch, D. (2004), *Deeper Integration and Trade in Services in the Euro-Mediterranean Region – Southern Dimensions of the European Neighbourhood Policy*, Washington, DC: World Bank.

Nadelmann, E.A. (1990), 'Global Prohibition Regimes: The Evolution of Norms in International Society', *International Organization* 44: 479–526.

NGO Monitor (n.d.), www.ngo-monitor.org (accessed 1 April 2005).

Nuttall, S. (1990), 'The Commission: Protagonists of Inter-Regional Cooperation', in Geoffrey Edwards and Elfriede Regelsberger (eds), *Europe's Global Links: The European Community and Inter-Regional Cooperation*, London: Pinter Publishers.

Nuttall, S. (2001a), '*Consistency' and the CFSP: A Categorization and Its Consequences*, LSE European Foreign Policy Unit Working Paper, No. 2001/13.

Nuttall, S. (2001b), *European Foreign Policy*, Oxford: Oxford University Press.

Occhipinti, J.D. (2004a), 'Justice and Home Affairs', in N. Nugent (ed.), *European Union Enlargement*, New York: Palgrave Macmillan.

Occhipinti, J.D. (2004b), 'Police and Judicial Cooperation', in M.G. Cowles and D. Dinan (eds), *Developments in the European Union 2*, New York: Palgrave Macmillan.

Olcott, M.B. (2005), *The Energy Dimension in Russian Global Strategy: Vladimir Putin and the Politics of Oil*, London: James A. Baker III Institute for Public Policy, Rice University, Houston.

Oldfield, J.D. et al. (2003), 'Russia's Involvement in the International Environmental Process: A Research Report', *Eurasian Geography and Economics* 44: 157–68.

Olson, M. (1965), *The Logic of Collective Action: Public Goods and the Theory of Groups*, Cambridge: Harvard University Press.

Ostrom, E. (2003), 'How Types of Goods and Property Rights Jointly Affect Collective Action', *Journal of Theoretical Politics* 15: 239–70.

Ottaway, M. and T. Carothers (2004), *The Greater Middle East Initiative: Off to a False Start*, Policy Brief 29, Carnegie Endowment for International Peace, Washington, DC, March.

Oye, K. (ed.) (1986), *Cooperation under Anarchy*, Princeton: Princeton University Press.

Pace, M. (2005a), 'The European Neighbourhood Policy: A Statement about the EU's

Identity?', Berlin: Friedrich Ebert Stiftung, www.fes.de/fes6/pdf/Pace.pdf.

Pace, M. (2005b) 'Imagining Co-presence in Euro-Mediterranean Relations: The Role of "Dialogue"', *Mediterranean Politics* 10:3 (November), 291–312 [Special Issue on Conceptualizing Cultural and Social Dialogue in the Euro-Mediterranean Area: A European Perspective].

Pace, M. (2005c), 'Conclusion: Cultural Democracy in Euro-Mediterranean Relations?', *Mediterranean Politics* 10:3 (November), 427–37 [Special Issue on Conceptualizing Cultural and Social Dialogue in the Euro-Mediterranean Area: A European Perspective].

Pace, M. (2006), *The Politics of Regional Identity. Meddling with the Mediterranean*, Oxford: Routledge, New International Relations series.

Padoa Schioppa, T. et al. (1987), *Efficiency, Stability and Equity – a Strategy for the System* of the European Community, Oxford: Oxford University Press.

Pardo, S. (2004), 'Europe of many circles: European Neighbourhood Policy', *Geopolitics* 9(3).

Paris, J. (2006), 'Making Sense of the Russian–Ukrainian Gas Spat', *European Tribune*, 20 December 2005, www.eurotrib.com/story/2005/12/30/5475/2215.

Patten, C. and J. Solana (2002), *Wider Europe*, joint letter to the EU General Affairs Council, August.

Pevehouse, J.C. (2002), 'Democracy from the Outside-In? International Organizations and Democratization', *International Organization* 56: 515–49.

Philippart, E. (2003), *The Euro-Mediterranean Partnership: Unique Features, First Results, and Forthcoming Challenges*, Brussels: Centre for European Policy Studies, Working Paper.

Pierson, P. (1993), 'When Effect Becomes Cause: Policy Feedback and Political Change', *World Politics* 45: 595–628.

Piper, J. (2004), 'Towards an EU–Russia Energy Partnership,' presentation, International Conference on Energy Security: The Role of Russian Gas Companies, November.

Pridham. G. (2005), *Designing Democracy: EU Enlargement and Regime Change in Postcommunist Europe*, New York: Palgrave Macmillan.

Prozorov, S. (2005), *The Structure of the EU-Russian Conflict Discourse: Issue and Identity Conflicts in the Narratives of Exclusion and Self-Exclusion*, EUBorderConf Working Paper, www.euborderconf.bham.ac.uk.

Prodi, R. (2002a), *Europe and the Mediterranean: Time for Action*, speech at Université Catholique de Louvain-la-Neuve, 26 November.

Prodi, R. (2002b), Speech at ECSA-World Conference, Brussels, 5–6 December.

Prozorov, S. (2005), 'The Structure of the EU–Russian Conflict Discourse: Issue and Identity Conflicts in the Narratives of Exclusion and Self-Exclusion', EUBorderConf Working Paper, www.euborderconf.bham.ac.uk.

Putnam, R.D. (1988), 'Diplomacy and Domestic Politics: The Logic of Two-Level Games', *International Organization*, 42:3, 427–60.

Regelsberger, E. (2003), 'The Impact of EU Enlargement on the CFSP: Growing Homogeneity of Views among the Twenty-Five', *CFSP Forum* (FORNET), 1:3.

RFE/RL (2003), 'EU proposals for future ties spark disappointment', 18 March.

RFE/RL (2004), 'EU to reconsider exclusion of south Caucasus states from "Wider Europe" program', 30 January.

RFE/RL (2005a), 'Ukraine, EU Sign Three-Year Action Plan', 23 February.

RFE/RL (2005b), 'Ukrainian President Lukewarm on EU Neighbourhood Policy', 24 February.

RFE/RL (2005c), 'Russia, United States, Spar over Belarus's "Dictatorship"', Vol. 9, No. 76, Part II, 22 April.

RFE/RL (2005d), 'US Provides Armenia with New Law Enforcement Assistance', Vol. 9, No. 132, Part I, 15 July.

Riedel, E. and M. Will (1999), 'Human Rights Clauses in External Agreements of the EC', in Philip Alston et al. (eds), *The EU and Human Rights*, Oxford: Oxford University Press.

Rosenau, J.M. (1992), 'Governance, Order, and Change in World Politics', in James Rosenau and Ernst-Otto Czempiel (eds), *Governance Without Government: Order and Change in World Politics*, New York: Cambridge University Press.

Rosenau, J.M. and E.-O. Czempiel (eds) (1992), *Governance Without Government: Order and Change in World Politics*, New York, Cambridge University Press.

Sagers, M. (2001), 'Developments in Russian Crude Oil Production in 2000', *Post-Soviet Geography and Economics* 42:3, 153–201.

Saprykin, V. (2002), 'EU–Ukraine–Russia: Further Gas Dialog as a Guarantee of Europe's Energy Security', *Central Asia and the Caucasus*, October, www.ca-c.org/journal /eng-05-2002/00.conteng5.shtml.

Sasse, G. (2004), 'Minority Rights and EU Enlargement: Normative Overstretch or Effective Conditionality?', in Gabriel N. Toggenburg (ed.), *Minority Protection and the Enlarged European Union: The Way Forward*, Budapest: LGO Books.

Schafer, A. (2004), *Beyond the Community Method: Why the Open Method of Coordination Was Introduced to EU Policy-Making*, European Integration Online Papers 8:13, http://eiop.or.at/eiop/texte/2004–013a.htm.

Scharpf, F. (2001), *What Have We Learned? Problem-Solving Capacity of the Multi-Level European Polity*, Max Planck Institute for the Study of Societies Working Paper, July.

Schimmelfennig, F. (2003a), *The EU, NATO and the Integration of Europe*, Cambridge: Cambridge University Press.

Schimmelfennig, F. (2003b), 'Strategic Action in a Community Environment. The Decision to Enlarge the European Union to the East', *Comparative Political Studies* 36: 156–83.

Schimmelfennig, F. (2005a), *The International Promotion of Political Norms in Central and Eastern Europe: A Qualitative Comparative Analysis*, Cambridge, MA: Harvard University, Centre for European Studies, Central and East European Working Paper 61.

Schimmelfennig, F. (2005b), 'Strategic Calculation and International Socialization: Membership Incentives, Party Constellations, and Sustained Compliance in Central and Eastern Europe', *International Organization* 59: 827–60.

Schimmelfennig, F. and U. Sedelmeier (2004), 'Governance by Conditionality: EU Rule Transfer to the Candidate Countries of Central and Eastern Europe', *Journal of European Public Policy* 11: 661–79.

Schimmelfennig, F. and U. Sedelmeier (eds) (2005a), *The Europeanization of Central and Eastern Europe*, Ithaca: Cornell University Press.

Schimmelfennig, F. and U. Sedelmeier (2005b), 'Introduction: Conceptualizing the Europeanization of Central and Eastern Europe', in F. Schimmelfennig and U. Sedelmeier (eds), *The Europeanization of Central and Eastern Europe*, Ithaca: Cornell University Press.

Schimmelfennig, F., S. Engert and H. Knobel (2003), 'Costs, Commitments, and Compliance: The Impact of EU Democratic Conditionality on Latvia, Slovakia, and Turkey', *Journal of Common Market Studies* 41: 495–517.

Schimmelfennig, F., S. Engert and H. Knobel (2006), *International Socialization in the New Europe: European Organizations, Political Conditionality, and Democratic Change*, Basingstoke: Palgrave Macmillan.

Schneider, E. and C. Saurenbach (2005), 'Kiev's EU Ambitions', *SWP Comments*, Berlin: German Institute for International and Security Affairs.

Sedelmeier, U. (2005), *Constructing the Path to Eastern Enlargement: The Uneven Policy Impact of EU Identity*, Manchester: Manchester University Press.

Sedelmeier, U. and H. Wallace (2000), 'Eastern Enlargement: Strategy or Second

Thoughts?' in H. Wallace and W. Wallace (eds), *Policy-Making in the European Union* (4th edn), Oxford: Oxford University Press.

Shaffer, B. (2003), 'US Policy', in Dov Lynch (ed.), *The South Caucasus: A Challenge for the EU*, Paris: EU Institute for Security Studies, Chaillot Paper No. 65.

Sissenich, B. (2003), 'State Building by a Nonstate', Ph.D. dissertation, Ithaca: Cornell University.

Sissenich, B. (2004), 'European Union Policies towards Accession Countries', presented at the conference 'Public Opinion about the EU in Post-Communist Eastern Europe', Indiana University, Bloomington, Indiana.

Smith, E.W. (1999), *Re-Regulation and Integration: The Nordic States and the European Economic Area*, University of Sussex.

Smith, H. (1995), *European Foreign Policy and Central America*, New York: St. Martin's Press.

Smith, K.E. (1998), *The Making of EU Foreign Policy: The Case of Eastern Europe*, New York: St. Martin's Press.

Smith, K.E. (2001), 'The EU, Human Rights and Relations with Third Countries: "Foreign Policy" with an Ethical Dimension?', in Karen Smith and Margot Licht (eds), *Ethics and Foreign Policy*, Cambridge: Cambridge University Press.

Smith, K.E. (2005), 'The Outsiders: The European Neighbourhood Policy', *International Affairs* 81.

Smith, M. (2001), 'European foreign and security policy', in S. Bromley (ed.), *The Governance of the European Union*, London: Sage.

Smith, M. (2003), 'The framing of European foreign and security policy: towards a post-modern policy framework?', *Journal of European Public Policy* 10: 556–75.

Smith, M.E. (2000), 'Conforming to Europe: The Domestic Impact of European Foreign Policy Cooperation', *Journal of European Public Policy* 7: 613–31.

Smith, M.E. (2001), 'Diplomacy by Decree: The Legalization of EU Foreign Policy', *Journal of Common Market Studies* 39: 79–104.

Smith, M.E. (2003), *Europe's Foreign and Security Policy: The Institutionalization of Cooperation*, Cambridge: Cambridge University Press.

Smith, M.E. (2004), 'Toward a Theory of EU Foreign Policy-making: Multi-level Governance, Domestic Politics, and National Adaptation to Europe's Common Foreign and Security Policy', *Journal of European Public Policy* 11: 740–58.

Snidal, D. (1991), 'Relative Gains and the Pattern of International Cooperation', *American Political Science Review* 85: 701–26.

Socor, V. (2005a), 'Putin–Schroeder Gas Deal Times to German Elections', *Jamestown Monitor*, 2:169, 13 September.

Socor, V. (2005b), 'Russo-German Gas Pact in the Baltic', *Jamestown Monitor*, 2:169, 13 September.

Solana, J. (2003), *A Secure Europe In a Better World: European Security Strategy*, adopted by the European Council, Brussels, December 2003 and reprinted by the EU Institute for Security Studies, Paris.

Solana, J. and C. Patten (2002), *Wider Europe*, joint letter to the Danish EU Presidency, 7 August.

Spencer, C. (2001), 'The EU and Common Strategies: The Revealing Case of the Mediterranean', *European Foreign Affairs Review* 6: 3–51.

Spongenberg, H. (2006), 'EU border agency begins work in Italy but is delayed in Spain', EUobserver.com (4 August).

Stålvant, C.-E. (2001), *The Northern Dimension A Policy in Need of an Institution?*, BaltSeaNet Working Papers, No. 1.

Stauffer, T.R. (2000), 'Caspian Fantasy: The Economics of Political Pipelines', *Brown Journal of World Affairs* 7:2, www.watsoninstitute.org.

Stein, A.A. (1990), *Why Nations Cooperate: Circumstance and Choice in International Relations*, Ithaca: Cornell University Press.

Stetter, S. (2004), 'Cross-pillar Politics: Functional Unity and Institutional Fragmentation of EU Foreign Policies', *Journal of European Public Policy* 11: 720–39.

Stulberg, A.N. (2004), 'Moving Beyond the Great Game: The Geoeconomics of Russia's Influence in the Caspian Energy Bonanza', *Geopolitics* 10: 1–25.

Sweet, A.S. and W. Sandholtz (eds) (1998), *Supranational Governance: The Institutionalization of the European Union*, Oxford: Oxford University Press.

Sweet, A.S. and T.L. Brunell (1998), 'Constructing a Supranational Constitution: Dispute Resolution and Governance in the European Community', *American Political Science Review* 92: 63–81.

Szymanski, M. and M.E. Smith (2005), 'Coherence and Conditionality in European Foreign Policy: Negotiating the EU–Mexico Global Agreement', *Journal of Common Market Studies* 43: 171–92.

Tanner, F. (2004), 'North Africa: Partnership, Exceptionalism and Neglect', in R. Dannreuther (ed.), *European Union Foreign and Security Policy: Towards a Neighbourhood Strategy*, New York: Routledge.

TACIS CBC (n.d.), http://europa.eu.int/comm/europeaid/projects/TACIS/publications /annual _programmes/cbc_2004_en.pdf (accessed 14 December 2004).

Tefft, J. (2005), 'Ukraine and the United States: The Challenges Ahead', Speech by the Deputy Assistant Secretary for European and Eurasian Affairs to the Chicago Council on Foreign Relations, 7 February, www.satte.gov/p/eur/rls/rm/42044.htm.

Torreblanca, J.I. (2001), *The Reuniting of Europe: Promises, Negotiations and Compromises*, Burlington: Ashgate.

Torreblanca, J.I. (2003), 'Accommodating interests and principles in the European Union: The Case of the Eastern Enlargement', in E. Barbé and E. Johansson-Nogués (eds), *Beyond Enlargement: The New Members and New Frontiers of the Enlarged European Union*, Bellaterra: Institut Universitari d'Estudis Europeus.

Treaty on European Union (n.d.), Brussels.

United Nations Development Programme (2004), 'Arab Human Development Report 2004', http://cfapp2.undp.org/rbas/ahdr2.cfm?menu=12.

United Nations General Assembly (2000), *International Convention on Transnational Organized Crime*, UNGA Doc. A/55/383.

United Nations General Assembly (2000), *Protocol to Prevent, Suppress and Punish Trafficking in Persons, Especially Women and Children, supplementing the United Nations Convention against Transnational Organized Crime*, UNGA Doc. A/55/383.

US Department of State (2003), *Trafficking in Persons Report*, Washington, DC, www.state.gov/g/tip/rls/tiprpt/2003/.

US Department of State (2004), *Trafficking in Persons Report*, Washington, DC, www.state.gov/g/tip/rls/tiprpt/2004/.

US Department of State (2005a), 'US, EU Cooperate on the Middle East Peace Process', Fact Sheet, Washington, DC, 17 February.

US Department of State (2005b), 'Background Note: Armenia', Washington, DC, April.

US Department of State (2005c), 'Background Note: Georgia', Washington, DC, September.

US Department of State (2005d), *Trafficking in Persons Report*, Washington, DC, www.state.gov/g/tip/rls/tiprpt/2005/.

Vachudova, M.A. (2002), 'Strategies for Democratization and European Integration in the Balkans', in Marise Cremona (ed.), *The Enlargement of the European Union*, Oxford: Oxford University Press.

Vachudova, M.A. (2005), *Europe Undivided: Democracy, Leverage and Integration After Communism*, Oxford: Oxford University Press.

Vachudova, M.A. (2007), 'Historical Institutionalism and the EU's Eastward Enlargement', in edited by Sophie Meunier and Kathleen McNamara (eds), *The State of the European Union Vol. 8*, Oxford: Oxford University Press.

Vahl, M. (2005), 'The Europeanisation of the Transnistrian Conflict', CEPS Policy Brief No. 73, Brussels, May.

Vahl, M. and M. Emerson (2004), 'Moldova and the Transnistrian Conflict', in Bruno Coppieters et al., *Europeanization and Conflict Resolution: Case Studies from the European Periphery*, Brussels: CEPS.

Vandeveer, S.D. and J. Carmin (2004), 'Assessing Conventional Wisdom: Environmental Challenges and Opportunities Beyond Eastern Accession', *Environmental Politics* 13: 315–31.

Victor, D.G. and N.J. Victor (2003), 'Axis of Oil', *Foreign Affairs* 82.

Waever, O. (2000), 'European Security Identities 2000', in J.P. Burgess and O. Tunander (eds), *European Security Identities: Contested Understandings of EU and NATO*, Oslo: International Peace Research Institute.

Wallace, W. (2003), 'Looking after the Neighbourhood: Responsibilities for the EU-25', Paris: Notre Europe, *Policy Papers* No.4.

Wallace, H. and W. Wallace (eds) (2000), *Policy-making in the European Union* (4th edn), Oxford: Oxford University Press.

Walt, S.M. (1988), *The Origins of Alliances*, Ithaca: Cornell University Press.

Weber, K. (1997), 'Hierarchy Amidst Anarchy: A Transaction Costs Approach to International Security Cooperation', *International Studies Quarterly* 41: 321–40.

Weber, K. (2000), *Hierarchy Amidst Anarchy: Transaction Costs and Institutional Choice*, New York: SUNY Press.

Weber, K. and M. Hallerberg (2001), 'Explaining Variation in Institutional Integration in the European Union: Why Firms May Prefer European Solutions?', *Journal of European Public Policy* 8: 171–91.

Webber, M., M. Smith et al. (2002), *Foreign Policy in a Transformed World*, Harlow: Prentice Hall.

White House (2003), 'President Bush Discusses Freedom in Iraq and Middle East', Remarks by the President at the 20th Anniversary of the National Endowment for Democracy, United States Chamber of Commerce, Washington, DC, www.whitehouse.gov/news/releases/2003/11/20031106–2.html.

White House (2004), 'Broader Middle East/N.Africa Partnership: Partnership for Progress and a Common Future with the Region of the Broader Middle East and North Africa', press release, 9 June, www.whitehouse.gov/news/releases/2004/06/20040609–30.html.

White House (2005) Bush–Putin meeting in Bratislava, Slovakia, 24 February, www.whitehouse.gov/news/releases/2005/02/20050224–9.html (accessed 1 March 2005).

Williamson, O. (1979), 'Transaction-Cost Economics: The Governance of Contractual Relations', *Journal of Law and Economics* 22: 233–61.

Williamson, O. (1981), 'The Modern Corporation: Origins, Evolution, Attributes', *Journal of Economic Literature* 19: 1537–68.

Williamson, O. (1985), *The Economic Institutions of Capitalism: Firms, Markets and Relational Contracting*, New York: Free Press.

Wolczuk, K. (2004), 'Ukraine's European Choice', Centre for European Reform, Policy Brief, 22 October.

World Bank (2005), *Belarus: Window of Opportunity to Enhance Competitiveness and Sustain Economic Growth*, Washington, DC: World Bank.

Yacoubian, M. (2004), *Promoting Middle East Democracy: European Initiatives*, United States Institute of Peace Special Report, October.

Youngs, R. (2001), *The European Union and the Promotion of Democracy. Europe's Mediterranean and Asian Policies*, Oxford: Oxford University Press.

Youngs, R. (2002), *The European Union and Democracy Promotion in the Arab–Muslim World*, Brussels: Centre for European Policy Studies, Middle East & Euro-Med Working Paper No. 2.

Youngs, R. (2004), 'Europe's Uncertain Pursuit of Middle East Reform', Washington, DC: Carnegie Endowment for International Peace, Carnegie Papers, Middle East Series No. 45.

Zaharchenko, T.R. and G. Goldenman (2004), 'Accountability in Governance: The Challenge of Implementing the Aarhus Convention in Eastern Europe and Central Asia', *International Environmental Agreements: Politics, Law and Economics* 4: 229–51.

Zielonka, J. (1998), *Explaining Euro-Paralysis: Why Europe is Unable to Act in International Politics*, New York: St. Martin's Press.